DISCARD

ONE CHILD

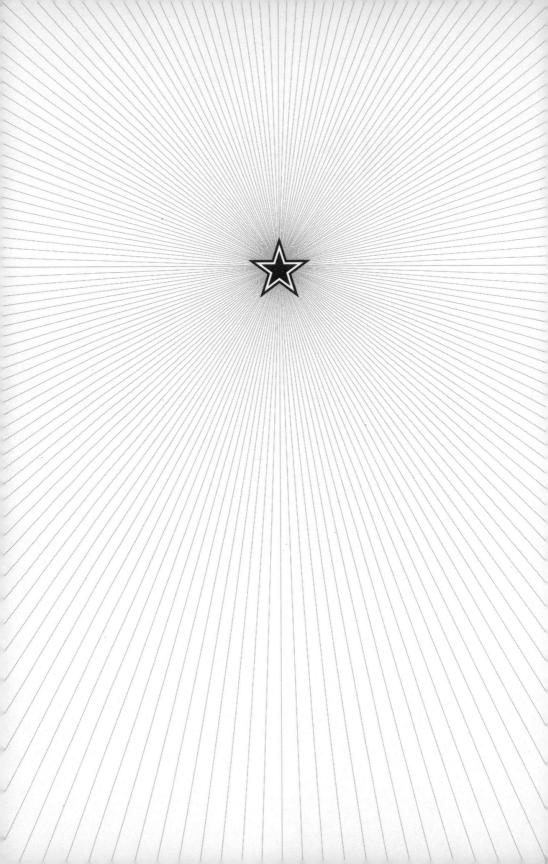

ONE CHILD

The Story of

China's Most Radical

Experiment

Mei Fong

Houghton Mifflin Harcourt

Boston   New York   2016

Copyright © 2016 by Mei Fong

For information about permission to reproduce selections
from this book, write to trade.permissions@hmhco.com or to
Permissions, Houghton Mifflin Harcourt Publishing Company,
3 Park Avenue, 19th Floor, New York, New York 10016.

www.hmhco.com

Library of Congress Cataloging-in-Publication Data
Names: Fong, Mei, author.
Title: One child : the story of China's most radical experiment /
Mei Fong.
Description: Boston : Houghton Mifflin Harcourt, 2016. | Includes
bibliographical references and index.
Identifiers: LCCN 2015037254| ISBN 9780544275393 (hardcover) | ISBN
9780544276604 (ebook) | ISBN 9780544815582 (pbk. (international edition))
| ISBN 9780544815605 (trade paper)
Subjects: LCSH: China — Population policy. | Family planning — Government
policy — China. | Family size — Government policy — China. | Families — China.
| China — Social conditions — 2000– | China — Social policy — 21st century.
Classification: LCC HB3654.A3 F66 2016 | DDC 363.9/60951 — dc23
LC record available at http://lccn.loc.gov/2015037254

Book design by Greta D. Sibley

Printed in the United States of America
DOC 10 9 8 7 6 5 4 3 2 1

To anyone contemplating the cost of parenthood

CONTENTS

AUTHOR'S NOTE

Whenever it made grammatical sense, I have tried to make a distinction between "China" and "Chinese," since one can be ethnically Chinese but not a citizen of the People's Republic of China.

In representing Chinese names, I've usually placed the family name first, though there are exceptions — mine being one. Readers may also note that I've used English translations for some Chinese names — for example, "Moon Lotus" — and not for others. I've done so to help Western readers distinguish various Chinese characters in books, since unfortunately in Romanized script many Chinese names can sound alike. In some older interviews I conducted, I failed to get accurate translations of the subjects' names at the time and do not venture to guess.

A last note on statistics. China sources such as Xinhua or the country's Bureau of Statistics have been used as indicators but should not be taken as gospel. (Even China's Premier Li Keqiang reportedly said China's GDP figures are "man-made.") The wise reader would assume that official numbers may be deflated when such figures have negative implications for China's prestige — such as fatalities or pollution indicators — and possibly inflated in cases where overstatement may benefit authorities — for example, GDP growth.

PROLOGUE

In the midst of the Cold War, China's rocket scientists came up with an ambitious plan that had nothing to do with missiles, or space exploration, or weaponry of any kind.

It concerned babies.

On September 25, 1980, China's Communist Party unveiled this plan through an open letter that asked members to voluntarily limit their family size to one child. The request was, in truth, an order.

Thus began the one-child policy, the world's most radical social experiment, which endured for thirty-five years and continues to shape how one in six people in this world are born, live, and die.

Like crash dieting, the one-child policy was begun for reasons that had merit. China's leadership argued the policy was a necessary step in its Herculean efforts to lift a population the size of the United States' from abject poverty. But like crash dieting, the one-child policy employed radical means and aimed for quick results, causing a rash of negative side effects.

The excesses of the one-child policy, such as forced sterilizations and abortions, would eventually meet with global opprobrium. Balanced against this, however, is the world's grudging admiration for China's soaring economic growth, a success partially credited to the one-child policy.

What we fail to understand is that China's rapid economic growth has had little to do with its population-planning curbs. Indeed, the policy is imperiling future growth because it rapidly created a population that is too old, too male, and, quite possibly, too few.

More people, not less, was one of the reasons for China's boom. The country's rise as a manufacturing powerhouse could not have happened without abundant cheap labor from workers born during the 1960s–70s baby boom, before the one-child policy was conceived.

To be sure, fewer births made investments in human capital more efficient — less spreading out of educational resources, for example. Many economists, however, agree that China's rapid economic rise had more to do with Beijing's moves to encourage foreign investment and private entrepreneurship than a quota on babies. Privatizing China's lumbering state-owned enterprises, for example, spurred private-sector growth until it accounted for as much as 70 percent of China's gross domestic product (GDP) by 2005. Arthur Kroeber, one of the most prolific and respected economists who specializes in China, said, "Let's say China grew 10%; I would be surprised if more than 0.1% of this is due to the one-child policy."

China's vast cohort of workers is growing old. By 2050, one out of every four people in China will be over sixty-five. And the one-child policy has vastly shrunk the working population that must support and succor this aging army. In recent years China has made great strides in rolling out nationwide pension and health-care schemes, but the social safety net is far from adequate, and the leadership will have to do much more with much less time.

I started reporting on China's economic miracle in 2003 as a *Wall Street Journal* correspondent. I was on the factory beat, covering the workshop of the world. Every little city in southern China's Pearl River Delta defined itself by what it made: I made regular stops at Jeans City, Bra Town, and Dollar Store center, wrote stories about the world's largest Christmas tree factory, and about a brassiere laboratory that birthed the Wonderbra.

Few envisioned a worker shortage then. But I was starting to hear stories about factory owners being forced to hike wages. Some resorted to offering previously unheard-of perks like TVs, badminton courts, and free condoms. Most economists at the time saw it as a short-term labor supply issue that would soon sort itself out. For how could you run out of workers in China?

As it turned out, the work force shrinkage happened faster than anticipated. The one-child policy sharply accelerated a drop in fertility. China's massive 800-million-person work force — larger than Europe's population — started to contract in 2012 and will continue doing so for years to come, driving up wages and contributing to global inflationary pressures.

After twenty years of below-replacement rates, China has officially moved to a two-child policy as of late 2015 to ease demographic pressures. It may be too little, too late. When Beijing loosened the policy slightly two years earlier, only about a tenth of eligible couples applied to have a second child, a take-up below even the most pessimistic projections. Many say it's simply too costly and stressful to raise multiple offspring in modern-day China. In that sense, the one-child policy can be judged a success, for many Chinese have thoroughly internalized the mindset that the one-child household is the ideal.

If Beijing is unable to reverse this thinking, then somewhere in the decade between 2020 and 2030, China's population will peak and decline. By 2100, China's population may have declined to 1950 levels, about 500 million, a startling reversal for the world's most populous nation. No other country has ever shed this much of its population without the aid of warfare or pestilence. And at the same time, the policy's enforcement was occasionally vicious, bordering on inhumane in certain cases, and it encouraged a number of baleful side effects, from a potentially explosive gender imbalance to what is essentially a black market for adoptable infants.

China's one-child policy was crafted by military scientists, who believed any regrettable side effects could be swiftly mitigated and women's fertility rates easily adjusted. China's economists, sociologists, and demographers, who might have injected more wisdom and balance, were largely left out of the decision making, as the Cultural Revolution had starved social scientists of resources and prestige. Only the nation's defense scientists were untouched by the purges, and they proved not the best judges of human behavior.

The sad truth is, the harsh strictures put in place by the one-child policy were unnecessary for economic prosperity. By the 1970s, a full decade before the policy, China already had in place a highly effective and less coercive family-planning policy, called the "Later, Longer, Fewer" campaign. In the ten years the "Later, Longer, Fewer" campaign was in place, women in China went from having six children on average to three.

Many demographers believed this pattern of falling fertility would have continued without the imposition of the one-child policy, a reasonable assumption considering similar fertility trajectories among neighboring Asian nations. After all, China's neighbors also managed to slow population growth — and turbocharge their economies in the bargain — without resorting to such traumatic measures. In roughly the same period of time China's one-child policy was in place, birthrates in South Korea, Taiwan, Singapore, and Thailand also plummeted, from six births per woman to two or fewer.

It is possible that if China had followed the path of these countries, investing in normal family-planning activities, fertility would be almost as low as current levels.

Certainly its people would be happier. "Even an extra 50 to 100 million people wouldn't have made a huge difference," suggested University of Washington professor William Lavely, an expert on China's fertility transition. "It wouldn't have greatly reduced overall welfare, and in fact it may well have increased it, as many families would have been able to have the second child they need. Higher GDP per capita can't substitute for the security and psychic benefits that some families gain from an extra child."

Will China be able to flip the baby switch on as successfully as it turned it off? Recent history suggests not. Asian countries that have tried to boost their population with pro-natal policies have largely failed; Singapore resorted to immigration to refresh its labor force. What China, the world's largest economy by size, decides to do to rectify its future labor shortage will have repercussions beyond its shores.

Despite all this, the various costs and consequences of the one-child policy are so poorly understood that it continues to get plaudits, especially from environmentalists. For years, the Communist Party has asserted that the policy averted between 300 and 400 million births, about the size of the American population. (Such claims are now suspect; some demographers estimate the real number of births averted was probably 100 to 200 million at most. That's a lot, but it's still dwarfed by the Communist Party's pronouncements.) Based on these possibly inflated claims, the venerable *Economist* magazine ranked the one-child policy as one of the most important stratagems to have slowed global warming, more effective than preserving the Brazilian rainforest or improved US emissions standards.

While sheer numbers contribute to carbon emissions, that's hardly the whole story. After all, the United States has less than 5 percent of the world's population but contributes about 15 percent of the world's carbon emissions. China, despite having drastically curbed its population, is still the world's top carbon polluter. The real culprit is the Communist Party's economic-growth-at-any-cost model. This mindset, which led to the imposition of the one-child policy, also prompted Beijing to erect the flimsiest of environmental protection measures. This has probably had a more detrimental effect on global carbon emissions than the number of children born in China.

Even now, the one-child policy has its global supporters. Brazilian environmentalist Charles Clement wrote that all governments should "adopt a one-child policy in some form ... rather than abolishing this policy in China and ignoring its world-wide importance." Prominent Canadian writer Diane Francis advocates "a planetary law, such as China's one-child policy." Berkeley academic Malcolm Potts told me he believes the one-child policy, though painful, yielded important economic benefits and is still "one of the most important social policies ever implemented."

It is worth noting that the system they advocate authorized forced abortions and sterilizations. It raises the question, What are we saving the planet *for?* It is possible to support population control without embracing anything so brutal as a one-child policy.

In writing this book, I have tried to examine the causes that led to this policy, and the wide spectrum of effects it has had on ordinary people's lives. For though China made international headlines by peremptorily moving to a nationwide two-child policy, the one-child policy's side effects will endure for several decades; many still pay a price.

In my quest to find the individual dramas behind the one-child policy, I traveled to "bachelor villages," rural hamlets with no females of marriageable age. I tracked down a former senior family-planning official hiding in an American suburb, who by her own reckoning was responsible for authorizing over 1,500 forced abortions, about a third during late-term pregnancies. I discovered a burgeoning industry that thinks it holds an answer to China's female shortage: custom-made, life-size sex dolls. I spoke to Americans who adopted babies from China, and Chinese who were having babies using American surrogate mothers. I underwent in vitro fertilization (IVF) treatment in a

Beijing clinic and spent time in a Kunming hospice, experiences that shed light on how the one-child policy has affected the most basic of human experiences, life and death.

Against the stark chiaroscuro of China's one-child policy, I would weigh the costs of parenthood and learn for myself the answer to the question, Why do we have children?

The ground moved. That was how it began.

ONE CHILD

After the Quake

Two sorts of errors are absolutely commonplace. The first of these is the idiotic belief that seismic events are somehow "timed" to express the will of God. People will seriously attempt to guess what sin or which profanity led to the verdict of the tectonic plates.

— *Christopher Hitchens*

I

The road to Huimei's school was red.

I blinked, wondering if my mind had conjured this mirage after three hectic days on the road. But there it was: not a comforting earthen red, but a scarlet gash made up of thousands of shredded fireworks, lit to honor the recent dead.

Huimei's mother tottered up the path. Four days before, Tang Shuxiu was working at a Beijing construction site when the building began to sway. Eight hundred miles away, a powerful earthquake was ripping through her hometown, tearing up major cities along the western Sichuan basin and unleashing as much force as the Fat

Man bomb in Nagasaki. Tremors were felt as far away as Bangkok and Bangladesh.

As news of the quake unfolded, Tang dialed home frantically, trying to reach her teenage daughter. There was no answer.

The next day, Tang and her husband, Liu, set off for home. I tagged along, a random reporter they'd met. My presence barely registered except as an extra set of hands to help with their luggage. All those weary miles home, the couple doggedly lugged bags crammed with instant noodles, charcoal cakes, gardening gloves, sanitary napkins, and floral quilts. There were shiny thermos flasks the color of Mao's *Little Red Book,* reams of tissue-thin toilet paper, disposable chopsticks, and a giant pack of cigarettes. Tang even packed a gallon of cooking oil over her husband's objections. Of course, the bottle leaked over everything—our clothes, bags, hands. Toward the end, we were covered with a film of grease, our faces glowing incongruously, like movie stars at a photo shoot.

Now Tang was unceremoniously dumping this precious cargo to race up that red path. Tin mugs and exercise books lay in the rubble of the school grounds, and a basketball hoop swayed at an impossible angle. A notice, written on torn-off exercise paper, said:

> The government has done a lot to save the children of this school.
>
> The government hopes parents coordinate with them to claim the bodies.

Tang and Liu made their way to the edge of the field, to a man with a plastic folder.

I remember her screams when they told her. The sound was a wound tearing open, a sound humans shy away from as instinctively as dogs from the scent of rotting meat. That sound meant, *Game over.*

II

In the beginning, the Sichuan earthquake, China's deadliest in years, was viewed as a simple tragedy. The earth moved, buildings crumbled, and about seventy thousand people died.

In time, I would see it as a devastating illustration of the tragedies of the one-child policy, writ large.

Many people had no idea Shifang, the area near the epicenter, was a test case for the one-child policy. Before the 1980 nationwide launch of the one-child policy, population planners had experimented in Sichuan, in particular Shifang County, using coercive methods to drastically lower birthrates. Scholars believed Sichuan was chosen first because it is the heartland of rural China, home to a tenth of China's people. It was also Deng Xiaoping's birthplace. Whatever the reasons, the methods worked astoundingly well. By 1979 Shifang County's population growth had drastically plunged, and 95 percent of couples there had pledged to have only one child. Sichuan gave China's birth planners "a sense of tremendous possibility" that Beijing could "achieve demographic miracles," wrote population scholar Susan Greenhalgh.

When the quake struck almost thirty years later, some eight thousand families lost their only child in the disaster, according to state-run news agency Xinhua. In Shifang, where over two-thirds of families are single-child families, the quake was said to have wiped out a generation in some villages, local media reported.

This lent a bizarre dimension to the tragedy. Mere weeks after the quake, parents were rushing to reverse sterilizations they had been forced to accept long ago under family-planning rules. They were desperate to conceive a replacement.

Soon after, they were pressured into signing documents pledging to make no trouble. Chinese media were expressly forbidden to write stories about grieving parents and the shoddy school construction that had caused many of these children's deaths. Locals who tried to probe were jailed. Lives were lost, families ruined, and protests steamrolled as Beijing prepared to host the Olympics, just months away.

Although Communist China is theoretically secular, many still believe in omens and portents. People interpret natural disasters as a sign of withdrawal of the mandate of heaven from China's rulers. After all, Mao had died six weeks after the 1976 Tangshan earthquake, ushering in a new era, which eventually led to socioeconomic reforms — such as the one-child policy — that shape today's China.

Some wondered if the 2008 earthquake was a judgment on the one-child policy and other practices that tampered with nature. There was speculation, for example, that the building of massive dams in highly seismic areas might have triggered the quake.

These were precisely the sorts of inferences Beijing did not want. The Communist Party had worked long and hard to ensure that the year 2008 would be associated with another set of omens, ones designed to suggest a glorious future for the Republic.

The 2008 Beijing Olympics was to be a multibillion-dollar event that would mark China's phoenix-like ascent from the ashes of the Opium Wars and the Cultural Revolution. It was no accident the leadership picked the year 2008 to host the Games, nor that they set the opening ceremony date for the eighth day of the eighth month, when the capital city would be at its hottest and most polluted, not at all conducive to peak athletic performance. The number 8 is auspicious, for in Chinese the word sounds the same as the word for fortune. When turned on its side, 8 represents eternity, certainly something any regime would aspire to. Eight is so popular that places with Chinese communities charge a premium for it, from phone numbers to license plates and house numbers. That year, a license plate with the number 18 fetched over $2 million in a Hong Kong auction.

I myself was born on August 8, and Chinese friends never fail to comment on the symbolism of my birthday when they find out. "Wah, you must be so lucky."

All across China, clocks were set on a countdown to the day of the opening ceremony: August 8, 2008, at, of course, 8:08 p.m. May's earthquake, and its attendant baggage, was not going to be allowed to upset this auspicious apple cart.

It was ironic because until the earthquake, the one-child policy had been receding from the news and national discussion.

As the descendant of southern Chinese who'd migrated to Malaysia, I was always grateful I hadn't been born in China. I am the youngest of five daughters, all conceived in hopes of a son that never was. Malaysia was by then too modern for practices such as abandoning unwanted girls, and in any case my parents were educated urbanites, not farmers. Still, my accountant father never ceased regretting his lack of a son, nor reminding his daughters they were liabilities, not assets.

They say *huaqiao* — overseas Chinese families — are more traditional than mainland Chinese, who were forced to abandon or hide the old ways during the Cultural Revolution. It was certainly true of my father's family. "Be glad we're not in the old country," my relatives would say. "*You*'d never have been born." That was my introduction to China's son-loving culture and the one-child policy. As a bookish child, I would come to see the one-child policy as one of the most fascinating and bizarre things about the land of my ancestors, equal parts Aldous Huxley and King Herod.

I certainly didn't anticipate that I would be living and working in China one day. By the time the *Wall Street Journal* posted me to greater China in 2003, the policy was well over two decades old and was by no means as monolithic as outsiders envisioned. Over time, exceptions were made. You could likely have more than one child if you were a farmer, or if you were Tibetan; if you were a fisherman or a coal miner. Or if you were handicapped, or were willing to pay the fines, which ranged from nugatory to wildly exorbitant and depended on whom you knew and where you lived. Given all these exceptions, the one-child policy should more accurately be called the "1.5-child policy," but nobody used such a clunky-sounding term. In China, the term of reference most used is the more anodyne *jihua shengyu,* which means "planned birth program," instead of a more straightforward translation — *yitai zhengce* — of "one-child policy."

Negotiations and rule bending are a way of life — some say art form — in China. To *xiang banfa* — find a solution — is second nature in a place where people are many, resources scarce, and regulations strict but erratically applied. That's why when you live in China you must quickly accustom yourself to full-contact bargaining, line jumping, and creative driving, all part of the *xiang banfa* ethos. Many Chinese *xiang banfa*-ed and came up with all sorts of creative ways to get around the policy — fertility treatments for twins or triplets, birth tourism, fake marriages, bribes. I had Chinese friends who had several children, though usually no more than two. I met a woman in a second-tier city who'd had *six,* all born during the years of the policy. (According to grisly family lore, she'd killed her first by plunging it in boiling water.)

By the time the one-child policy entered its third decade, experts estimated that only about a third of the population faced strict one-child limitations, and it had become increasingly easy for people to afford the fines for a second or third child. By 2013, China's one-child policy was "slipping into irrelevance," wrote my colleague Leslie Chang, a well-respected China watcher.

It would take an earthquake, a miscarriage, and a journey of a thousand births for me to fully realize that curbing China's masses had serious implications beyond its borders.

III

Far from courting irrelevance, the one-child policy had irrevocably shaped the face of modern China and set in motion a host of social and economic problems that will endure for decades.

In fifteen years' time, if you throw a stone anywhere outside of Beijing or Shanghai, statistically speaking, you will probably hit someone over sixty. Chances are high that person will be male, to boot. China's one-child policy so tilted gender and age imbalances that in a little under a decade there will be more Chinese bachelors than Saudi Arabians, more Chinese retirees than Europeans.

Everything in China is about scale and speed. China doesn't just face the prospect of being home to the world's largest number of old people; proportionally, too, its population is aging faster than anywhere else, meaning there will be far fewer working adults to support a retiree population. The speed of this transition will strain China's rudimentary pension and health-care systems. By 2050, pension funding shortfalls could be as much as $7.5 trillion, or equivalent to 83 percent of China's gross domestic product in 2011, according to one estimate by Deutsche Bank.

This is a pretty bleak outlook, and yet the policy's future repercussions may be difficult to reverse. Over the past decade, most people in urban China have accepted the reality of smaller families and, indeed, prefer it. After all, China had leapfrogged from socialism to full-blown capitalism, so costs of services like schooling and health care are relatively high. Throw in things like melamine-tainted milk powder, lead in toys, and lung-searing pollution, and child rearing in urban China becomes quite a daunting proposition.

Besides, authorities had done a good job with messaging: the one-child policy, they insisted, had played an integral part in China's economic resurgence. It seemed churlish not to rejoice in better living standards for a country that had, not too long ago, seen great famine and tremendous political turmoil. This is, after all, my ancestral homeland.

Anyone over the age of sixty in China will have a hardship tale to tell, but one that still sticks in my mind is an anecdote by Chinese journalist Xinran Xue. She once visited a family so poor, they rotated one set of clothing among four children. The rest would lie naked under a blanket, happily dreaming of their turn to "wear the clothes."

China was like a terrier puppy that had been brutally mistreated by history's vicissitudes. It was hard not to cheer a little to see it lick its wounds and limp along gamely. Starting in the late 1990s, there was much to cheer. Children of peasants became the first in their families to enter college. Infant mortality rates fell. Starbucks outlets bubbled up like so many foamy lattes. A veritable fleet of Bentleys, Beemers, Hondas, and Hyundais took to the roads, and local Xinhua bookstores were crammed with travel guides for China's first generation of group tourists.

When my Mandarin teacher excitedly recounted her first trip to Europe, I asked her to name her favorite European country. "Germany," she said promptly. I was surprised. Why not France, Italy? She paused a beat, then said, "It's so orderly."

In 2005, I spoke to a contractor who built dormitories for factory workers. He complained of having to put in more electrical outlets, as workers now had so many gadgets to charge. In 2007, I witnessed the opening of Beijing's first Hooters, or "American Owl" in Chinese. As I eyed waitresses with jacked-up décolletage dishing out overpriced chicken wings, it seemed, strangely, like another milestone had been reached.

People used to joke that a year in China was like a dog year: so much changed that it would be as if seven years somewhere else had passed. In the four years I lived in Beijing, the city's subway lines expanded fivefold. IKEA opened its largest-ever store outside of

Stockholm in Beijing, with extra-wide aisles to accommodate the multitude of first-generation homeowners. The car population quadrupled. Despite the growing pollution and the corruption, it was hard not to feel the quickening excitement, echo the prevailing sentiment: *Jiayou, Zhongguo, Jiayou!* "Go, China, Go!"

It took me a while to realize that, contrary to popular thinking, the one-child policy had very little to do with China's double-digit economic growth of the past thirty years, and will actually be a drag for the next thirty. That the Chinese government's claim that the one-child policy had averted 400 million births was an exaggeration based on faulty math and wishful thinking. Or that the one-child policy was, in the final sum of things, a painfully *unnecessary* measure, since birthrates had already fallen sharply under earlier, more humane measures.

More intriguing are the future effects of the one-child policy on the economy: Could it prove detrimental, stalling future progress? The answer here is: most likely, though how much remains to be seen. Predicting long-term economic growth is a chancy business, and few economists, if any, anticipated that the country's economic rise would be so swift, so spectacular, or so prolonged. Equally, these experts' basis for predicting a future economic slump is the premise that what goes up must, at some point, come down, a prognosis that would perhaps be more useful if we knew when, and by how much.

Clearly, though, a large graying population in China will likely mean a less productive China. It will also mean the China that global companies currently see — world's largest cell phone market, world's largest car market, soon-to-be world's largest luxury sales, home of KFC's biggest customer base even — will change. With the manufacturing boom in its last days, the country is now trying to move to a consumption-driven model of growth, with increased domestic spending and growth in the service sector. A large population of retirees will likely prove as helpful in this transition as the Great Wall was in repelling northern invaders.

There is also a growing body of evidence suggesting that China's population would have fallen significantly — exactly how much is in dispute — even *without* the one-child policy. A family-planning policy that predated the one-child policy, called *wanxishao,* or "Later, Longer, Fewer," had already halved family sizes successfully using less coercive tactics.

In 2009, demographers Wang Feng, Cai Yong, and Gu Baochang challenged the Communist Party's assertion that the one-child policy averted the births of more people than the entire US population. Until then, the 300 to 400 million number had been pretty much taken as gospel truth. It was, and continues to be, a key part of the central government's claim of the global good wrought by the one-child policy. Without the one-child policy, Chinese officials argue, the world would have reached the 7 billion population mark in 2006, instead of five years after. Wang et al. contend that the real number of births averted was probably no more than *half* of what the Communist Party claims.

How did this huge gap occur? They argue that the original calculations used a simplistic extrapolation method that projected what China's future birthrate would be in 1998, based on birth trends between 1950 and 1970. The number arrived at was 338 million, which was subsequently rounded up to 400 million. But this method was flawed. First of all, it was based on the assumption that people's reproductive habits would roughly trend the same from the 1950s to the 1990s, a period when changes such as urbanization, feminism, and advances in infant mortality dramatically altered social behavior. This is patently as absurd as modern-day tour companies drawing up itineraries on the assumption people still travel by steamship. Second, the Communist Party's method counted birth reductions from the 1970s. The one-child policy didn't start until 1980. In Chinese parlance, this kind of misrepresentation is called *zhiluweima* — pointing at a deer and calling it a horse.

Even as the policy loosened up, many were still adversely affected. Yang Zhizhu, a law lecturer in Beijing, lost his job because he had a second child. In 2010, the peppery Yang advertised himself as a slave for anyone who could help him pay the $36,000 fine. "Whoever decides to buy me, I will become their slave and serve them until I die. I reject donations as I don't want to become a parasite for the sake of my child," wrote Yang in his tongue-in-cheek ad. Yang was eventually reinstated at his university, but at a lower position. His wages were garnished, and university administrators took away his spacious university-assigned housing and made him live in a smaller flat. "The policy is just an ingenious way to tax people without giving any kind of service in return. What could be more natural than having children? Might as well tax for breathing and eating," Yang told me.

I met a girl, Li Xue, or "Snow," who spends her days fruitlessly lobbying for the all-important *hukou,* or household registration, that authorities will not allow her because she is an out-of-plan second child. Her parents were laborers who couldn't afford the birth fine. Without a *hukou,* she hasn't been able to attend school, get proper medical treatment, or so much as apply for a library card. Without a *hukou,* Snow is a nonentity, without the ability to legally hold a job or get married. Any future children she might have might also be locked in this limbo. An estimated 13 million people share her predicament as an undocumented *hei haizi,* literally, "black child."

During the summer of 2008, as the country geared up for the Olympics, the fifteen-year-old Snow bravely showed up at Tiananmen Square every morning, holding a sign that said, "I want to Go to School."

She was never there for more than five minutes before being seized by authorities. Tiananmen, the Gate of Heavenly Peace, is one of the most tightly policed places in the world. In 2008's Olympic year, security was tighter than usual. Still, she managed to doggedly show up there all summer long. Sometimes, public security officials would try to grab her just outside her house. There'd be frantic chases as Snow and her motorbike-mounted mother weaved through Beijing's narrow warrens, all in a mad attempt to get to Tiananmen for those brief few minutes.

Her actions filled me with both admiration and exasperation. So much risk, so little yield. It all seemed so valiant, so *futile;* whatever did she hope to accomplish?

"I just wanted someone to notice me," said Snow.

Years later, I met a man who'd had an affair with his teenage co-worker in the factory where they worked. She became pregnant, so he brought her to his village to have the baby. They couldn't legally marry because she was underage, and their baby was born without a birth permit. Later, family-planning officials used this as a pretext to seize the child, who was sold into adoption. This man has now spent the last five years in search of the child, whom he believes is living in an Illinois suburb.

Such were the costs of the one-child policy.

IV

I was on a flight returning from Kunming, the nearest major Chinese city bordering Myanmar. A sour taste of failure was in my mouth, for I'd failed to get a visa into the country. Myanmar was in a news blackout after a cyclone, and they weren't letting in foreign aid workers, let alone journalists of any stripe or color. I flew back to Beijing unaware that the earth was ripping apart thousands of miles under me.

The Sichuan quake measured a cool 8.0 on the Richter scale. This was China's most serious quake since Tangshan, which happened thirty-two years before, measured 7.6, and is accounted one of the world's deadliest disasters. For years, the Communist Party covered up the severity of the Tangshan quake, which happened at the tail end of the Cultural Revolution. State-run news agency Xinhua eventually put the number of fatalities at 250,000.

Nearly every family in Tangshan had a casualty. Every year, on the quake's anniversary, "paper money burnt for the dead is like black butterflies flying low on the Tangshan streets and alleys," wrote resident Zhang Qingzhou. "People are used to this kind of quiet and speechless way of mourning rather than speaking out their sorrows."

Since Tangshan, building standards had improved somewhat, but it was a fair bet Sichuan would have huge casualties. With over 80 million inhabitants, Sichuan is one of China's most populous provinces, with a mountainous terrain that would complicate rescue efforts.

At the Beijing airport, I turned on my BlackBerry and watched in disbelief as dozens of messages scrolled by. My colleagues were already in the air headed to Chengdu, Sichuan's capital.

I stomped to the office, cursing. Why, oh why did I have to return so quickly? If only I'd lingered in Kunming. There's roughly only 400 miles between Kunming and Chengdu, about the same distance as between New York City and Buffalo. I could have *driven* to Chengdu and be reporting now, I fretted.

Meanwhile I banged out a couple of bread-and-butter stories, including one recounting how Chinese citizens were using a newfangled, Twitter-like service called Weibo to report the disaster. It was one of the first instances of citizen journalism in China. Looking back, the piece seems as quaint as a story about ancient drumming techniques.

I cudgeled my brains thinking of other ways to cover the story.

There are a lot of Sichuan migrant workers in Beijing, and just about everywhere else in China. Most Westerners know the province as home of China's cuddly mascot, the panda bear, but the region is also China's Appalachia, poor and populous.

More than half of its natives labor as guest workers, powering factory assembly lines and cleaning crews, the kinds of menial tasks

most urban Chinese no longer want to do. Factory owners and construction crew bosses quickly learn to include spicy Sichuan dishes on
cafeteria menus in order to retain these hardy workers, who are likened to the tiny peppercorns they so love: diminutive, fiery, and with
boundless ability to *chi ku* — eat bitterness.

Since the earthquake, many were frantically trying to return.
What would it be like, I wondered, to have to fight your way across
the quake's wreckage to your remote home? And what would you
find there?

I headed to the railway station.

I spotted Tang first. Her face was a series of *O*s, a smooth oval
face, dark circles under the eyes, her mouth a half circle of misery, lips
chapped and bitten. She was in her best gear: jeans embroidered with
glittery butterflies, a coral satin coat. Railway journeys were a rare
thing for her, and she was observing the formalities by dressing up,
even though she was dizzy with worry.

She hadn't heard from her fifteen-year-old daughter, Huimei.

Tang's husband, Liu Jishu, was a wiry five-footer. He looked a little like a Dutch doll: small, with glossy black hair and round apple
cheeks. It was an immobile face but for his red-rimmed eyes, which
glared with fierce intensity.

Tang and Liu worked on a construction crew in Beijing, roaming
from work site to work site. They were now frantically trying to return home with a group from their village.

The quake had ripped through railways and highways, so it wasn't
clear how far they'd be able to travel, but there was no alternative.
They couldn't afford to fly. Liu sketched out a rough trip scenario
that might include twenty-hour bus journeys, days of hiking and
sleeping in the open, to get to their remote mountain village.

I wavered. How could I keep up with manual laborers on a physically taxing journey? I rang my editor.

"Can't we just hire a car and give them a ride home?" I asked tentatively, already knowing the answer. The journey was the story.

We boarded the train two days after the quake. The third-class compartments were packed. Most slept wedged standing up, or perched on tiny seat barriers. During the Spring Festival period, when the whole country is on the move, sales of adult diapers inevitably shoot up. I could see why, for there was no way of getting to the toilet in this crush. Take a train journey in China, and you will know absolutely, indubitably, that the Middle Kingdom is the most populous nation on Earth.

Liu grinned at me fleetingly as I mashed his toes. *"Ren tai duo,"* he muttered. "China has too many people." I heard that all the time.

Despite the No Smoking sign, Liu puffed away furiously. Tang said little and ate less, sitting stoically as tears crept down her cheeks.

By the third day, she was so dehydrated no more tears flowed. Liu forced sips of tea down her throat, dampening her blouse in big Rorschach blotches. It looked pretty, like a design that was meant to be.

Their story was like that of many other migrant workers. They couldn't make a living farming rice on a tiny patch of land, especially not with their daughter's school fees to pay, so they left and became *liudong renkou* — literally, "flowing population." It's a poetic name for China's migrant workers, who drift from the countryside to the city, going from menial job to menial job. Without the city *hukou* household registration, they cannot access urban social services like schooling and health care. That's why Liu and Tang couldn't bring Huimei with them to Beijing.

The *hukou* is a form of economic apartheid that creates a permanent underclass and prevents the population of China's teeming cities from overflowing to unmanageable numbers. It is also a cleaver that cruelly separates families like the Lius for months on end. Liu and Tang hadn't seen their teenage daughter for more than a year.

When I asked them for a description, Liu couldn't remember if she had long or short hair. What did she like? What was she like? Tang said, vaguely, "She loves to watch TV, but she is a good girl."

There are about eight hundred miles between Beijing and their home village, the formidably named Iron Gourd Village. The distance is in some sense helpful to note — it is roughly equivalent to, say, the distance between New York and Chicago. But economically and culturally, it is like a trip to the moon.

There's no running water in Iron Gourd. No villager has sat on a plane. Everybody under the age of forty eventually makes the trek to a city — any city — forced by poverty or boredom, returning to brag, or breed, or both. Everyone in Iron Gourd is named Liu, or married to someone named Liu. Infanticide and bride buying are things of yesterday and not the distant past, and the spring rains that tunnel through the earthen roads make the place impassable for parts of the year.

And yet the place has beauty, with craggy hills and velvety blue lakes that match the skies above. On days when she coughed black phlegm in Beijing's sooty air, Tang would dream of those faraway blue skies and wonder why she ever left. Life on a work site was even more primitive than life in Iron Gourd. With no washing facilities, you wore the same clothes until you threw them away and bought new, a stunning piece of extravagance she marveled at. They cooked on a smuggled hot plate, drank water from buckets once used for paint. Tang had saved that rose-colored coat in her bedroll — no mean feat as they trudged from work site to work site, everything they owned on their backs — so that she'd have something tangible to show the folks back home, some shiny emblem of their adventures.

Now, as the train chugged homeward, she cursed the curiosity that made her leave. "It wasn't all money," she said wistfully. "We just wanted to go out and have a look."

Now she was mentally flogging herself for leaving Huimei behind. She said, "We all avoided this tragedy. But my baby didn't," again and again, like an incantation.

It was hard to hold a good conversation or build up any kind of rapport. The carriage was crowded, they were worried and disinclined to talk, and their accents were difficult to understand.

I was also ducking in and out of the carriage in an effort to evade railway officials, who found out I was a reporter and forbade interviews. This made Tang and Liu even more stiff and self-conscious.

I had always liked train journeys for the lulling sound of rails, the flashing landscape, and the feeling of being inexorably borne to a certain destination. But this was a prickly ride, sour with tension and fear. Everyone kept their phones by their sides like expert gunslingers, cocked for any new information.

Bit by bit, the news seeped through.

Casualties estimated at twenty thousand. Then thirty thousand. The earthquake's epicenter had occurred in the city of Wenchuan, where some 80 percent of the buildings were destroyed in the first three minutes.

Tremors were still shaking the region. Whole towns were being evacuated.

They were pulling more dead bodies from the rubble than live ones.

Twenty-four hours into the journey, Liu and Tang heard that 183 bodies had been pulled from Huimei's school.

"She's dead," sobbed Tang.

"You can't say that yet," insisted Liu. "You can't say that yet." His eyes glared.

The uncertainty left hope alive. One man sat nearby with an ashen face. He had just gotten a call telling him that his child was dead.

Somewhere between then and Xian the water ran out in the toilets. The rank smell of urine drifted out, mingling with clouds of cigarette smoke.

Liu and I fell into conversation with another villager, Ding Wan-long, who was considered an outsider because he was one of the rare few not born in Iron Gourd. He'd been relocated there after his first home was razed to make way for a dam. Ding was proud because he'd managed to build a second home from money squirreled away from construction jobs in far-flung cities.

"It's a two-story building, very comfortable," he said, puffing a Diamond brand cigarette.

He paused a beat. "I'm going to have to rebuild all over again."

A few hours later, he got a call. The quake had in one stroke orphaned him and made him homeless. His mother was buried in the rubble of his ruined house.

We chugged past Xian, home of the terra-cotta warriors, and were told the rails had been repaired enough for the train to forge on. This was a welcome bit of news, saving the Iron Gourd group a ten-hour bus journey. After the last train stop, we would take a ferry and hike up some hills.

At this point, almost everyone in the group had bad news — some relative killed or maimed, some home wrecked, some both. Tang and Liu had heard nothing from Huimei though.

Liu unbent a little as the trip went on. As we chugged on, sipping beer, he told me about a relative who'd bought a wife. The bachelors of Iron Gourd were finding it hard to find brides. Few women, especially with ever-increasing prospects of factory jobs in cities, were willing to brave the hardships of life in the small village. Years of family-planning policy had also contributed to a staggering gender imbalance. If you had to choose to have a boy or a girl, you chose a boy and gave the girl away, or looked away tacitly while the midwife took care of your problem. So there were almost no young women of marriageable age in Iron Gourd, unless she was your sister or your cousin.

This relative, said Liu, was so lonely and so harangued by his family for his failure to add to the family line that he succumbed to the blandishments of a town matchmaker, borrowing and scrimping for the bride price.

"So, what happened?"

"She ran off, that's what!" he said, chuckling, using his teeth to rip off a beer bottle top.

We laughed, then stopped when a phone rang. Another death was announced.

The train tunneled its way south through Hebei, Shaanxi, and Shanxi, China's heartland, a landscape that looked like it was steeped in tea. Coal dust pollution. For Americans, the car is the American way. Jay Gatsby roars through capitalism, individual freedom, and the good life. For China, the train is the metaphor. Everyone's on board, there's no chance to steer, and it's clickety-clack to collectivism's dream. Years later I was reminded of this reading Dickens: "The power that forced itself upon its iron way — its own — defiant of all paths and roads, piercing through the heart of every obstacle, and dragging living creatures of all classes, ages and degrees behind it, was a type of the triumphant monster, Death."

Once we got off the train, things sped up like one of those montage sequences in the movies. It was a nightmarish dream sequence. Rows of suddenly homeless people sleeping on the streets. Us, hunkering down in line at the ferry terminal as the loudspeakers blared: *We are here to help you. We are here to help you.*

We were boarding the ferry when a woman shrieked. She'd just heard: someone she loved was killed. They carried her on board, stiff as a corpse.

And then we were on the water, chugging past dramatic craggy mountains, Alpine-style scenery.

Tang stared blindly, running through her mind countless scenarios that ranged between hope and despair. In the best scenario Huimei was untouched, though somehow inexplicably unable to reach a telephone or a relative. Then there were the possibilities of injury, memory loss, crushed limbs — painful to a parent, but still tolerable. Or perhaps Huimei was buried in the rubble somewhere, drinking her own urine, calling for her mother in weak croaks.

"There's still hope," counseled Liu. "We don't know anything until we get home," he said.

When we landed, we hiked miles up the mountain. It was there that I began to see the damage the quake had wrought. We clambered past landslides, crushed cars, and caved-in buildings. A group of People's Liberation Army soldiers marched by, shovels on their shoulders.

After seeing Tang and Liu stagger to the hills in search of their daughter's body, I left. In truth, I ran. I ran because I had a deadline. I ran because I thought there was nothing more I could do for them. I ran because I didn't want to be there. I ran, and I will always feel guilty for the unseemly haste with which I abandoned them on that ruined road.

Weeks later, I would try to make reparations by journeying back. I met Liu on top of a windy cemetery. It wasn't where Huimei was buried, for she had been hastily interred in a mass grave not far from the school. Rather, Liu had chosen that spot because its vantage point made it easier to detect the approach of informers and spies.

By this time, authorities were in full cover-up mode. Many children had died in crumbled schoolhouses — called "tofu schools" for the way they'd crumpled under the tectonic onslaught. Scores of parents were calling for a probe of corruption in school construction. They would show up at devastated school grounds, clutching pictures of their dead children — including some of their mangled corpses — calling on authorities to take notice, to investigate, to do something, anything. So the authorities did: they shut the protests down.

Liu didn't look well. The wiry frame that I had seen carry enormously heavy bags with ease seemed shrunken, tentative. He smoked incessantly. Tang wasn't there. She rarely left the house, didn't see anyone, he said.

He asked, "Those pictures you took of us, can you destroy them?"

Reluctantly, I told him we had already run the story.

His face fell.

"Don't worry, most readers aren't even in China," I said hastily.

I didn't tell him the photo I took of him and his wife, looking resolute, had been on the front page of the *Wall Street Journal*.

I remember taking that picture, carefully positioning my camera to capture Tang on the boat, gazing into the distance. She had looked so weary, so hopeful. It was before they reached journey's end.

"We don't want to talk anymore," he said. "We have no words left."

Suddenly, an explosion of sound. We jumped. Peering around the headstones, I saw mourners lighting firecrackers. No matter happy or sad, Chinese ceremonies have a certain similarity. Fireworks explosions precede the birth of babies, weddings, New Year celebrations, and funerals. We exchange money when people are born and when people die. Red packets at birth become white packets at funerals. The same observances give some kind of comforting sameness to the rituals of birth and death, a sense of circularity, of coming home.

Liu showed me a document he'd been forced to sign. It acknowledged he was accepting money for the death of his daughter and absolved officials of culpability.

It said: *I pledge to come back to normal life and normal production as soon as possible.*

A great wave of indignation washed over me.

"So, you see . . ." He shrugged.

He hesitated, turned, and began trudging down the hill, a figure that grew smaller and smaller until it was swallowed by the countryside.

I never saw him again, but his life and mine developed a strange symmetry.

For when I began my journey with them, I had been pregnant.

And the Clock Struck 8/8/08

Being a mother must be the saddest yet the most hopeful thing in the world, falling into a love that, once started, would never end.

— *Yiyun Li,* A Thousand Years of Good Prayers

I

I returned from Sichuan sad and weary. I had covered the aftermath of 9/11, as well as car crashes, assaults, murders — all the other, more ordinary acts of beastliness that humans inflict by design or careless will. Nothing made sense. I was tired of being a professional voyeur. At night, I tossed and turned, dreaming in odd snatches of Tang, Liu, and others I'd talked to.

There was a woman, I remember, who had come to me saying, "See my child, my beautiful, beautiful child." She'd thrust two pictures at me. One was a smiling teenager. The other was a mangled tiny form, unrecognizable. In Sichuan, people colloquially refer to children as *wawa,* the same word as "doll." On and on it floated in my dreams. See my *wawa*. My *wawa* is dead. Can you help me find my *wawa*?

And then, on a hunch, I took out an at-home pregnancy kit.

I couldn't believe it when the pink line showed. I made my husband, Andrew, get another kit. And another.

An hour later we had five sticks, all testing positive.

At first, I was afraid to let myself feel anything but cautious joy. I have polycystic ovarian syndrome, a common but little-understood hormonal disorder that is one of the leading causes of infertility. I'd been diagnosed in my early thirties, and I remember reading about the symptoms with wry disbelief. If you had PCOS bad, you could be *both* hairy and bald, or develop severe acne and yo-yo weight gains.

Until recently I'd been ambivalent about children, uncertain how they'd fit in my peripatetic life. The transition from reporter at a Singapore tabloid to journalist for one of the world's largest newspapers hadn't been easy. To climb the ladder, I'd lived in four cities and three countries within six years. As an ethnic Chinese woman in Beijing, I was constantly mistaken for the secretary, interpreter, or girlfriend of some white foreign correspondent. I remember during an interview with Politburo member Wang Qishan — then mayor of Beijing — he'd shaken hands with my white colleagues, then turned away from my outstretched hand. Doubtless, he thought I was their assistant.

I loved my job, but it was a demanding one, with bosses who woke up in a different time zone just as I was longing for bed. Being a parent requires time, attention, energy. Could I juggle? Yet, at thirty-six, my age and my condition made it imperative I make a decision soon.

Then came the bombshell. Without much engineering, my biological defect appeared to have been overcome. I would finally be having a child, even as I was chronicling the deaths of many. This much unexpected happiness amid misery — it felt obscene.

About a month after the quake, a phosphate miner called Zhu Ji-anming had his vasectomy reversed. His teenage daughter had been killed in the quake, along with two-thirds of her classmates. Strictly speaking, Xinyue — her name means "New Moon" — was not an only child. She had an older brother who had been born mentally handicapped. Because of this, her parents were given permission to have a second child, on the condition that Zhu be sterilized after the second birth. Their son drowned a few years before the quake, leaving New Moon the sum of her parents' hopes and dreams.

New Moon was killed by falling masonry when her school collapsed. Ten days after her death, her grieving parents started thinking of trying for another child. Zhu was fifty, his wife forty-five. They worried it was already too late, but the thought of a childless old age was unbearable. Three weeks later Zhu, having scraped together enough money for the procedure, went under the knife. There wasn't enough money left for Mrs. Zhu to consult a doctor about *her* fertility chances.

Sichuan is one of the few places in China where sterilizations were largely done on men. In most other parts, chauvinism prevails, so it's mostly women who are sterilized, even though doing it on men is easier, faster, and less likely to result in complications. (A village head in Shanxi told me, rather grandly, that he was the first to be sterilized in his village. "I did it to set a good example," he said. Further questioning revealed it was actually his wife who'd had the procedure. "It was me! He'd never have a knife near his male parts," she sniffed.) Why was Sichuan an outlier? Largely because of the efforts of a Chongqing doctor called Li Shunqiang. In 1974, Dr. Li pioneered a surgical technique for vasectomies that is still widely used in many countries. Called the No-Scalpel Vasectomy, it involves using a clamp to puncture the scrotum, instead of the traditional method of making an incision. An American anthropologist who'd seen it done in 1981 in Chongqing described it to me thus: "You take a crochet hook, stick it into the scrotal sack, wiggle it about. It's very quick, about five minutes."

So swift and easy was the procedure, it was sometimes performed in Sichuan's public spaces as an advertisement for family planning. The wide use of this sterilization technique played a major role in making Sichuan the model province for family planning. The talented Dr. Li went on to head Chongqing's Family Planning Research Institute and later retired as a senior family-planning official.

Zhu, who'd had this procedure done years before, was fortunate because doctors were able to successfully reverse the effects. The fertility clinic that had performed the procedure put me in touch with him. I asked a staff member there if they specialized in doing vasectomy reversals. Her answer was a swift and emphatic *no*. There was no money in it. Their clientele were yuppies, many experiencing infertility because of delayed childbearing, like me. They had many cases of clients having difficulties conceiving, having scarred their tubes through multiple abortions. This was an unexpected byproduct of the one-child policy, because many use abortion as a form of birth control. For a nation so open about controlling *one* of the aftereffects of sex, the Chinese were surprisingly prudish when it came to teaching youngsters about the birds and the bees. Fewer than 1 percent of China's schools provide sex education.

The one-child policy regulated births on the assumption that all this procreation was going on between married couples. There was little leeway for underage pregnancy, or unmarried mothers, or women who'd simply gotten pregnant before the official waiting period elapsed. If it didn't fit the rules, the policy's answer was almost always: pay or abort.

I remember once consoling a friend who'd discovered that her husband, who had been her college sweetheart, was cheating on her. They hadn't been married long. "To think I had three abortions because of him," she wailed.

So much of childbearing is a question of timing. With rising infertility, timing became even more crucial. You had to be rich or lucky to battle the forces of time. Zhu certainly wasn't rich. Would he be lucky? I went to meet him in his hometown of Shuanglin, a remote village in an area famed for the towering Leshan Buddha, the world's largest Buddha face. It is carved into a stone cliff overlooking the churning Dadu River.

Built in the eighth century, the serene-looking deity had been miraculously undamaged by the quake, although pollution caused by rapid economic growth had blackened his nose. It also caused the stone curls of his hair to droop.

Driving to Zhu's home, I saw plenty of examples of one-child propaganda. One mural showed a launching rocket and a handsome family trio — father, mother, and child of indeterminate gender — with the slogan, "Late marriage, late childbirth benefit both country and people." Another read, "Fewer births, swifter prosperity."

I met Zhu and Mrs. Zhu at a friend's place. Their dwelling was even more remote and involved a boat crossing, so Zhu picked a friend's more luxurious and accessible home. Unfortunately, there was a power cut, so we spoke in the growing darkness.

Zhu was a small man who swam in his coat, cheekbones sharp as a knife. Mrs. Zhu had a face as sweet and rosy as a persimmon, but her eyes were stricken.

Life in the village was painful. Neighbors and friends avoided them. Mrs. Zhu thought it was because the neighbors feared the now-childless couple would be increasingly dependent, borrowing money, asking for help, and generally being pathetic hangers-on, since "we can never depend on our children now."

Zhu had initially supported the one-child policy. The idea of having fewer mouths to feed was attractive to a man who grew up with memories of hunger. "We ate grass, worms. There was never enough," he said.

There were also other deterrents. In his area, those who violated the policy had to pay almost $150, an unimaginable sum for a newlywed Zhu, who at that time made only a few cents a day as a porter. In Sichuan, porters are called *bangbang jun* — literally, "stick stick army" — for the sticks they sling across their shoulders to balance heavy loads. This job is one of the hardest and poorest paid in the district. As a lowly *bangbang jun,* Zhu could not afford harassment from family-planning officials, who frequently came to the homes of people who broke family-planning rules, smashing things "just to teach them a lesson," he said.

Now they were filled with regret for following the rules, even though they could not imagine how they could have done things any differently.

"When we see some of my former classmates have become grandparents," said Zhu, voice trembling, "it's really hard for us to get through."

The Zhus weren't just emotionally bereft and worried about their future financial security. The loss of New Moon also created a sense of social failure and insecurity. I could easily imagine how they spent their days, sitting in their darkened home, surrounded by increasingly hostile neighbors, feeling vulnerable.

As I was leaving, I kicked myself for not having brought along some small gift. I wanted to give them a small token, some kind of good-luck talisman. I rummaged around in the car, finally coming up with a small packet of biscuits, which I pressed on a bemused Mrs. Zhu. I saw her clutching it in her hand as I waved goodbye. They waved back, two gallant figures.

A few days after the story ran, I received an e-mail from a doctor in America. This woman had undergone fertility treatments and had several fertilized embryos in storage. She offered to give the Zhus one, or several, of her embryos. She didn't know how they would deal with raising a white child in a small Chinese village, she wrote, but would they be interested?

There were too many complications for this strange, generous offer to work, but I, too, wonder what could have been. Medical advances have allowed us to stretch our fertile years beyond what Mother Nature intended, but they are still finite, something the one-child policy does not take into account.

Soon after the following Spring Festival, the Zhus, still childless, left their village in search of work. They changed phone numbers, and we lost touch.

II

All this is very unfortunate, one might say, but how is it the Communist Party's responsibility? It's very sad that so many people died, and so many of them the only children, too — but why should we see this as anything more than a senseless accident?

Which brings me to the Olympics. I see the two events, earthquake and Olympics, as two sides of the same coin. Sichuan and all its connotations — the one-child policy, the ruthless cover-up of the schoolhouse collapses — represent the dark side of China's nationalism. On the other side was the Beijing Olympics, fruit of the country's growth-at-all-costs model, of rebirth after more than a century of humiliation following the Opium Wars.

As a sporting contest, the Olympics were another area where authorities exercised a form of population control designed to bring glory to the country. Indeed, selective breeding to raise more talented humans — a mindset that verges on eugenics — is at the heart of *both* the one-child policy and China's elite sports program.

Chinese authorities were never shy about stating this aim of the one-child policy: fewer births, higher-quality births. In the same vein, leaders of China's Soviet-style sports program informally arranged marriages between athletes, partly to foster the genetic transfer of talent. The success of this would be tested in the crucible of the 2008 Games.

The whole nation was ticking toward August 8, 2008, until, with the flip of a coin, the earthquake reminded us of the dark side of Chinese nationalism and threatened to overwhelm Beijing's carefully orchestrated narrative. China's official machinery swung into action.

Three days after the quake, seventeen bloggers were arrested for circulating "malicious" rumors. Grieving parents were given hush money. Public security officials followed me when I was covering a schoolhouse demonstration, chasing my car and pulling me over. They claimed they were worried about my safety and offered to escort me to a "safer place." I fobbed them off.

Other journalists I knew were detained, harassed, or had their cameras smashed. Huang Qi, a Chinese cyber-dissident who criticized quake relief efforts, was jailed. Liu Shaokun, a schoolteacher, was sentenced to labor camp for a year. Liu had been taking pictures of collapsed schools and questioning the shoddy construction online. Environmentalist Tan Zuoren, who coined the phrase "tofu dreg project" to describe the collapse of the schools in the earthquake, was detained. He served five years in a labor camp.

I began to get phone calls from bereaved parents, telling me they were being threatened and roughed up. I longed to investigate, but I was hamstrung by my pregnancy. Once I knew, I cut back on travel, hoping to wait until I was safely past the first trimester.

I spent those few months in a strange hormonal cocktail of emotions: sadness for all that I had seen, an itch to get back to the stories, joy for the growing child that I hadn't known I could have, and, despite myself, rising excitement as the Olympic machinery swung into gear.

In contrast to Sichuan's chaos, the Olympic show was all about control. Even the skies had to submit to Beijing. To cut down the pollution, the Orwellian-sounding Weather Modification Bureau peppered the sky with rockets laced with silver iodide, making short bursts of rain to wash away the city's ever-present smoky pall.

A forest of fancy buildings, designed by grand architects, few of them Chinese, sprang up. In the years before the Games, all of Beijing was a massive construction site. Thousands of migrant workers like Huimei's parents lived in primitive squalor on work sites, safely hidden from the public by giant billboards saying things like "Olympics for a harmonious society."

Thereafter, the scent of concrete dust would always evoke this city, this period, for me.

Now these billboards were coming down, unveiling elaborate structures like the National Stadium's tangled steel carapace, the opera house's dome, and state broadcaster CCTV's square doughnut of a tower. Locals irreverently dubbed them Bird's Nest, Egg, and Underpants, but for all that, they were awe-inspiring monuments, built with great ingenuity and human cost.

Underpants Tower, for example. It didn't look like any other building I had ever seen and was an architectural contradiction: a square building that somehow looked aggressively phallic. Perhaps it was because one of its sections — basically, the Underpants's crotch — jutted 250 feet into nothingness.

It was an engineering marvel. They built the two gargantuan legs first, then, like some mythic love story, united the towers at dawn. (Engineers prosaically explained this prevented the sun's heat from distorting the steel and creating structural instabilities.) Underpants's design had been a prizewinning entry in a competition, praised by one of the judges for its "fearless, can-do spirit" that appeared to represent the New China.

Yet it was impossible to escape the fact that Underpants was also the grandest propaganda office in the world. Pulitzer Prize–winning critic Inga Saffron blasted architect Rem Koolhaas for giving China's

TV monopoly "the architectural equivalent of a bomb." The tower's size and structure, she wrote, would "always remind you of how small you are, and how big the state."

I remember interviewing those who'd been evicted for Underpants's erection. They had lived in low-rise redbrick buildings, mostly empty by the time I visited. All the windows had been smashed, some etched with messages like "Want human rights." Many apartment dwellers complained they were given inadequate compensation and forced to move. One woman recounted how she'd returned from a trip to find her apartment padlocked, her belongings cast to the ground four stories below. She was so distraught she tried to jump down herself, only to be saved — and subsequently jailed — by local police.

A multitude of mistranslated English signs that had been part of the city's crooked charm disappeared, replaced by irreproachably boring and correct translations. "Dongda Anus and Intestine Hospital" became the uninspiring "Hospital of Proctology." "Racist Park" transformed into "Park of Racial Minorities." No longer would the handicapped be forced to seek "Deformed Man" toilet cubicles. Millions of cars were kept off the roads, factories ordered to stop production. Even the city's arid beige grass was spray-painted emerald green.

While this was going on, I went for my first pregnancy checkup. The technician bustled in and rubbed lotion over my still-flat stomach.

"What's that — *oh!*" said my husband, gazing at the heartbeat, pulsing so strongly. It was impossible not to feel excited. We clutched hands, as excited as little children at the beach. Despite myself I started running through possible names, picking out books I would read, stories I would tell, to that pulsing peanut. Seeing the heartbeat made it real.

"Soon you will know the sex," she said cheerfully.

I knew she wouldn't be telling me this if I were a Chinese national. To prevent sex-selective abortions, medical staff are prohibited from revealing the gender to expectant parents. Of course, you can get around it. I might make oblique hints, give a red packet "donation," perhaps be handed a pink sweet, or a blue. The physician might cough, signifying a girl, or nod, for a boy. That is how things work when the state regulates your womb.

III

The narrative that China's leaders wanted — China's coming-out party, China's global ascendance — was taking over.

Beijing city was setting up invisible cordons to prevent troublemakers from ruining the party. That included bereaved quake parents who tried to make it to the capital to petition authorities for justice, a time-honored tradition. Unfortunately, most were detained long before they made it to the city. They were escorted off trains or banged up in detention cells. Some were even billed for the cost of their meals and lodging while locked up.

Some parents who'd tried to take a tour to nearby Kunming ended up being shadowed the whole time by public security officials. "They can't even let us take a holiday in peace," said one father, bitterly. Another said, "My child is dead. Heaven agrees I have a right to scream and shout, but this government, it thinks it is bigger than heaven!"

The count ran down. Thirty days. Twenty-one days.

Online rumors began floating about the Beijing Olympic mascots — Teletubby-like creatures — hinting they represented coming disasters for China. Jingjing, the panda, stood for the Sichuan earthquake. Huanhuan, the flame, and Yingying, the Tibetan antelope, symbolized the Olympic global torch relay, which had been beset by protests over China's crackdown in Tibet. Nini, the swallow, was linked to a plague of locusts from Inner Mongolia.

The mascots were collectively dubbed *fuwa* — "good-luck dolls" — but online wags took to calling them *wuwa* instead — "witch dolls."

Censors, of course, quickly shut this down.

Fourteen days. Ten days.

I was in the hospital for my official first-trimester checkup. My doctor was reassuring. "You're past the hump," he exclaimed cheerily. He passed a transducer lightly over my belly, frowned, did another pass.

"Never mind, you'll see it all better when you do the scan," he said, and smilingly sent me down to Radiology.

After gazing at the monitor, the man in Radiology bit back an exclamation.

"Who's your doctor?" he demanded. He left abruptly.

I clutched Andrew's hand.

They told me the heartbeat — the same one that I had seen pulsing so strongly a few weeks earlier — had stopped. I hadn't felt it, hadn't known.

Game over.

Later, in my bedroom, I heard the same sort of choking cries I'd heard from Tang. How odd, I thought, before realizing it was me.

Eight days.

I was in the hospital for a D&C. The next day, I was back at work. I was going to act like it had never happened. What happened to me was just a small taste of what happened to the parents in Sichuan. The dream had ended, that was all. Morning had come.

Despite my best efforts, the guilt bubbled up. Did I hurt the pregnancy by traveling to a seismic zone? Carrying heavy bags? Looking at dead bodies? Or maybe it was breathing the polluted Beijing air, or riding a bicycle . . . I told myself sternly not to be irrational. Miscarriages are common in the first trimester. Still, the little voice remained. *Your fault, your fault. See what you did to your* wawa.

Zero days.

The opening ceremony was held at the Bird's Nest Stadium, the world's largest steel structure and very likely its largest folly too, for after the Games the costly building would serve almost no practical purpose. To cut costs, they scrapped plans to build a retractable roof. With no cover, the stadium would be too hot or too cold most of the year.

On this day, the air smelled of rain, and we nervously fingered the rain ponchos placed inside our Olympic grab bags. The Weather Modification Bureau had deployed twenty-six control stations to fend off rain clouds before they got to the Bird's Nest.

With temperatures in the nineties, the Bird's Nest was more like a wok. Everyone — China's Politburo, George W. Bush, and David Beckham — was cooking. Raising my binoculars, I zoomed in on athletes on the field, picking out seven-footer Yao Ming. Sweat stains bloomed all over his scarlet blazer. The basketballer had walked in to thunderous applause with an adorable nine-year-old. Lin Hao, a quake survivor, had pulled two classmates from the rubble. Two-thirds of his classmates had been killed.

Of the two, it was really Yao whose existence said more about the one-child policy and what might have been. Born in 1980, Yao belonged to the first generation affected by the policy. He was the eleven-pound child of towering basketball players. Spotting his potential early on, sports officials fruitlessly lobbied for Yao's parents to be given an exemption to the policy. They'd wanted more Yao champions.

Increasingly sports recruiters complain that Chinese parents are reluctant to subject their precious one-and-only to this system, where young athletes are plucked away from their families and relentlessly drilled. Looking at the parade of athletes, I thought it was funny that the one-child policy could eventually spell the end to this sports system.

One Olympic gymnast told my colleague her meal portions were so tiny, "it was like cat food." She said, "I never realized until I traveled overseas that other athletes did this for *fun*." Guo Jingjing, known as the "Goddess of Diving," suffered from extremely poor eyesight, a common condition among China's elite divers, who start high-impact diving before their eyes are fully developed.

Yao himself believes the one-child policy fostered selfishness, a lack of trust, and "may be one reason why we struggle in team sports." Certainly the Chinese have a sporting inferiority complex because, although they periodically win medals in Ping-Pong, diving, and gymnastics, they don't fare as well in commercial sports like soccer and basketball.

Sports insiders call this the "Big Ball, Small Ball," theory, arguing that China can do well only in sports that emphasize precision and mechanization — "Small Ball" — but not in sports that need creativity and teamwork — "Big Ball." Beyond sports, it's become a metaphor for everything from China's education system to its economic prowess.

On this night, it was clear China was gunning for Big Ball status.

I was live-blogging the opening ceremony and trying not to think about miscarriage, or children, or the earthquake, which had all linked in my mind to become one giant lump of misery. I thought the Olympics, with its relentless push to celebrate China's glory and bury the history of its excesses, would be a good venue.

But even here, it was impossible to escape reminders.

Take the venue itself. Ai Weiwei, China's most famous dissident artist, likened to Warhol, had been a consultant on the Bird's Nest design. He ended up disavowing his role in its creation, saying the Chinese government had turned the Olympics into a sham.

Ai had gone to Sichuan ten days after the quake to film the disaster and was a vocal critic of the school collapse cover-up. Later on, he tried to create a database of the names of all the children killed in the quake. For his efforts, he was beaten, detained, and slapped with a $2 million fine for unpaid taxes.

At 8:08 p.m., the show began in a deafening burst of fireworks, floating fairies, spacemen, and synchronized tai chi performers. There were 2,008 cherubic children, representing China's different tribes. It was all a lavish spectacle choreographed by Zhang Yimou, who had once been persona non grata for making films with themes critical of the regime. In recent years the director had toned down and was now considered safely rehabilitated. Detractors now called him China's Leni Riefenstahl.

Zhang had certainly pulled out all the stops, with set pieces giving spectators a quick romp through five thousand years of Chinese culture, touching on the Silk Road and Great Wall. In one set piece, the word *harmony* blazed brightly.

An angelic little girl sang the popular "Ode to the Motherland": "Our future is as bright as ten thousand radiating light beams."

A giant globe rose from the floor of the stadium. Was this China's Big Ball moment? Balanced on top, a Medusa-locked Sarah Brightman kicked off with syrupy sweetness, singing the Olympic theme song "You and Me": "... from one world ... we are one family ..." The lyrics are overwhelmingly banal.

I dashed away a tear. How absurd! To be moved to tears by Sarah Brightman!

And then, my heart broke.

IV

Nothing was what it seemed.

Those 2,008 children representing China's tribes? They were all Han Chinese.

That little singer? She was lip-syncing, a last-minute replacement because the actual singer wasn't considered pretty enough.

The fireworks viewers saw on their TV screens? Computer-generated imagery.

Zhang, the ringmaster, would fall from grace for violating the one-child policy after online rumors floated that he had sired several children. Family-planning officials ended up slapping a $1.2 million fine on him. The man who orchestrated China's biggest show would end up the man with the biggest fine in the history of the one-child policy.

China's coming-out party did mark the country's ascendance as a global superpower, especially after the Lehman Brothers collapse on Wall Street a few months later, which set in motion a chain of events that underscored America's shaky economic status. But far from displaying a can-do, fearless spirit, China would become increasingly paranoid about maintaining control, clamping down on media and displaying increasingly territorial behavior with its neighbors.

A few months after the Olympics, activists unveiled Charter 08, a manifesto advocating reform along democratic lines. China responded by jailing one of its authors, Liu Xiaobo. In 2010, Liu was awarded the Nobel Peace Prize but was unable to collect it since he remains incarcerated.

Influential Tsinghua University academic Sun Liping wrote, "The Olympics marked a beginning, it can be said, of the stability preservation regime in China. Looking back now, it might be said that the Olympics were something we did that we ought not to have done."

V

Six years later, I arrived in Anren, a little town southwest of Chengdu. Anren is a fairly prosperous-looking little place, with an expensive prep school and lots of new buildings imitating the old Chinese style, with curved sloping roofs, just like in kung fu movies. Signs indicated a Four Points Sheraton was imminent.

Anren is the pet project of Fan Jianchuan, a real estate tycoon and history buff. In a country that has institutionalized the art of collective forgetting, Anren is a chimera. Fan has built a Xanadu of museums documenting modern Chinese history. All in all, there are fifteen museums, spanning the period from the Japanese Occupation to the Cultural Revolution — the touchy bits that have been mostly excised from other, more orthodox collections in the country. (Beijing's National Museum, the world's largest museum, has room for only three lines of text alluding to the ten-year Cultural Revolution.)

I went to Anren because it boasts two museums on the Sichuan earthquake. I was curious to see how they have memorialized the event. It is always a source of frustration to me that Chinese museums, stuffed with so many exciting artifacts from five thousand years of civilization, are mostly curated by a clutch of didactic, prosy bores with no sense of drama or storytelling. Would this be the same?

At first, it seemed that propaganda was going to win the day. One building was stuffed with dioramas, diagrams, and pictures praising the government's swift response to the quake. Beijing's swift response was admittedly praiseworthy — especially contrasted with the Bush administration's Katrina response — but it all made for dull viewing.

Statistics were offered up, as numbing as Sichuan peppercorns:

Confirmed deaths: 69,226.
Injured: 374,643.
Missing: 17,923.
Roads damaged: 53,295 km.

The quantities of water conduits and power lines damaged in the quake were recounted to the exact kilometer, but nothing was said about the number of children killed in the quake, or school buildings destroyed.

I was strolling around the museum compound, flagging, when I saw a sign: TOUGH PIG. It was next to a pigpen, purportedly the home of the quake's most famous porcine survivor. Zhu Jianqiang, or "Tough Pig," was a hardy hog that survived under the earthquake rubble for thirty-six days without food and water. I was just wondering if this was the actual pigpen, transported to the museum, when a perfect chorus of shrill grunts burst out behind me.

There was Tough Pig himself, a huge creature strolling the grounds majestically. He was a massive dirty gray animal, easily dwarfing his keeper. Judging by the alacrity with which people whipped out their cameras, it was definitely a case of four legs good, two legs bad. Hands down, Tough Pig was easily the most popular exhibit I had seen so far.

Tough Pig had been castrated before the quake, but in 2009 scientists used his DNA to clone six piglets, hoping to study whatever genetic markers he might have that made him so hardy. Even the swine hero of Sichuan could not escape the long arm of family planning. Of course, unlike humans, he was encouraged to multiply. Four legs good, two legs bad.

Behind Tough Pig's pen was an annex.

Here, at last, were the real reminders of the quake, as poignant as Pompeii. There were clocks permanently stuck at 2:28 p.m. There was half a shoe and the ripped remains of a bridal veil, from newlyweds who perished when disaster struck.

There was a red motorcycle, used by a man to take his dead wife home. He'd lashed her two-day-old corpse to him for their last ride.

There were murals from Shejiantai, a village famous for producing painted New Year pictures — called *nianhua* — since the Song dynasty. These *nianhua* are hand-painted pictures of chubby, rosy babies frolicking around carps, peaches, and peonies, all symbols of plenty. It was a sort of rural, more durable version of Hallmark. People put *nianhua* up at the start of the New Year as a way of bidding goodbye to the past and welcoming the future. Shejiantai had been completely destroyed in the quake, though was later rebuilt.

The saddest exhibits were artifacts from the collapsed schools, all conveying an unspoken message of time stopped, life quenched in medias res. Among battered school desks, badminton rackets, backpacks, and Ping-Pong paddles, there was a copy of a seventeen-year-old's diary. The last entry was dated a week before the quake: "Today the midterm report came out. It's bad, it's bad . . . I am so sad. How come I am so useless? How come I didn't really study hard, spend time reviewing? I'm sorry Father. Really, truly, sorry."

From Xuankou Middle School, there are handwritten menus laying out meals for the week. On Monday, the students lunched on pig head in spicy oil, shredded potatoes, and cauliflower with ham. On Tuesday, they had stir-fried pork and lettuce. Many were having a post-lunch siesta when the quake struck. A third were killed.

I was strongly reminded of the Holocaust Museum in Washington, DC, where a haunting display of thousands of old shoes from victims brings home the tragedy in a way no statistic could. There is very little narration in Anren's quake museum — I suspect to avoid censorship — but the voices are nonetheless strong.

The pièce de résistance is an air shaft entirely covered with black-and-white pictures of parents, who are in turn holding pictures of their dead children. This picture-within-picture is blown up, replicated, and pasted onto all four sides of the narrow shaft, which stretches upward.

Standing there, I was surrounded on all sides by mourners. My eye was drawn upward, a portrait of loss stretching into infinity, pressing down on me. It was hard to breathe.

I had not thought to see this remembrance in China. So many horrors have happened in modern Chinese history, people have become polar opposites of the citizens of Gabriel García Márquez's fictional Macondo, who are chained to nostalgia. In China, they are chained to forgetting. Radio journalist Louisa Lim called her book on the 1989 Tiananmen Square massacre *The People's Republic of Amnesia.* On the twenty-fifth anniversary of the Tiananmen Square killings, Internet censors busily excised even the word *nostalgia.*

At the Anren museum, there were reminders everywhere of the importance of the family—witness all those *nianhua* pictures. You could see how children represented so much in rural China. Not just love, but economic security, societal acceptance, affirmation that life holds meaning.

When the earthquake happened, there was no real way to describe parents who lost their only child. The term *shidu* had not yet come into popular usage, but it surfaced in later years. *Shidu* comes from the words *shi*—"lose"—and *du,* or "only." Sichuan's parents became one of the earliest examples of the *shidu* phenomenon, a by-product of the one-child policy.

By 2014, there were an estimated 1 million *shidu* parents, and an additional 76,000 set to join their ranks yearly. They had become a loose-knit organization, commiserating among themselves and petitioning Beijing for higher compensation, priority in adoptions, as well as plans that cater to their specialized pension, medical, and burial needs.

Shidu parents say the death of a child—if it is your only one—is, in the Chinese context, by far a greater and deeper injury than the loss of one of several children. This truth is unpalatable to Western ears—as though a child's death could be anything but ruinous and painful for any parent!—but with no progeny, *shidu* parents have trouble getting accepted into nursing homes and buying burial plots. They are also more financially vulnerable than ordinary retirees, and more prone to depression, studies show. Everything in Chinese society is geared toward marriage and family. Even if the government limited you to one child, you are still a parent, like almost everyone else you know. The unmarried and the childless are very low on the societal totem pole.

That was why Zhu Jianming had gone out just three weeks after New Moon's death for a reverse vasectomy. That was why his voice had trembled when he thought of the lonely years ahead. There are no Florida retirement homes, no colonies where you can lose yourself in craftwork or good works or composing poetry, for a man of his background and income.

I read an Internet post once by a retiree who'd lost his only child. He didn't want to move into a retirement home. He couldn't face weekends, when the halls would fill with visiting family.

The Sichuan earthquake was not just a tragedy caused by a natural disaster. Like the shadowy outlines of the kraken beneath the sea, it showed the tragic proportions of that great *un*natural disaster, the one-child policy.

Cassandra and the Rocketmen

It is a very good thing that China has a big population. Even if China's population multiplies many times, she is fully capable of finding a solution; the solution is production.
— *Mao Zedong*

I

After fifteen hours on a very slow, very old train, followed by a bone-jolting bus ride, I stumbled bleary-eyed into Yicheng.

It didn't look worth the trip. Yicheng is a dirty little place in landlocked Shanxi, coal country with smog levels that are appalling even by China's standards. It's the kind of place even KFC and Starbucks wannabes don't bother with. Yicheng has pretty parts, but they were all blanketed by the fug of pollution. When I drove to the hills flanking the city, I found cave dwellers living in quaint, Hobbit-like splendor, and fields of sunflowers, their great golden heads drooping, exhausted, in the dust.

Yicheng's locals joke that it is so named—"City of Wings"— because everybody wants to fly away to bigger, cleaner places. But

Yicheng's name also has another meaning for those interested in population studies. It provides a vision of a China that never took flight.

For over a quarter of a century, Yicheng and several other rural counties were part of a secret experiment. They were zones where, with remarkably few conditions, residents could have two children. For example, while many rural parts of China allowed couples a second child if their first was a girl, only in Yicheng and a few other places could residents have two children regardless of gender.

Overall, these secret two-child zones affected roughly 8 million people in the time since their creation in 1985 — a drop in the bucket for China. Nonetheless, they offer a tantalizing glimpse of the road not taken by family planners. With fewer restrictions, people in these counties were not driven to resort as much to infanticide or sex-selective abortions for unwanted daughters. Today, Yicheng and its sister counties have gender ratios that are closer to global norms. Birthrates are also below the national average. The two-child allowance also made enforcement of birth quotas — always an unpopular task — easier for Yicheng's officials. "We didn't have to use force. We could hold our heads high and live in peace with our neighbors," said village chief Huang Denggao.

Years later in their fight to overturn the one-child policy, a group of demographers would hold up Yicheng as an example of a future China. In doing so, they would also throw into prominence the man behind the Yicheng experiment, Liang Zhongtang. Liang, a little-known economics instructor, holds the distinction of being publicly the only vocal critic of the one-child policy at its inception over three decades ago.

In a seminal population conference in Chengdu, held just a few months before the one-child policy's 1980 nationwide launch, Liang warned that the policy would be a "terrible tragedy," leading to a "breathless, lifeless society without a future."

He foresaw an aging population with little familial support and coined the phrase "4:2:1" — now commonly used — to refer to the situation where two adults would have to support four elderly parents and one child. "Simple though it was, this numerical figure served as a powerful rhetorical device," wrote scholar Susan Greenhalgh.

I met the Cassandra of China's one-child policy one blustery autumn day at his apartment in Shanghai's Hongkou university district. The wind was whistling mournfully around his top-floor, book-lined eyrie, an appropriate setting for the unsung hero of China's population movement. Liang was now a retiree, an erect, silver-haired figure with a distinctly tart edge to his tongue.

Some of China's current crop of demographers eventually came around to Liang's way of thinking, calling him "hero" and "national treasure" for his prescience. Liang, however, sees his role as small, his resistance nothing compared to the force of the one-child policy. "I don't think I meant anything," said Liang, who, in all our conversations, would frequently describe his efforts as "useless" and "a waste of time."

Year after year, Liang was unable to persuade Beijing to adopt his two-child proposal nationwide. Nonetheless, he was able to interest reform-minded party elders like Hu Yaobang and Zhao Zhiyang to allow the series of experimental two-child zones. As a result, thousands born in these places owe their existence in some part to Liang.

Liang said wryly, "It's much more helpful than just sitting here doing nothing," adding, "It's better doing it as a demographer than a peasant." He was both.

One of six children born to peasant farmers, Liang finished high school in 1966, intent on studying philosophy at Beida, or Peking University, China's premier higher-education institute. The year 1966 was a bad time to hold such ambitions, for that was of course the year Mao launched the Cultural Revolution. The Great Helmsman closed all schools and launched his Red Guards on a decade-long war against intellectuals.

Liang lost his chance for higher education and never regained it — a factor that would count against him when he tried to get China's family planners to take his proposals seriously. He became a soldier, whiling away his years in the People's Liberation Army, teaching himself political theory and devouring Marx and Engels. Eventually, he ended up as an instructor at a local party cadre school in Taiyuan, Shanxi's provincial capital. In the late 1970s, he was asked to teach demography, a subject he initially knew little about and initially had no interest in.

The study of demography — and, indeed, of all social sciences — had been viewed with suspicion and removed from university curriculums after the Cultural Revolution. Demography as a subject was revived only after China was restored as a permanent member of the United Nations General Committee, and the Chinese Association for Population Studies was founded only in 1981 — a year after the launch of the one-child policy.

In the early days, said Liang, China employed a system learned from the Soviet Union, which focused on productivity and economic statistics, without (as Western countries did) incorporating social and economic elements. China's demographers did not even know how to construct life tables — projections of life expectancy, considered essential to the field — until the early 1980s.

In 1980, when Beijing decided to impose drastic population curbs, leaders still weren't sure how many people there were in China. The country's last population count had been fifteen years before and had provided "only rather crude numbers," according to population scholar Thomas Scharping. It seemed incredible to me that China launched the world's most ambitious demographic experiment on such a shaky foundation. In retrospect, I asked Liang, was this not a little like a definition I'd once read of a critic: "a legless man teaching running"?

True, Liang said. "But you have to remember, at that time there was a sense we were drowning in people, and we would never stop being poor unless we did something. *Ren tai duo.*" Too many people.

Ancient civilizations like China and India have long been populous. In the 1200s, the prosperous lakeside city of Hangzhou was the world's largest, with 1.5 million inhabitants. It dazzled the Italian traveler Marco Polo, who came from that relative backwater known as Venice.

But population growth in the latter half of the twentieth century was unprecedented, thanks to medical advances that pruned infant mortality rates and lengthened life spans. In China, population growth took a great leap forward from 540 million in 1949 to over 800 million twenty years later. Another ten years and Monty Python was singing, "There's nine hundred million of them in the world today / You'd better learn to like them, that's what I say."

China had been practicing population curbs in fits and starts since the 1950s, mainly through legislating early marriage, as well as distributing condoms and IUDs. In the 1970s, it ramped this up in earnest with the "Later, Longer, Fewer" (*wanxishao*) campaign which encouraged couples to marry later, space out their childbearing, and have fewer children altogether. The propaganda slogan of the time was "One child isn't too few, two are just fine, three are too much."

Almost all population scholars agree that "Later, Longer, Fewer" was a huge success in curbing China's soaring numbers. In that decade, the average woman in China went from having six children to three. Such stunning results could not have been achieved without some level of coercion, of course, but nothing near the kind inflicted during the one-child policy years. So why didn't authorities stick to "Later, Longer, Fewer" instead of ramping up?

Politics was key to this decision. Mao's death in 1976 led to a power struggle. The country struggled to get back on its feet after disastrous policies like the Great Leap Forward and the Cultural Revolution. New leaders like Hua Guofeng, Hu Yaobang, and Deng Xiaoping needed to shore up their legitimacy and steer the demoralized population onward and upward. They staked their legitimacy on providing economic revitalization, and the decade-long *wanxishao* was felt to be too slow for turbocharged growth.

The logic of curbing births was fairly simple: to grow its per-capita GDP quickly, China would have to raise output and slow down population growth. The latter was obviously easier to do than the former.

Deng set a goal of quadrupling China's per-capita GDP to $1,000 by the year 2000. Working backward, population planners calculated that China could not reach this goal with a two-child policy and needed to tighten restrictions to a one-child-for-all policy. That, in essence, was how the one-child policy came about: an arbitrary economic goal that altered the course of millions of lives.

By the time the year 2000 rolled around, China's population had edged past the 1.2 billion goal by only 60 million. Not too bad, considering per-capita GDP had more than tripled past Deng's original $1,000 mark. Even so, authorities continued to stress the need for maintaining population controls. "Economic development is like a cake," said the head of the National Population and Family Planning Commission. "We need to slow down the growth of the number of people eating the cake."

Liang was not the only one to foresee the kinds of problems the one-child policy would lead to: aging, son preference, a vastly diminished work force over time. But those bent on pushing the policy brushed these issues off as things that could be easily fixed. Song Jian, a scientist whose calculations were instrumental in the one-child policy's implementation, publicly dismissed these concerns. In a 1980 article he made vague reference to scientific developments that could easily avert the aging issue before it became a serious problem "in the distant future" and suggested authorities could "adjust women's average fertility rate in advance" to keep population growth stable.

If Song's prognostications on the human condition seem incredible — aging and fertility dialed up or down, like levers on a machine — perhaps it is because his area of expertise *was* machines. Specifically, rockets.

How did a rocketman become involved in determining how many babies women in China could have? To answer that, we have to look at the peculiar set of circumstances that birthed the policy, both within and without the Middle Kingdom.

II

Born in haste, dragging on past its sell-by date, China's one-child policy was never meant to last forever. When it was launched in 1980, China's leaders promised these painful family restrictions would be temporary. "In thirty years, when our current extreme population growth eases, we can then adopt a different population policy," read the announcement from the Communist Party Central Committee.

In fairness, Chinese leaders were not alone in their fears of a population time bomb. It was an idea du jour of the 1960s and 1970s, like bell-bottoms and est therapy. After World War II, population numbers had crept up everywhere, not just in China. People made love, not war, and babies, predictably enough, followed. Conservationists and ecologists began sounding the famine alarm.

In 1968, Stanford professor Paul Ehrlich's unlikely bestseller, *The Population Bomb,* dramatically proclaimed that "the battle to feed all of humanity is over," and "hundreds of millions of people will starve to death." No preventive measures would avert "a substantial increase in the world death rate," wrote Ehrlich.

In 1969, the United Nations launched the UNFPA, or Fund for Population Activities (renamed the United Nations Population

Fund in 1987), with the objective of curbing population growth in third-world countries.

In 1972, the Club of Rome, an organization of prominent academics and politicians, published *The Limits to Growth,* which, like *The Population Bomb,* argued that economic growth was ecologically unsustainable. Using Massachusetts Institute of Technology computer simulations, the Club of Rome came up with several scenarios gaming out the distribution of global resources among the world's hypothetical population. Most predictions were gloomy, and some expected global collapse around the mid- to end of the twenty-first century.

The battle to control global population — particularly those darker-skinned bits of it — kicked into high gear, with a significant amount of Western aid funneled to population control activities.

For a brief period, India had a forced sterilization program, an unpopular move that led to Indira Gandhi's ouster (though she later regained power); South Korea had a "Two's Too Much" campaign, and near me, even the tiny island nation of Singapore — whose population today is smaller than New York City's — had a "Stop at Two" campaign. As a child, I grew up with stories of those propaganda drives. One poster, I remember, featured many hands reaching for one loaf of bread.

This was the world into which China emerged after a decade of isolation following the Cultural Revolution. It was in a unique position. While places like India and Indonesia also imposed population curbs, only China had both the authoritarian political structure and the social and cultural readiness to push through these ideas on a grand scale. While Western scientists like the Club of Rome were expounding theories of population control as intellectual exercises, Chinese scientists were prepared to put these ideas into practice on a *real* population, with few to no fail-safe mechanisms.

The country had been so beaten and demoralized, its intellectual capital so sapped by the Cultural Revolution, the idea of rationing children, in the same way coal and grain were rationed, made sense.

There was also no adequate political mechanism for those affected to signal their outrage when the full brunt of the one-child campaign kicked in — unlike in India, for example. China also had no deep-seated religious beliefs on birth control or abortion to root out.

In retrospect, the country was fertile ground for reducing fertility.

There is evidence that some Western ideas on population reduction found root in Chinese soil. In 1975, Song Jian joined a Chinese delegation to the Netherlands, where he met a young Dutch mathematician called Geert Jan Olsder. "He seemed like a regular guy, very friendly," recalled Olsder, who is still bemused, years later, by his inadvertent role in China's population movement. Over beers that day, Olsder told Song about a paper he'd cowritten. It laid out a problem: how to prevent overpopulation on a fictional island. Olsder and his colleagues had come up with "an elegant mathematical solution," which he recounted to Song.

"In hindsight, he seemed to perk up at this point," said Olsder. "His eyes lit up."

Olsder thought he was talking to a fellow academic. He had no idea Song was one of China's super-scientists, an elite band whose military work had protected them during the Cultural Revolution, when all other intellectuals had suffered greatly. After the Revolution, they were virtually the only technocrats who emerged with their intellectual and social capital intact.

The Russian-trained Song was a ballistics missile specialist and a special protégé of Qian Xuesen, the brilliant cofounder of NASA's Jet Propulsion Lab, who had quit the United States in disgust after several humiliations during the McCarthyite Communist witch-hunts. Qian, of course, was welcomed by China with open arms. He went on to lead China's rocket program and mentor acolytes like Song, who would play a major role in the one-child policy rollout.

Through Qian's patronage, Song was given access to top-level political-military leaders. Over the next few years, he and colleagues Li Guangyuan, Yu Jingyuan, and Tian Xueyuan would use Olsder's and other European scholars' research as a basis for creating a formula for controlling China's birthrate. Unlike Olsder, they did not view this merely as an intellectual problem. They sought real-world application.

Song and company's mathematical formulas would clash with Liang's human-centric proposals at the 1979 population control symposium in Chengdu.

III

The Chengdu conference was a milestone, for this was when various academics unveiled their proposals for how to curb China's masses. It's unclear at this point how it shaped the events that followed. While some historians believe the conference marked a turning point that weighed decisively in favor of the missile scientists' radical one-child proposal, others believe Communist leaders had already locked in their decision at this point, and Chengdu was just so much scholastic sound and fury. But the discussions at Chengdu showed that alternative points of view existed. The one-child policy was not the only solution on the table, though it was the most extreme.

A team of mathematicians from Xian Jiao Tong University presented a paper demonstrating that the government's goal of zero population growth by 2000 could not be reached. It was not what authorities wanted to hear, and the paper disappeared from view. Liang got worse treatment when he voiced concerns over the one-child proposal. Li Xiuzhen, director of the National Population and Family Planning Commission, dismissed his viewpoint, saying, "It's unlikely that problems are really that serious.

"Chinese people have long been used to listening to one voice at one time," said Liang. "When they suddenly hear something different and critical, it's like oil blasts in the pot."

Liang was unusually courageous in his candor, for there were many China scholars who suffered adverse consequences for voicing opinions contrary to the Communist Party's. Two decades before, Peking University president Ma Yinchu had killed his career that way. Ironically, Ma, who argued for population curbs in 1959, is now credited as the father of the one-child policy. Unfortunately, Ma's ideas were contrary to those of Chairman Mao. His erratic stance on population control would vacillate between "More is merrier" and "Less is more." Ma had the bad luck of pushing for curbs at a time when the Great Helmsman was in the "More is merrier" camp. Ma was summarily removed from his position as head of one of China's top universities. It would be twenty long years before he was politically rehabilitated, around the time Liang unveiled *his* objections to population curbs.

At Chengdu, Liang would clash with the rocketmen, who impressed the crowd with their complex calculations, making Liang's projections seem like caveman scribbles in contrast.

Li Guangyuan represented Song's team at the conference. He was in his mid-thirties, a talented speaker and a graduate of the well-regarded Chinese University of Science and Technology. Li spoke of his team's use of cybernetics — the science of control and communications in complex machine systems — to make calculations of China's future population. For the scholars — many of whom didn't even have access to personal computers at the time — this was "something so mysterious and unheard-of to most people," remembered Liang, "the atmosphere at the whole conference was kindled."

China's rocket scientists argued that even with a two- or three-children-per-family quota the population would continue to balloon. According to their projections, even with "the most drastic policy measure, one child per couple, the population would keep expanding for a full quarter century," wrote Susan Greenhalgh.

Soon after the conference, Liang remembers Li Guangyun asking him, "How did you calculate the population numbers in the next twenty years?"

"With my pen," said Liang.

"That's so slow! It's much easier if you use the computer. For example, it takes less than an hour to calculate the population statistics in the next century, and it's absolutely correct!" cried Li, according to Liang.

A few months later, Song's group's findings began to make their way into mainstream media. At the same time, in many internal conferences the one-child policy was interpreted as the only solution to China's population problems.

On September 25 that year, the Communist Party published an open letter to its members asking them to voluntarily limit their family size to one child. Thus began China's most radical and longest-running social experiment.

Liang returned from Chengdu disappointed and depressed. He bitterly resented what he saw as the arrogance of these scientists, "asking more than 700 million people of China to use their lives to practice their inadequate calculations, in a condescending gesture." He raged at how scholars, "using science as a disguise to stoke the fire," became cheerleaders for the central government's plan.

It would be twenty more years before a group of reformers would emerge, academics who would try to use the tools of logic and research to undo the one-child policy's Gordian knot.

IV

Looking back, it seems amazing how confident China's rocketmen were in their projections of population growth, refusing to factor in how human behavior or technology might change their projections. They appeared utterly sure of the correctness of their solution.

This Masters of the Universe mindset is clear in a 1988 book Song and Yu published explaining their theories. Wrote the authors:

Since human beings appeared in the world millions of years ago, they have been battling with Nature. Now they have finally conquered it by their wisdom and social strength, and won brilliant victories.

We have placed the whole vegetable kingdom under our control. ... We have become the rulers of the entire animal kingdom and conquered all kinds of ferocious beasts that once killed or injured large numbers of our ancestors. ... Now we have got our revenge on them, using their lives to repay the blood debts they owe us from history. ...

We have tamed the rivers and controlled lightning ... roam in outer space, land on the Moon, and send messengers to Venus, Mars and other planets. ...

In short, we have been the victors, we have mastered the world, we have conquered outer space and we have won freedom.

The rocketmen calculated that China's optimal population a century hence would be about 700 million people, but they based their calculations on a variety of questionable assumptions. For example, they presupposed that the ideal Chinese diet would involve Western-style protein consumption. There was no way China's agricultural production could ramp up to allow for this sudden change, so, to meet this goal, the population would have to be drastically reduced. The whole project entailed making "countless heroic assumptions" on the basis of "little more than educated guesswork," said Greenhalgh.

The rocketmen's calculations did not factor in how quickly fertility would decrease as modern educated Chinese women opted for fewer children. By 2010, census results showed that average annual population growth had been at half the rate of the previous decade.

In the course of many conversations with demographers, I learned that predicting population growth is a tricky business. Forecasts are reasonably accurate only up to a twenty- to thirty-year time frame. Demographers base their predictions on three factors: how many people are born, how long people live, and how they move around.

Out of these three, only one — mortality rates — can be predicted fairly accurately today. Migration and fertility patterns have been much harder to foresee, because they are deeply intertwined with individual decision making and agency. "There is no good theory to explain, much less predict, why fertility rates change over time," said population scholar Matthew Connelly. By the end of this century, the world's population could be anywhere between 8 billion and 13 billion, depending on which demographic projections you choose to believe. The difference between the two numbers is as many people as there were on Earth in the 1950s. Demographers know the world's population in 2030, but for 2050, "we are in uncharted waters," and for 2100 — "well, science fiction," said demographer Nicholas Eberstadt.

Olsder, now a retired professor, says his original problem was just a "wonderful kind of mathematical exercise. The social, economic aspects were not factored in.

"I don't know, we lived in a university, in a tenured position, and I was trying to keep myself fresh in a math way. It was a competition with colleagues to show off, to show you were active. I never anticipated this long chain of events," he said.

The Club of Rome's doomsday predictions did not come to pass, but "for many people it was an awakening, to be careful with Earth and our resources," he said. Olsder believes that "all things equal, we should do the same and have a one-child policy."

Out of curiosity, I asked him how many children he has. I was not surprised to learn he has three daughters and five grandchildren, for

I had begun to notice, over the course of many interviews, that those who do support the one-child policy tend, if they live outside China, to have more than one offspring.

By contrast, people like academic Wang Feng, who has called the one-child policy the worst policy mistake China made — more terrible than the Great Leap Forward or the Cultural Revolution, even — well, Wang has just one child, even though he lives in America. Absent government restrictions, the one-child policy seems for many to be an issue of "Do as I say, not as I do."

Olsder would see Song a few more times in conferences. In 2004, Song would visit him in Delft again, this time accompanied by a private secretary, a chauffeur, and two bodyguards.

By this time, Song had risen to be a member of the State Council, China's highest state administrative body. As vice chairman of the Three Gorges Project Construction Committee, he was also involved in another controversial major project, only instead of erecting a dam against human fertility, the Three Gorges sought to dam the massive Yangtze River and create a major hydropower source.

Like the one-child policy, the Three Gorges project was also dogged by criticism for causing unintended side effects. In the case of Three Gorges, it was flooding, landslides, increased seismic activity, and the acceleration of the extinction of a rare dolphin species locals called "the Goddess of the Yangtze." Ironically, Song also headed the State Council's Environmental Protection Committee at that time.

Song presented Olsder with a copy of his 1988 English-language book, *Population System Control.* In one section, Song elaborates on his thoughts about conservation, describing how the banks of the Three Gorges used to be a "paradise for monkeys" over a thousand years ago, before population increases led to deforestation. "Dear animals, you should understand that the kindness of humanity is limited, and we can provide a corner in the zoo or the reservation to prevent your species from extinction. You should thank human beings for such generosity and kindness."

V

In understanding the origins of the one-child policy, it is important not only to ask *how* it came about, but also why it lasted so long.

In 2000, an ad hoc group of China's top demographers, as well as some former officials, got together to seek changes in the one-child policy. Prime movers included people like Gu Baochang, head of Renmin University's demographics unit. As a former senior adviser to the National Population and Family Planning Commission, Gu was a major player in family-planning circles, with strong ties to the Communist Party leadership.

Another well-connected member was Zhang Erli, currently a retired top official from the National Population and Family Planning Commission. Some reformers were also China's first generation of Western-trained demographers, like University of California–Irvine professor Wang Feng. The goal: to collect and collate compelling evidence to show that the one-child policy no longer served China's purposes economically or socially. It was a brain trust of some of China's best and brightest social scientists.

The group felt the time was ripe, as the one-child policy was approaching its third decade, supposedly the end of its life span.

The reformers hoped to convincingly answer questions that had been floating around China's population circles for years, questions such as: What was China's real fertility rate? Was population growth in China still strong, or was it falling, and if so, how much? And, most provocatively, what if authorities loosened or even lifted the one-child policy? Would this lead to a baby boom, undoing all the policy's effects?

For answers, they turned to the secret two-child experiments advocated by Liang some fifteen years before. These communities provided evidence that loosened restrictions did not lead to a baby boom. Yicheng and its sisters all had below-average birthrates, as well as less marked gender imbalances and fewer cases of infanticide and gendercide, compared to the rest of China.

In 2004, the reform group distributed a report on its findings to the National Population and Family Planning Commission and other government agencies. It declared it was time to loosen the one-child policy. Aside from the social costs of a lopsided gender balance and an aging population, they presented evidence indicating that China's fertility had plunged to below-replacement rates. They lobbied Beijing to expand the number of experimental two-child zones, allowing more of China greater freedom in deciding the size and makeup of their families.

But authorities weren't convinced. Many still believed China's population could rebound with another baby boom. Critics of the reform group argued that Yicheng and the rest of the two-child experimental clusters weren't really representative of China. There was some truth in this. Jiuquan, one of the zones, is located in an area between Xinjiang and Inner Mongolia, with nomadic traditions and without deep-rooted clan ideology. Enshi is mountainous, with a strong local tradition of equality between the sexes.

So it was back to the drawing board. In 2006, reformers went to Jiangsu, north of Shanghai, to an area that permitted couples to have two children under the *dandu* policy. (The term *dandu* refers to couples in which one spouse is an only child.) Only about a tenth took advantage of this freedom to have a second child.

In 2008, reformers once again submitted a proposal to China's government agencies with these updated findings. The tone was more urgent: aging was moved higher up the agenda. Cross-country comparisons were included. But "it was still the same reaction," said Cai Yong, a professor at the University of North Carolina–Chapel Hill.

After that, the reformers decided to take the debate public and no longer rely on internal lobbying. They started publishing their findings and commentary in the nation's top news media.

Liang, who had been serving as a sort of emeritus professor for the reformers, started stepping out more into the limelight. When the reform group started trumpeting Yicheng's demographic success, Liang would escort scholars and journalists there, using his connections to arrange interviews with officials. *Christian Science Monitor* correspondent Peter Ford remembers accompanying Liang. "He was treated like a god," says Ford. "It was clear I would not have had the access I had if he had not gone with me," he said.

The reformers also decided to enlist the support of economists, many of whom had been debating the effect of the one-child policy on China's labor markets. One boldface name that joined the cause was billionaire Internet entrepreneur James Liang, founder and chief executive at Ctrip, one of China's biggest online travel sites. Liang, who holds a PhD in economics from Stanford, had written a book called *Too Many People in China?* arguing that the policy would quench entrepreneurism and innovation.

Still, the group kept hitting a brick wall. Authorities reiterated time and again that there would be no major changes to the policy. Liang Zhongtang, furious, said China had become "like an armored car," with the driver proceeding "without paying attention to what is happening outside."

In 2012, the debate heated up. Feng Jianmei was a twenty-two-year-old factory worker who was pregnant with her second child. Feng, who already had a four-year-old daughter, believed she qualified for a second-child exemption. Local officials deemed otherwise and demanded that Feng and her husband pay about $6,000 in fines.

Quite possibly, Feng hoped that even if the legalities weren't clear, she could carry the child to term. But until the child was born, Feng risked being forced into an abortion. So she played an obstetrical game of hide-and-seek, hiding out in relatives' homes.

Once, she spent several hours on a dark rainy hillside in an attempt to evade authorities. To no avail. When she was seven months along, officials caught her and dragged her to the hospital with a pillowcase over her head. They demanded that her husband, Deng, pay about $16,000. Deng managed to negotiate the payment down to about a third of this. He rushed to the hospital after borrowing a portion of the money from his work mates. He hoped officials would accept an IOU for the rest. But he received a text message from them demanding payment in full, "and not a penny less."

Feng, meanwhile, was made to sign an agreement saying she voluntarily consented to the abortion. On June 2, she was injected with a substance to kill the fetus. She later said, "I could feel the baby jumping around inside me all the time, but then she went still."

What happened to Feng was outrageous but not unheard-of. Horrific stories of forced late-term abortions had been making the rounds since the early 1980s, when Stanford anthropology student Steve Mosher personally witnessed several while doing fieldwork in southern China. Mosher published his findings in his book and was kicked out of Stanford's program. Stanford said it was because Mosher violated anthropological tenets by publishing pictures and names of abortion victims. (A reporter friend of mine said caustically, "Those women's rights were being violated in a much bigger way.") Many believed Stanford had caved to pressure from the Chinese government to expel Mosher.

Such stories receded in the late 1990s as China's rapid economic rise made it possible for more to afford these fines. But Feng's case reignited the question and exploded in social media. Her sister-in-law used her cell phone to snap a picture of a dejected Feng lying next to the seven-month-old fetus's almost perfectly formed body. The graphic image went viral and took the one-child policy debate nationwide. Hundreds of thousands posted online comments calling the family-planning officials barbarous, thuggish, and murderous, although censors quickly deleted most postings. Even many urban Chinese who supported the one-child policy were appalled.

The reform group seized this opportunity to send an open letter to the National People's Congress arguing that urgent changes needed to be made to the policy. It came on the heels of a similar appeal sent by a think tank affiliated with China's Politburo.

Zhang Erli, the retired family-planning official from the group of reformers, was particularly affected by Feng's case. He went on television and tearfully apologized to women who'd had to end their pregnancies because of the policy. He said, "I feel quite guilty. Chinese women have made huge sacrifices. A responsible government should repay them." It was an extraordinary public admission from a former senior government official, especially one who'd worked in the very agency responsible for causing those abortions.

I met Zhang in Beijing. He had just undergone a course of chemotherapy but looked alert and vigorous. Before joining the National Population and Family Planning Commission, he had been an electronics engineering professor at Tsinghua University, dubbed "China's MIT."

"It could have been a better policy," Zhang said. "I could say this now, but it is already useless."

After more than a decade of behind-the-scenes lobbying, Beijing announced in 2013 it would fold the Population and Family Planning Commission into the Ministry of Health. This move cut the institutional legs out from under the commission and was widely interpreted as a prelude to the slow phasing out of the one-child policy.

Later that year, the government announced it would further loosen nationwide one-child restrictions by allowing all *dandu* couples to have a second child.

It was the first major change made to the policy in well over a decade. Business analysts confidently predicted a new baby boom and a corresponding rise in sales of diapers, milk powder, cars, and even pianos, as if two children couldn't share a musical instrument.

Shares at Japanese diaper maker Unicharm shot up 4.2 percent on the first trading day after the *dandu* announcement and went on to gain 44 percent over the year. (Those analysts turned out to be massively wrong. The number of people who applied for the *dandu* exclusion was far below official projections.)

I visited Liang again soon after the *dandu* announcement. He was peppery.

"When the policy was published the other day, I received a lot of phone calls. Some are from foreign media. They all sound cheerful. But I asked, 'What if this policy exists in your country? Will you be cheerful because it's loosening up a little bit?'" he said. "It's one step forward, two steps backward."

The *dandu* exclusion would affect only a small group of people, he said, and would do little to solve the problems caused by the one-child policy. Many of China's urban couples are both singleton children, making them already eligible to have two children under then-existing rules.

"The only time when China talked about how family decides your future was during the Cultural Revolution. After thirty years, we don't talk about this anymore. Instead, we seek equality and free will. That's progress. But with this *dandu* policy, we fall back to the ages when parents' decisions decide everything. You cannot have a second child because your parents made the decision decades ago to have more than one. It's not your choice."

We sat in silence.

I glanced at his bookshelves, where there were several pictures of his grandchildren. Both his daughter in England and son in Shanghai opted to have one child each. He had nothing to do with their decisions, he said. I pointed to a picture of Liang in the park with his young grandson. Liang is in a white singlet, looking relaxed. It's a far cry from the bitter, angry person I saw before me. How would he explain the one-child policy and his legacy to them? I asked.

He responded promptly, "I will tell them the truth, if they are interested. From how this policy was established, and how it has been applied. I will also tell them the existence of it indicates our country is still at a very low status. That's why ridiculous policies like the one-child policy exist."

The man who once advocated a two-child plan no longer believes there should be any restrictions at all. "I gradually realized it is not about giving birth to one or two children. It is about people making their own decisions."

A year later, official numbers showed that only 35 percent of eligible couples had applied for a second child under the *dandu* exclusion, far fewer than official estimates. So far, the baby boom's been a bust. Many couples cited the high costs of child rearing as a reason.

Once again, Cassandra was right. He also had another prediction: the one-child policy would end in less than ten years.

The Population Police

Birth planning in China is practiced on a voluntary basis.
— *Zhao Zhiyang*

Civilization is sterilization.
— *Aldous Huxley,* Brave New World

I

Ma Qingju, or "Green Chrysanthemum," used to have a board on her wall telling her which of her friends were pregnant. It showed what kind of contraceptives they used; whether they had one or two children; if they were sterilized, pregnant, married, or single. This took the saying "Know thy neighbor" to a new level.

Green Chrysanthemum was a cheery forty-five-year-old woman who ran the snack shop in a tiny village called Huangjiapu, Yicheng County. Until recently, she also earned an extra $60 a year as a "cluster leader," keeping track of ten households' reproductive habits and reporting these details to the village's family-planning commission.

"It's not a difficult job, everybody knows each other so well," she said. Not one person in her group exceeded the two-child limit, she proudly told me.

In addition to cluster leaders like Green Chrysanthemum, Huangjiapu, population five hundred, had fifteen full-timers tasked with family-planning matters.

These village-level offices are the most basic building blocks of China's birth-planning machinery, a bloated behemoth that goes from some 85 million part-time employees at the grass-roots level all the way up to half a million full-time employees at the National Population and Family Planning Commission. The commission also has its own archives and statistics and propaganda departments; affiliate centers for pharmacological research, film production, and publishing; and a consulting company that handles exhibitions and conferences. Other state organizations such as the military and police have their own internal family-planning units, as do state-owned companies.

The complexity of this machinery and its reach are partly why Beijing took its time winding down the one-child policy, say analysts. Birth planning had been so baked into the business of ordinary governance, its revenue contributions so necessary, that unwinding all this posed a challenge.

I went to Yicheng to understand how such a vast machine worked at the basic level. Given the county's more liberal birth quotas, I was able to get some retired family-planning officials to speak on the record. Many officials had been doing the work since before the onset of the one-child policy in 1980, continuing through the introduction of Yicheng's special two-child status in 1985. They were able to explain to me the vacillations of the policy, which they themselves found dizzying.

Green Chrysanthemum, for example, explained that family-planning work was practically unnecessary nowadays, since younger members in her group didn't even want a second child because of the expense.

"Everybody wants just one," she said. Since 1985, only one family in Huangjiapu has had a third child, she said, a relatively wealthy couple with an auto parts business.

But even with a looser two-child limit there were still rules people found onerous, such as a requirement throughout the 1990s that women be sterilized after the birth of a second child, or a requirement that births must be spaced at least five years apart.

What if a woman didn't want more children but would prefer not to be sterilized? What if a couple got pregnant with their second child, say, three years after the first, instead of five? That was when even Yicheng's benign machinery would show its ugly side, according to Huangjiapu's former village head Huang Denggao.

The usual mode of punishment was fines: parents of children born out of plan would be hit with fines between five and ten times their annual disposable income. "If the couple is too poor to pay, we'll take things from their house, but only in a few cases," said Huang. TVs were a favorite, he said — worth a villager's whole annual income — as were tables, bicycles, and washing machines. These items were usually collected by a team of ten part-time enforcers (usually "strong healthy young men") and sold off, and the proceeds were kept by the township. To Huang, these actions did not count as coercion. Rather, he called such tactics "persuasion."

One of the most difficult tasks Huang had to do was persuade women to be sterilized, he said. Many women feared the procedure. Side effects such as excessive bleeding were not uncommon, especially given the conveyor-belt manner in which some of these procedures were done. The village women tried to bargain, said Huang. Some asked to use barrier contraceptives instead, or promised not to have more than two children. "But it was my job to get people to do the operation, or else I would not be able to accomplish my target," said Huang. "I can't possibly guarantee they won't have another baby with just a promise."

China in particular favored sterilization because it was a virtually foolproof way of lowering fertility. Nonpermanent barrier methods like condoms, the Pill, and IUDs, which gave individuals more choice and control, were not so trustworthy, even though the IUD used—a stainless steel ring with no string—was specially modified so women could not remove it themselves. In one year alone, 1983, China sterilized over 20 million people, more than the combined population of the three largest US cities, New York, Los Angeles, and Chicago.

Nowadays, sterilizations are no longer mandatory in Huangjiapu. Such methods are unnecessary, for the little village's population has fallen from its peak in 1983, when there were almost six hundred inhabitants. In 2008, Huangjiapu's elementary school was forced to merge with another because there were just seven students, down from fifty in the 1980s. Some of this is due to migration of workers to cities, but most of it is due to dwindling family size, said Huang.

Throughout my interviews with Yicheng's family-planning officials, many said they consoled themselves with the thought that they were doing their duty and carrying out an important national directive. Some of this, I felt, was lip service, justification for doing what had to be the most unpopular job in China. There appeared to be few true believers. I felt this strongly talking to Che Yuelian, the local village medic and family-planning officer in Xiheshui, another small village in Yicheng.

Che, whose Chinese name means "Moon Lotus," had been in family-planning work since the 1970s. In those early days, her job consisted of teaching birth control techniques and encouraging people to have smaller families. Many families took exception to a pert twenty-three-year-old giving them advice on sterilization and abortion. "They said, 'We'll be grateful to have you help deliver babies, but it is unacceptable for a young woman like you to tell people not to have babies. Mind your own business,'" she said.

Now in her late sixties, Moon Lotus continues to work in the village clinic, a small courtyard building with maize spread out on the rafters to dry. After administering an intravenous drip to an elderly patient, Moon Lotus, a rotund, deeply tanned woman with piercing eyes, settled down to a cigarette. It was the first of many during a difficult conversation. She was evasive and made it clear she didn't enjoy my questions.

Like Huang, she constantly referred to her task as one of "persuasion." I asked her if she ever persuaded any women with late-term pregnancies to abort. Moon Lotus first replied by saying this was illegal. Later, she said no, she hadn't. Then she recalled persuading a woman six months along to have an abortion. "She didn't even know she was six months pregnant, but I could tell just by looking," she said triumphantly.

Her first successful case of persuasion was a twenty-seven-year-old mother of two daughters. The woman wanted the operation but feared her in-laws' disapproval. Moon Lotus secretly escorted her to the operation and gave her a ride back on her bicycle. For her pains, she was verbally abused by the woman's relatives. "Her mother-in-law cursed me, 'It's your own business that your family does not have a son. But I want a grandson to pass down our family name.'" Even Moon Lotus's parents yelled at her. "But I said, although this job is troublesome, somebody's got to do it. At that time, people held the old concept of preferring boys to girls and said nobody is going to bury you if you don't have a son."

Even family ties gave way to family-planning imperatives. Moon Lotus's nephew's wife became pregnant at twenty-two, two years before the permitted age for a first pregnancy. Get an abortion, said Moon Lotus. "I told her you should set an example for other women, people are watching us."

While talking, I learned to my surprise that Moon Lotus herself had four daughters and a son. To be sure, her son, her youngest, was born in 1978, before the one-child policy. But Moon Lotus's job all these years has been to encourage smaller families and discourage son preference. How did she explain the discrepancy between what she preached and what she practiced?

At first, she ignored my question. "My circumstances were special," she finally said, stubbing out her fifth cigarette. "My adoptive parents weren't in good health. Me neither. They don't have any children, so I wanted to have a boy so he can take care of me and my parents. I tried to wear an IUD but that made me bleed badly."

After the birth of her son, Moon Lotus finally did what she spent years convincing others to do. She had her tubes tied.

II

The closer I looked at the workings of the population police, the messier they seemed.

When the one-child policy was launched in the 1980s, it was clear that enforcement of such a hugely unpopular policy would be difficult. In the beginning, execution of the one-child policy ranged from lax to excessive across China. In some parts of the country, pregnant women without birth permits were marched off in handcuffs to undergo forced abortions. In others, officials ignored or paid mere lip service to these strictures from the central government.

It didn't help that other national regulations undercut the one-child policy's intentions. A new marriage law, also launched in 1980, lowered the legal age of marriage to twenty for women and twenty-two for men. This was done to combat illegal marriage and sex crimes, but of course it also encouraged more unions and, by extension, babies. The move toward agricultural decollectivization also undermined official efforts to enforce the one-child policy. Under collectivism, pay, rations, and other benefits were meted out by village leaders, and bad behavior (having an out-of-plan child, for instance) could be punished directly; new reforms loosened official control over peasants' livelihoods.

By 1984, the nationwide one-size-fits-all measure proved so unpopular that the central government was forced to decentralize a large portion of the one-child policy. It circulated new provisions enshrined in what population scholars call Document 7. Document 7 gave each province more power to adapt the one-child policy to local circumstances.

This was the beginning of a raft of exclusions that made it hard for people within China — never mind outside China — to understand the policy in anything but the broadest strokes, because conditions really were different from place to place. For example, residents in many rural areas were allowed to have a second child, provided their first was not a son — a tacit acknowledgment of the son hunger that was rampant in the countryside. Places like Tibet and Yunnan, with large ethnic minorities, had vastly more liberal policies than more populous provinces like Sichuan and Henan.

Document 7 was a nod toward making enforcement easier for local authorities. It was not intended to make things easier for the general populace. Authorities called this tactic "opening a small hole to close a big gap," making small concessions to ensure overall compliance.

Document 7 did not remedy the lack of transparency and accountability within the system. Local officials had wide discretion in determining how much to fine violators. Sums could range from a multiple of two to ten times annual household income. People had no way of figuring out ahead of time what they were liable for, and two sets of violators, under similar circumstances, might pay vastly different penalties. In 2010, a family-planning official apparently imposed a fine of 5 million RMB, or over $800,000, on a violator.

When that person protested, the official allegedly increased the fine, saying, "You are just a piece of meat on the chopping block," according to local media reports.

In essence, the central government gave local provinces the message, "Meet your birth quotas; we don't really care to know how." They also expected provinces to fund the bulk of population planning on their own. This created a system ripe for corruption.

Even though Feng Jianmei's explosive forced abortion story rocked the nation in 2012, no birth-planning official involved actually served a criminal sentence, though several laws were broken. I asked Zhang Erli, who had been a high-ranking, national-level family-planning official, why this was so. He explained the national-level family-planning commission lacked the right to punish local-level family-planning officials. "We can only investigate them and report to the provincial leaders. They have the power to punish or even fire the officer involved, not us."

Most on-the-ground family-planning officials told me there was a tacit understanding that they would never face criminal charges for their actions, because maintaining birth control targets was considered a top priority.

"As long as we kept the quotas, we could do anything: destroy homes, property, jail people, even threaten to confiscate people's children, and no one would say anything," one former Sichuan County official told me. (As it turned out, officials in another province did actually confiscate children, which I'll elaborate on in chapter 8.)

Adding to the chaos was an internal battle that raged throughout most of the 1980s within China's leadership. Liberal-minded leaders, who leaned toward a more humane two-child approach, argued with hard-liners, who urged the need to stay the course.

In 1988, a circular from the National Population and Family Planning Commission spoke of a "crisis in birth planning," outlining problems such as increasing attacks on overworked birth-planning personnel. Corruption was also a huge issue, with many provinces falsifying reports. There was a growing realization that the 1.2 billion target simply could not be reached, for in 1988, 80 percent of China's provinces had already breached population targets.

The 1989 student protests at Tiananmen, and the subsequent harsh crackdown, marked the triumph of the hard-liners. Leaders like Zhao Zhiyang, who had championed the two-child experiment at Yicheng, were purged. There would be no softening on birth quotas.

In 1990, the central government instituted a nationwide account-ability system. Called *yipiaofoujue* (loosely translated as "one-vote veto"), it made birth-planning targets a major objective for all provincial authorities. Officials — not just family-planning specialists but also garden-variety administrators — who did not meet their area's birth quotas would face sanctions in the form of wage deductions, demotions, or even dismissal. It didn't matter, for example, if officials met other performance targets. That one black mark from not meeting birth quotas would blot out everything else they'd accomplished.

Yipiaofoujue became the stick the central government held over provincial officials, and this in turn incited them to harsher acts. Some provinces would impose even tighter quotas, just to be on the safe side. One official told me there were times they would get decrees that made no sense, like "no births within the next hundred days," which they were obliged to enforce.

Fines intensified, and not just for unauthorized childbirth. Women were fined for living with a man out of wedlock; for not using contraception, even if it didn't lead to pregnancy; or simply for not attending regular pregnancy checkups. In Jiangsu, women had to line up twice monthly for pregnancy tests and publicly pee in cups. The birth police weren't squeamish about how they got the job done, and their methods produced results.

III

The woman who really explained the workings of the population police to me was a midlevel family-planning official who fled to the United States over fifteen years ago.

Gao testified before a congressional hearing in 1989, providing a trove of documents, video, and pictures detailing the inner workings of birth planning in her district, Yonghe Town, in southern China's Fujian Province. She laid bare a system of coercion that ranged from detaining those who resisted and their relatives, to property destruction and late-term forced abortions.

Gao described how she once turned in a woman without a birth permit who was nine months pregnant. "In the operating room, I saw how the child's lips were moving and how its arms and legs were also moving. The doctor injected poison into its skull and the child died and it was thrown into the trash can."

Gao now lives in a West Coast suburb. She agreed to meet me provided I did not reveal where she lives, for her neighbors don't know her past.

After her testimony, Gao said, some colleagues and relatives were beaten and arrested. She claimed one colleague was beaten to death, and another was raped. I could not independently verify these claims. Soon after her testimony, state-run news agency Xinhua ran a report saying Gao and her husband had defaulted on loans and were wanted for suspected fraud.

Gao maintains these charges are trumped up. "If I have a lot of money, why would I live such a miserable life now? I work as a domestic helper and my hands can hardly lift heavy things anymore," she said.

It was just after Halloween, and the woman who once described herself as a "monster" was talking about giving out candy to the neighborhood children. "They just kept ringing the doorbell all night long," she said good-humoredly.

Gao lives in a double-story home decorated with cartoon posters and Taiwanese lucky-knot wall hangings. A massive leatherette massage chair holds pride of place, next to a Lion King poster proclaiming that immortal what-me-worry message, "Hakuna Matata."

It's a far cry from the stark cell where she used to lock people up. Her detainees were usually relatives of women with unapproved pregnancies, whom Gao would imprison until these women turned themselves in. Jailing elderly parents was most effective, she said. "Few people could feel good, knowing their old mother was in prison because of them," she said. Detainees were kept in "black jails" in a building adjacent to the birth-planning office and charged a little over $1 daily for food. They were not allowed to make phone calls or mail letters and were sometimes kept for months at a time.

Gao also described a wage incentive for birth-planning officials, which was tied to how many sterilizations and abortions they were able to achieve. These bonuses could amount to as much as half their base pay, which was relatively modest. "That's why everyone is so keen to arrest people. The more you arrest, the more bonus you earn," she said. (Officials I interviewed in other parts of China also described similar bonus systems.) Even doctors would be incentivized to perform more abortions to increase the size of their bonus, said Gao. "Some girls were forced to get surgeries even though they weren't pregnant at all," she claimed.

With such a system, surely there was vast potential for bribery? Yes, said Gao, though she claimed she herself never took any bribes. A common form of bribery was to pay officials for a certificate stating that its bearer was not pregnant. This was needed by people traveling or working outside Yonghe. Since officers had discretion in determining the magnitude of fines, it was common to siphon some of this money away, or take fines without issuing receipts. Gao remembers a colleague who "lost" an entire book of receipts.

Throughout her litany of horrors, Gao reiterated that she had no choice, that she was just doing her job. At the time, she tried to compartmentalize her life. There was her job, where "I was a monster in the daytime," and her personal life, where she was a wife and mother. Even there she could not entirely escape, for she herself was in violation of the one-child policy. After the birth of her daughter, she secretly adopted a son. For years, she hid him in relatives' homes and never allowed him to call her "Mother" in public.

Now Gao's family is with her in the United States. Since leaving China, she has given birth to another son, cementing her ties to America. Still, she considers herself hard done by, and her residency situation is still precarious. She was brought into the country through the help of pro-life lobbyists, her testimony part of their efforts to get the US administration to defund the United Nations Population Fund. After her testimony, Gao sought but was denied political asylum, since US law grants asylum only to victims of persecution. With the help of her sponsors, she has the right to work in the United States but does not have a green card or a US passport. Speaking little English, she can only hold menial jobs and isn't able to travel outside the country. She cannot visit her mother, who is very old and very sick, she said.

"In the end, I tried to do the right thing. Must I always be punished?" she said, eyes swimming.

As expiation, she recounted how she stepped in to save the lives of three infants. These were babies born alive even after their mothers were injected with chemical solutions to induce late-term abortions. "I would secretly wrap them up and give them to their fathers. I told them to put the child in their bags, as if it was a thing, not a baby, and not to open the bag when they left, so they could get away," said Gao, sobbing.

Against those few lives, Gao, by her own reckoning, was personally responsible for about 1,500 abortions, of which about a third were late-term.

IV

The coercion Gao described is wrenching, but is it just one extreme example, far from the norm? How widespread were such tactics? And how long did they persist?

Up until the early 2000s, at least, many international actors chose to believe that adherence to the one-child policy was voluntary, despite growing evidence to the contrary. In 1983, the first-ever United Nations Population Award medals, for individuals who had made "outstanding contributions" to solving population issues, were conferred on Indira Gandhi — she of the forced sterilizations — and China's minister of population planning, Qian Xinzhong.

As awards go, it was akin to the Nobel Peace Prize committee giving Yasser Arafat the nod. It is still a source of embarrassment to the UNFPA, but it did not stop former head Nafis Sadik from accepting an award from the Chinese government in 2002. Dr. Sadik said she believed harsh enforcement of the one-child policy to be rare, thanks in large part to the UNFPA's collaboration with Beijing. Because of the one-child policy, the US government seesawed between giving and withholding contributions to the UNFPA.

Former UN and other nongovernmental officials I spoke to privately said they worked hard behind the scenes to get China's birth planners to move toward a more service-oriented system. When I spoke to them, Beijing appeared to be cautiously exploring these avenues, including a pilot project to turn enforcers into parenting counselors. But such efforts were still limited.

Logic dictates that as long as the one-child system endured, and quotas and targets were imposed, coercion continued. As recently as

2010, a mass sterilization campaign for close to ten thousand people was held in Puning City, Guangdong. According to Amnesty International, almost 1,400 relatives of couples targeted for sterilization were detained, to pressure these couples to consent.

I believe, however, that the nature of this abuse increasingly shifted away from forced abortions and sterilizations toward stiffer enforcement of fines. This was partly because these so-called social compensation fees (*shehui fuyangfei*) grew to become a major source of revenue for many counties, especially poorer ones. Over the past decade China implemented land tax reforms, requiring provinces to hand over income to the national treasury for redistribution. In practice, this meant that lower-level county and village governments lost almost all independent sources of income. The one exception was birth fines, which did not have to be handed over to the central government. "It's a common saying, for money, 'Big cities depend on land, small towns depend on birth planning,'" said journalist Matthew Pang, who exhaustively documented such abuses by family-planning officials in a small town in Hunan.

In 2013, lawyer Wu Youshui took advantage of a provision in Chinese law, similar to the US Freedom of Information Act, to request that each province account for how much it collected in social compensation fees. The total came to $2.7 billion, an amount that is almost certainly an underestimation, says Wu.

"The numbers are definitely fake. Few of them are real," he said. Lending credence to his assertion is the provinces' refusal to account for how the money was spent, information he has also repeatedly requested and no province has yet supplied.

The term *social compensation fee* is a relatively new one, adopted in 2000. Before that, fines were called "excess birth fines" or "unplanned birth fees," but the new term suggests the money would be put to use to help cover the costs of extra children to society. But family-planning officials I spoke to say the money from birth fines — no matter what they are called — was spent on office maintenance, personnel, sometimes entertainment expenses, or funneled to other departments. A detailed accounting is almost impossible.

I met Lawyer Wu in his offices in a suburb of Hangzhou, the city that in Marco Polo's time held the biggest population in the world and is now home to a variety of tech companies, including e-commerce giant Alibaba. That sheen has not rubbed off on Wu's practice. It is a small one, located on a floor along with many small real estate businesses, some covered with Out of Business signs.

Wu, a small, erect man with a whisper of a mustache, is someone whose personal history has intersected with China's family planning in a variety of ways. As a teenager, he remembers walking home and seeing women rounded up for a mass sterilization run. Some resisted by stripping off the local official's pants. "They said, 'You sterilize me, I sterilize you,'" he recalled. "But they were all sterilized in the end, forcibly."

The youngest of eight children — three of whom died during the Great Famine years — Wu has a brother whose fourth child was forcibly aborted, as well as a sister who worked in the family-planning sector. "She helped to bury all the dead babies."

Wu, a Christian, said he first became interested in the issue of social compensation fees during a business trip to a neighboring province. He noticed that many people there appeared to have three or four children. Locals told him that authorities actually encouraged violations so they could collect more fines.

In 2013, spurred by a belief that the family-planning commission's power was waning following Beijing's decision to fold the department into the Ministry of Health, Wu submitted his requests for information to each province. After that, he began doing pro bono work for clients who wanted to challenge the one-child policy.

Wu admitted his requests were by nature something of a Trojan horse maneuver, designed to challenge the issue of social compensation itself and draw focus to a wide variety of illegal practices within the family-planning policy. Wu said his actions were intended to "open up the space for discussion about family-planning policy." "I raised questions with this application. It is a start."

For example, it was technically illegal for the population police to use force or promote late-term abortions. Nor was it legal for authorities to deny household registration, *hukou,* to children born out of plan. But without such punishments it would have been impossible to enforce the one-child policy, said officials.

In the past three years, legal challenges to the one-child policy mounted, something that was previously almost unheard-of. About a third of these lawsuits protested the social compensation fee amounts incurred, while the rest involved out-of-plan children who'd been denied *hukou*s, as well as people who'd lost their jobs over one-child policy violations.

Most cases were dismissed and never made it to court. Claimants, however, saw glimmers of hope in a 2013 ruling. Two provinces, Shandong and Jiangxi, ruled that *hukou*s must be issued regardless of whether social compensation fees had been paid or not. (This was actually a reiteration of an existing nationwide regulation that was obviously not always followed.) It is a contentious issue for crowded cities like Beijing and Shanghai, anxious to limit the number of residents drawing on their social services and resources. (A Beijing *hukou,* for example, is much coveted and can be worth over $100,000 on the black market.) With an estimated 13 million people without *hukou*s in China—most related to violations of the one-child policy—resolving this will be a major headache for authorities in years to come.

Wu said he was not worried about official repercussions. I reminded him of the fate of activist Chen Guangcheng. In 2005, Chen filed a class-action lawsuit against the city's family-planning staff challenging coercive measures endured by pregnant women in his home province. Chen, who is blind, served jail time and was under house arrest for years before making a dramatic escape to the US embassy in 2012. He now lives in America, but his family members in China are still persecuted, he says.

Wu thought he can avoid Chen's fate by carefully picking "safe" topics, such as social compensation, which in general was hugely unpopular and, he believed, less politically volatile than abortions. He called the one-child policy "anti-human, illegal, and unreasonable," but added, referring to the then-powerful family-planning apparatus, "I need to come up with ideas to talk about the issue in a nonsensitive way, but still make a fuss."

In July 2015, Beijing began a crackdown on human rights lawyers, detaining over two hundred lawyers and associates over charges that they have exploited contentious issues and destabilized society. At the time of writing this book, Wu is still at liberty but says he faces strong pressure to tone down his legal challenges. He now says, "All who pursue rule of law" are at risk. "Because from the present situation, you can never tell where is the government's bottom line. Moreover, the line itself is ever-changing."

V

The most memorable discussion I had on the workings of the population police came during a chance discussion with a man I'll call Uncle Li.

Uncle Li was a relative of a friend, a businessman who'd volunteered to give us a ride to a neighboring town. He'd come to pick us up in his black Audi, a man in his late forties dressed in the uniform of moderately prosperous urban Chinese men — polo shirt, collar modishly flipped up, big clunky watch with many complicated dials, leather man-bag. I was just admiring how well kept his car was, with tiny pouches holding sunshades, tissue boxes, and mineral water, and little bow-shaped pillow headrests, when we started talking.

It turned out that in 1994, Uncle Li's first job out of college was as a county-level administrator. He became quite chatty talking about it. Meeting population targets was part of his job, and the most important one because of *yipiaofoujue,* he said.

"If they couldn't pay, then you would confiscate some things of value in the home, but they were never such expensive things because villagers were poor — just things like grain, or homespun cloth," he remembered. "Sometimes, we would climb up the roofs and make a hole, to show we meant business, or knock down some windows," he recounted. In his province, the one-child policy was taken very seriously, so fines were heavily punitive.

We stopped for lunch, and he continued talking, quite cheerfully, about property damage, confiscations, and pay scales. I didn't want to interrupt the flow, but at the back of my mind I was dying to ask the big question: How could you bear to be so beastly every day?

Finally, I ventured, "Doing this job must be hard, since people don't want to do as you say."

He fell silent. Then he said, "There's this one incident I'll never forget.

"I was twenty-four, and we had heard of a woman pregnant with an out-of-plan baby who had run away to a neighboring village. So we made preparations to catch her at night. I got together a team of six or seven people. We surrounded the house. We were very quiet, but I don't know, somehow she must have heard something — maybe voices — because she ran."

"How many months was she?" I asked.

"I don't know, but she looked pretty big. She ran and ran and ran until she came to a pond. Then she ran in, until the water was at her neck" — his hand sliced his Adam's apple. "She stood there and began to cry."

I was transfixed by the picture he'd painted. The woman with her bellyful of child, keening in the dark, officials circling the water hole like predators.

"What happened?"

He looked away. "Please, wait a moment," he said. The cheery insouciance was gone.

"She said a lot of things. She said she needed to have this baby. She would never have any peace, and her husband and her mother-in-law would never treat her well, until she had a son."

He lit a cigarette, clearing his throat.

"Finally, two women officials waded in and took her away."

We were silent.

"Why did this one incident stay with you, when you must have had so many of these encounters?" I asked.

"Maybe it was because I was young," he said, slowly. "I felt we were doing wrong, but I had no choice. Later, I was promoted and left the area."

That night, I was so moved by the story that I related it to a former student of mine whom I was meeting for drinks. She had grown up in the area and was now a PhD student in America. I thought the anecdote was powerful, but I figured she must have heard similar stories all her life.

She listened, her eyes widening.

"But you must have heard these stories before. What about your schoolmates? Surely some must have come from the countryside and told these stories?" I asked in surprise.

She knew, of course, the contours of the one-child policy. But the brutal vividness of this tale was something else. "You must understand," she said. "I went to Renmin University. To get there I had to go to a top high school, and a top middle school, and those kinds of places are not easy for children from the countryside to get into. Most of my friends and classmates were like me, middle-class, children from the city."

I was reminded yet again that despite the Internet and an increasingly globalized world, many Chinese people's perceptions of recent historical events can be sketchy.

While writing her book on the 1989 student protests at Tiananmen, National Public Radio correspondent Louisa Lim visited four top Chinese universities and showed students a picture of "Tank Man," the iconic picture of a single person stopping an oncoming line of tanks. To the Western world, it is one of the most recognizable images of the event. Lim found that only fifteen out of a hundred students recognized the photo.

It struck me as ironic that people of my former student's generation would know so little about a policy that birthed them and will continue to shape their reality. Yet to my student, such a story was a tale from another country.

Little Emperors, Grown Up

People born in the 1980s are now, at most, 28 years old, and they exercise no real power to speak of, so the damage caused by abuses of power cannot be their fault. If you haven't wiped your ass properly, don't try to use the younger generation's baby hair as toilet paper.

— *Han Han,* This Generation

If from infancy you treat children as gods, they are liable in adulthood to act as devils.

— *P. D. James,* The Children of Men

I

One of the most common sights in any Chinese public space is a staggering infant surrounded by a gaggle of hovering adults. This is, of course, the Little Emperor, a Chinese phenomenon more precious than pandas, though reproductively not as rare.

I was curious: What happens when this scenario reverses itself?

What happens when the Little Emperor grows up and has to return this attention sixfold, no longer the pyramid's apex but the base?

Over 90 percent of China's urban households were subject to the one-child policy at the time it was revised, which makes for over 100 million only children who will eventually have to shoulder the burden of aging parents, grandparents, and all the accompanying financial and emotional baggage — dementia, cancer, brittle bones, broken hips — with limited help from China's still-nascent social safety net.

In 2007, I began searching for a way to report this. It wasn't easy because the oldest children of the one-child policy were just thirty, with parents in their fifties, most still enjoying good health. I was trying to write about something that hadn't happened yet.

I started looking around for someone in the unusual position of having an ailing parent while still in his or her twenties. That's how I met Liu Ting, who became a minor national celebrity for a strange reason: he took his mother to college.

Now, when I say "took his mother to college," I don't mean that he physically brought her along to classes. Liu Ting's mother had kidney disease and required careful nursing. His father, a gambler, had decamped, worn out by years of marital acrimony. Liu Ting was off to college in a different town, and there was no one to care for his mother, Yong Min. In an engaging bit of role reversal that happened to catch a nation's fancy, he brought his mother to live with him on campus.

In another country, this might have been no big deal. But China has a long history of revering parents. The words *xiao shun* are translated into English as "filial piety," or respect for one's elders, but that's a dry facsimile of what it really means. *24 Paragons of Filial Piety,* a medieval set of stories still told to today's children, demonstrates filial piety in a variety of self-sacrificial ways. One "paragon" eats vegetables while the parents eat meat. Another, little Wu Ming, exposes himself to mosquitoes so they bite him, not his parents. One tastes his father's fecal matter, to judge how sick he is. Such solicitude even extends to in-laws; one notable paragon, Lady Tang, breast-feeds her toothless mother-in-law. At its most elevated, filial piety means putting parents ahead of children; as the thinking goes, you can always have another child, not another mother.

During the Cultural Revolution, filial piety and other cornerstones of family life took a hit. Mao's government encouraged children to rise up against their parents and other figures of authority in the name of smashing the four "olds" — customs, culture, habits, and ideas. In one instance, sixteen-year-old Zhang Hongbing turned in his mother for defacing Mao's portrait. She was shot two months later. Decades later, a guilt-ridden Zhang published a lengthy public confession, calling himself a son "who could not even be compared to animals."

In 2007, the Communist leadership, alarmed by the changes brought about by rapid economic growth as well as the family structure breakdown the party itself had engineered, sought to revive such traditional values. One of the ways it did so was by launching a series of National Moral Hero awards, a sort of Nobel for noble values: honesty, patriotism, and, of course, respect for elders. Liu Ting was honored in the first batch, one of the youngest winners.

It brought the lonely twenty-something a kind of fame he hadn't bargained for. Books, newspaper articles, and comics were written about him. National broadcaster CCTV aired a song, "Mother," composed especially for him. Someone else wrote a play. A local developer let Liu Ting live in a luxury apartment, rent free. His mother got a free kidney out of his National Moral Hero status; money for her operation was raised through donations. There's even a statue of him in Guangzhou's Cultural Square for Filial Piety, though he's never seen it.

Who is this modern-day paragon, and how does he speak for his generation of only children? Were his trials and tribulations somehow a foreshadowing of tensions to come?

I went to meet him in Lin'an, a small town four hours west of Shanghai. Slight, with a pointed chin and smooth skin as pale as rice, Liu Ting was quiet and deferential. He immediately linked hands with me and started calling me "Sister Fong." I noticed he kept his nails short except for his thumbnail, which jutted out. This was a common affectation among older men in China but rare in people of his age. Much like a Rolex or a fancy cell phone, the lone long fingernail signals affluence and gentility, for no peasant farmer can afford to maintain this kind of manicure. When I asked Liu Ting about it, he blushed and hid his hands behind his back.

Liu Ting was genuinely taken aback by the attention showered on him.

His days were a juggle of classes and nursing. Everything he did was constrained by the need to care for his mother, who had uremia, a disease that manifests itself in constant fatigue and nausea. He rose at six to prepare the family's breakfast of hot green bean congee. He headed to the wet market every day after class to buy fresh produce and ensure that his mother ate well. I went with him once, observing as he expertly threaded his way through the crowds to buy spring onions and tofu, which the vendor skillfully sliced from a trembling white slab the size of a small table. At the time supermarkets like Walmart and its local imitator, Wumart, were already making inroads even into small towns like Lin'an, but Liu, ever mindful of bills, rarely visited those air-conditioned bastions of comfort.

"It's not always pleasant," he said, delicately picking his way past a tubful of croaking frogs. "But you get the freshest and cheapest this way." He averted his glance from a corner where a dog shivered, paws and muzzle bound, destined for the pot.

A wet market in China is not at all like a genteel farmers' market in the West, with cheese tastings and organic olive oil. Instances of casual brutality are everywhere: Pick an eel slithery from a bucket, and the vendor will smash its head in for you with a large stick. Blood and entrails from newly slaughtered chickens slop onto the floor. Vendors stomp around in rubber boots, as sprightly as folk dancers, wearing colorful sleeve protectors — elasticized cloth tubes reaching from wrist to elbow. You can get almost anything in a wet market: meat off the hoof, fresh flowers, hand-rolled noodles, sticks of incense, Hello Kitty underwear, whippy little bamboo canes for disciplining children or pets.

All through the market, I saw people shoot Liu the sidelong glance, the lot of a small-town celebrity. Lin'an has a population of only fifty thousand, small by China's standards. (Even by 2013, the town was still so non-noteworthy it couldn't be found on Beidou, China's GPS system.) In such a small place, Liu's celebrity resulted in heightened focus. He couldn't put a foot wrong. Throughout his shopping he bobbed and ducked, courteously replying to queries about his mother's health, the state of his studies, and whether or not he was dating anyone. Shoving onto a crowded bus, Liu said, "Of course at times I want to be rude, but I can't. Everyone's watching." Back home, Liu scrambled to cook dinner: steamed fish, soup, and rice. Then the dishes, his mother's nightly back and foot rubs, and, finally, homework.

Liu's happiest memories were his first six months on campus, when he was unencumbered by family cares. He lived in a dorm, went to parties, indulged his interests in photography, art, and drama. Then came news his mother would die without a kidney transplant, an operation they couldn't afford. Liu Ting moved out of the dorm to a rundown apartment. He used his student loans to pay for his mother's medication. He also took a part-time job as a janitor on campus.

A local reporter learned about Liu's predicament and wrote the article that changed Liu's life. The next day, readers jammed university phone lines offering donations. A hero was born.

II

When China launched the one-child program in 1980, one of the big questions was whether a generation of only children — dubbed *xiao huangdi,* or "Little Emperors" — would mean a nation of overindulged, spoiled children. If so, what implications for China?

The nation's worst fears appeared to be realized in a famous, though controversial, 1992 study of a group of Chinese and Japanese children on a camping trip to Inner Mongolia. Conducted by Sun Yunxiao, deputy director of the China Youth and Children Research Center, the study described Chinese children as whiners and complainers. Unlike the Japanese group, Chinese kids did not know how to ration or prepare food, and they wanted adults to cook for them. The parents, Sun said, were no better — the Chinese rushed to help whenever their kids needed assistance, while Japanese parents held back to let their children learn independence.

The study was criticized as being unscientific, but it cast a long shadow. When I taught at the University of Southern California — the college with the largest proportion of Chinese nationals in America — virtually all my China students knew this experiment, which they disputed vigorously. They did not feel themselves to be more selfish or narcissistic than normal, but they did acknowledge one important benefit of not having siblings: most of their parents couldn't have afforded USC's hefty tuition otherwise.

In the years since then, a score of more rigorous studies have been conducted looking at China's only-child phenomenon, with mixed results.

While some supported the Little Emperor hypothesis — China's singletons tended to be more self-centered, with weaker life skills and less self-control — there are many others that indicate no significant differences between only children and children with siblings. Some showed that these antisocial differences disappeared over time, as singleton children are socialized through school and other institutions. Other studies showed that only children in China have an edge over children with siblings when it comes to academic achievements and sociability. In a massive 2007 study covering over eighty-five thousand children, run by the National Science Institute, a survey of only children compared with children with siblings concluded only that singletons were on average heavier, taller, and had poorer eyesight.

Measured against children with siblings, China's Little Emperors didn't look that different at first glance. Measured against other age cohorts, however, China's only-child generation displayed marked differences.

In 2012, a group of economists headed by Lisa Cameron recruited over four hundred people from two groups, one consisting of those born between 1975 and 1978, before the start of the policy, and the rest born after 1980. Over half of the pre-one-child group had at least one sibling. Only 15 percent from the so-called Little Emperor group had siblings.

Subjects took tests and played games designed to measure traits such as extroversion, agreeableness, and negativity. The contrasts between the two groups were striking. In a game where players decided how to split a pot of money, the Little Emperor generation were less generous. In another game that tested players' willingness to rely on others, Little Emperors exhibited less trust and trustworthiness. In games that measured risk taking, they favored safe bets over high-risk, high-reward propositions.

They were also more pessimistic. When asked to rate the probability of sunshine the next day, the Little Emperor group tended to expect gloomy weather. In a game that tested players' willingness to engage in competition, the Little Emperor group were also more likely to back away from competition.

While the sample size of 421 people was relatively small, the study stood out from other Little Emperor studies because it wasn't primarily based on behavioral surveys, nor did it compare single children with kids with siblings. Instead, it employed relatively new concepts from game theory to observe differences in behavioral patterns. Since Cameron et al. compared test groups that were only a few years apart in age — thus keeping large socioeconomic conditions fairly constant — the results suggest that the Little Emperor cohort's differences are a result of family structure.

Lisa Cameron admits when presenting the study results, "I did feel uncomfortable painting a cohort with such a negative brush as being less trusting and more neurotic."

The news that China's Little Emperors view themselves as unlucky and pressured may come as a surprise to others, if not themselves. This generation is the most affluent in recent Chinese history. Unlike their grandparents and parents, they didn't have to deal with the turmoil of the Cultural Revolution or the 1950s Great Famine. In the thirty years since the launch of the one-child policy, aspirations have morphed from the humble "three rounds and a sound" — bicycle, sewing machine, watch, and radio — to private home ownership, cars, and college degrees. Unlike their parents, the Little Emperor generation have never known anything but soaring economic growth.

I spent two days with Liu and his mother, Yong Min, in their apartment. Liu's Moral Hero award has scored him this two-bedroom rent-free apartment for the duration of his college years. It has security guards and landscaping, a beautiful little man-made creek, blossoming plum trees. We flipped through old photos: his mother in her youth, with soft parted lips and an ingénue look; his now-absent father in a loud checked sport coat and modified Afro; Liu's school pictures. Year after year, it was always a large crowd of boys and not very many girls. Everyone's gender is nearly neutralized with baggy tracksuit uniforms.

We paused before a studio shot of Liu Ting dressed up in yellow emperor robes. "I was *never* a Little Emperor," he said emphatically.

Yong Min's frail health made him protective. When he was ten, he remembered, he had a rare argument with his mother over a long-forgotten issue. Yong Min said, "Well, I've raised you for ten years, you dare stand up to me?" Liu Ting retorted, "It's normal for parents to take care of kids for a decade. When I'm grown up, I'll take care of you."

III

In 2005, academic Mei Zhong studied a series of letters from only children. They had been sent to radio talk show host Danyan Chen and published in a book called *The Only-Child Declaration.* Zhong analyzed the letters and broke them into categories that revealed these children were mostly preoccupied with a sense of living under pressure, excessive parental love, and loneliness. "In general, the writings have a common blue tone in them. Stress and pressure are a main theme," wrote Zhong.

Children expressed embarrassment and guilt for the huge sacrifices their parents made. One father offered to sell his blood for college fees. Another set of parents cooked magnificent feasts every weekend when their daughter returned home from school, only to live on leftovers the rest of the week. One teenager recounted how his mother, before heading to work, would travel across town every day to his dorm room to bring him breakfast and make his bed. "Before long, my roommates became upset because they're not used to having a woman in the room as they get up. What's more, my roommates, and later on, all my classmates gave me a nickname, 'Baby,' and called me as my mother does with a long inflection at the end."

With these sacrifices came great parental expectations. Many parents from this only-child generation had been deprived of an education or had theirs interrupted because of the Cultural Revolution, said Zhong. "They felt their dreams were crashed and the only hope to realize those dreams was through their only-child. There was a sense of urgency for them to push their child toward success, and in every possible aspect."

One child wrote, "Our generation of only-children is very self conscious. For historical reasons, we must shoulder all of our parents' goals and their ever-bigger dreams. Compared to previous generations, we don't have our independent future, but rather, re-walk the path our parents didn't finish; we live for it and struggle for it." The Little Emperor generation label themselves the "sandwich generation" and *kubi*.

Kubi (rhymes with "ruby"), combining the words for "bitter" and "pressure," is Internet slang, a term of self-mockery. Kids use it the way Americans say "It sucks": "I've got term papers due; my life's too *kubi*."

A former student of mine said the Little Emperor generation feel *kubi* because, compared with cohorts born in the 1970s and 1990s, they are unable to fully reap the benefits of China's economic growth but bear the brunt of its development.

Too young to take advantage of private-sector expansion or the privatization of the real estate market, they deal with skyrocketing property prices in China's major markets.

They also experienced China's expansion of higher education, which resulted in floods of graduates hitting the job market and high rates of unemployment. At the end of the Cultural Revolution in 1977, there were just 270,000 college spots available. Now 7 million college graduates flood the market yearly.

A typical *kubi* lament on Baidu, China's Google, goes thus: "When we were elementary school students we had missed the free college education at that time. We became college students eventually with the expensive tuitions, increasing enrollment, and worse teaching. We were not ensured a decent job after graduation because of the frequent education and social reform during our student days." While the one-child generation have it better than any other previous generation, they are competing in a fierce market economy. Yet their expectations have been fostered by their parents, who came from a background in which lifelong employment was a guarantee. It is this clash of expectations, I suspect, that is at the root of this malaise.

Another reason is growing restrictions on social mobility. When I first started writing about China in the late 1990s, there was a Horatio Alger–like sense that anybody could rise, provided they worked hard and were smart enough. People could look to examples like consumer electronics billionaire Huang Guangyu, who had risen from a peasant to become China's richest man.

Ten years later the landscape had changed radically. Huang is now serving a fourteen-year sentence for bribery and insider trading, as are a handful of other newly minted billionaires lacking the right political backers. Gaps between rich and poor grew so wide, China for years stopped publishing its Gini coefficient, a measure of income disparity. (In 2013, China started publishing it again, but many dispute the official figures.) In just a decade, that sense of limitless opportunity appears to have been vastly diminished.

The members of the one-child generation who feel this most are those not fortunate enough to be born in China's major cities. After graduation, they are drawn to these places in search of work, but lacking parental homes and big-city connections, they camp out in cramped lodgings with few amenities like running water or heat. In 2009, Peking University sociologist Lian Si coined the term *ant tribe* to describe these overworked and underpaid graduates.

Yet on the other end of the spectrum, employers also complain that Little Emperors have been raised with such high expectations, they make poor hires. In job ads, some employers expressly state a preference for candidates with siblings. China Railway Construction

Group, the country's second-largest state-owned construction en-
terprise, put out a want ad stating, "Non-only children college grads
from rural areas have priority."

A human resources manager quoted in Nanjing's *Jinling Evening
News* said, "We don't hire two kinds of persons, the wealthy ones
and single children." An employee at a geological survey company in
Henan said hires who were single children were quick to complain
the job was too tough and quit. Also, parents of single children were
quicker to object to the travel requirements of the job.

Another name associated with the Little Emperor generation — specifically male members of the tribe — is *diaosi,* a term for
male genitalia that is slang for "loser." The term is used by low-paid
office drones who "take an ironic pride in their lack of prospects,"
notes *Wall Street Journal* writer Josh Chin. *Diaosi* has become mainstream so quickly that Internet portal Sohu broadcasts an online com-
edy show called *Diaosi Man.* Since its 2012 debut the show's episodes
have been streamed over 1.5 billion times. The increasing popular-
ity of this term — and all it represents — has alarmed the Communist Party, which, in a recent editorial in the flagship *People's Daily,*
called for an end to its usage. Entitled "Self Deprecation — It's Time
to Stop," the essay said, "The danger it represents to the spirit of our
youth cannot be ignored."

I never ended up writing Liu's story for the *Wall Street Journal.*
Gentle forbearance did not make dramatic front-page material, and
other news cropped up. In 2008, however, I bumped into Liu again at
the Bird's Nest Stadium on Olympics opening night. He was wearing
his National Moral Hero medallion and snapping pictures. "Sister
Fong! How nice to see you." He beamed. We took a picture together.
Of all the nation-building symbols and emblems present that night,
Liu was probably one of the most representative, I mused.

"You should be out there on the field," I joked.

He giggled. "I don't think the country is ready."

IV

One year after the Olympics, I left Beijing and moved to California. While there, I met game developer Jenova Chen, a baby-faced thirty-something who is a cult figure in the gaming world.

Chen made his name creating thoughtful, lushly designed products that are worlds away from typical gaming shoot-'em-up fare. His games are more like movies, meant to evoke complex emotions like nostalgia and awe instead of pure adrenaline surges. Chen has often been compared to Japanese cartoonist Hayao Miyazaki, one of his games is on permanent exhibit at the Smithsonian Institution, and *MIT Technology Review* named him one of the world's top young innovators.

Despite this early success, Chen, product of the one-child generation, describes a state of constant pressure trying to live up to parental expectations. In traditional Chinese families, each sibling had a role to play, he said. "Being the single child meant I had to do all of them. I can't fail because that's all my family is counting on."

Chen Senior was a civil servant, someone who'd grown up poor but managed by dint of hard work to make it to Peking University (Beida), the pinnacle of Chinese academic achievement. On his child's first trip to Beijing, they skipped typical tourist sights like the Great Wall. Instead, the younger Chen was taken to Beida and Tsinghua, a move akin to taking an American child to visit Harvard and MIT. "That's the only two places we went," he recalled.

When Chen was fourteen, his father, sensing the coming Internet revolution, bought a personal computer for the teenager's use. For mid-1990s China, this was a huge investment, like buying a Stradivarius for a kid just starting violin lessons. "Nobody had a computer at the time," said Chen. His parents hoped to encourage Chen's interest in computer programming, but all the teenage Chen wanted to do was to play computer games.

For Chen, playing computer games was a welcome escape from academic life, which he made sound like a bruising scholastic version of the Hunger Games. At the time, he was not only enrolled in one of Shanghai's top high schools, he was in a special class for gifted students. "Every champion and medalist" in the city was in that class, he said. Each semester, the lowest-scoring students were cut and sent to the normal, nongifted class. They were deemed "losers." Chen spent every semester's end figuring out what his classmates' scores were, calculating how safe he was from elimination. He made few friends.

His parents wanted to steer him to a safe, prosperous career working for a prestigious company like Microsoft. Chen, however, longed to create games like *Legend of Sword and Fairy,* the first game that ever made him cry. "Nobody expected video games to make you care, to talk about sacrifice and love," he said. But telling his parents he wanted to be a game designer would be "like telling them I want to be a pornography director."

After graduation, Chen went to USC for graduate studies, one of the school's first batch of students to major in game design. For a student competition, he designed a game, *Cloud,* where players could simulate a sick child in the hospital — the asthmatic Chen had passed many such days — looking out of the window, fantasizing what it would be like to fly. So many people downloaded the game, it crashed USC's servers and made local news.

"Most games are about primal feelings like violence, competition," he said. He enjoyed those games growing up because they gave him a sense of power at a time when parental and academic pressures made him feel helpless. "But now I'm older, I want something more intellectual and relevant."

Chen eventually founded a small studio in Santa Monica and secured a three-game deal with Sony. Chen spent years developing *Journey,* a game depicting a nameless being's lonely pilgrimage across a barren landscape. Sony executives had expected the game to be done in a year. Chen, a perfectionist, took three. In the process, his company ran out of money. Chen was forced to lay off a substantial portion of his staff while the rest were forced to take 50 percent pay cuts. *Journey* eventually went on to critical and commercial success, winning the D.I.C.E. Awards, the gaming industry's equivalent of the Oscars, and becoming one of Sony PlayStation's top sellers.

Even so, Chen feels his non-mainstream choices trouble his parents. He hasn't, unlike some of his peers, made a killing on China's burgeoning Internet market. He is in the precarious world of entertainment.

"There are only three jobs for Asian kids: lawyers, doctors, and engineers," mocked Chen, ticking them off with his fingers. Such a narrow viewpoint is understandable in China, though. There, "your retirement plan is your child. When you're the only child, your parents want to make sure their investment is well vested," he said.

Several years later Chen's mother had glaucoma surgery in Shanghai. The procedure was not a success, so Chen brought her to the United States for a corrective procedure. Chen's mother's insurance didn't cover medical treatment outside China, so the operation ended up costing half of Chen's savings.

In late 2014, he married. His bride, born in China but raised in Hawaii, is also an only child. Despite their reservations about the burdens imposed on an only child, the Chens will likely be a second-generation only-child family. "I don't feel like I dare to have more than one child. I feel I can barely take care of my parents," he said.

At the time I first met Chen, I was teaching a class at the University of Southern California's Annenberg School that prepped graduate students for summer jobs in Asia. Although it was titled "Global Journalism," half the class consisted of students vying for a master's in public relations.

Before the class started, I would get everyone to do an introductory spiel about their career goals: "In five years, I hope to be doing..."

My students from China, who were mostly female, and mostly PR students, invariably said the same thing: in five years' time, they hoped to be working in in-house PR. I was mystified by these near-uniform replies. Why in-house PR? Why not agency work? Why not running their own business? I was accustomed to the soaring confidence of people in their mid-twenties, who had not yet begun to realize their limits, whose shiny new edges hadn't yet been worn down by nasty bosses, impossible deadlines, and crushing mortgages.

They told me: Well, in five years' time, they would likely be married, with families. In-house PR, with its more predictable hours and routine, was easier.

Such answers made me wonder if there was some truth to the Little Emperor stereotypes. I didn't believe that China's one-child generation were significantly more spoiled than other generations. I did, however, suspect that they struggled with a weight of heavy expectations, not only because many were single children, but also because China's rapid transformation and societal structure had shaped them to narrow their horizons early on, precisely at the time when they should be open to trying new things. Some of the problems stereotypically associated with only children appear true of this generation, not simply because they are only children, but because they are only children interacting with expectations and institutions unique to China.

Start first with the *gaokao,* the most searing, soul-destroying experience of any Chinese teen. In 1977, after the end of the Cultural Revolution, China reinstated the National College Entrance Exams, continuing a long tradition of test taking that began in the Song or Tang dynasty, with the world's first civil service exams. While a civil service exam is not the same as a college entrance exam, this long tradition of test taking has fed the Chinese belief that this is the only meritocratic way to advance.

Exam taking became so ingrained in Chinese culture that in Yunnan Province, a local dish called Crossing Bridge Noodles was said to have been developed specifically for cramming scholars. As the story goes, a wife used to walk across a bridge to deliver a nocturnal noodle snack to her husband, who was up late studying. The noodles, however, cooled before she crossed the bridge. So she devised a way of keeping the dish hot with an insulating layer of oil. True or not, the story says a lot about national obsessions. Consider, by comparison, the English, whose contribution to the culinary world — the sandwich — came about through a desire to gamble unimpeded.

With success in examinations, a well-established form of social mobility, the *gaokao* became a be-all and end-all examination for every Chinese school-going person, starting in their early teens.

When I lived in China, I always knew when *gaokao* season arrived. Colleagues would take a couple of weeks, sometimes even a month, off work in order to help their kids through this crucial time. Traffic would be lighter. Heavy construction around test areas halted. Beijing's smoggy skies would magically turn blue. I'd heard of parents who put their daughters on the Pill during *gaokao* so their focus wouldn't be diminished by menstrual cramps. Parents would put toothpaste on their child's toothbrush, just to save them those precious seconds to study.

In the year or two leading up to the *gaokao,* my Chinese students had twelve-hour school days and cram school on weekends, and they slept on average only four to six hours each night. The only children of China may not have had to compete with siblings, but they faced even fiercer competition with their peers.

While suicide rates in China among the young and college-going lag behind those of Japan, the United States, and Russia, test-taking pressure does take its toll. A 2014 Chinese government report looking at seventy-nine cases of suicide among students concluded that over 90 percent were caused by the pressures of China's test-oriented educational system. Sixty-three percent of the suicides occurred between February and July, when the *gaokao* and other important exams are held.

My students who said they wanted to work in in-house PR weren't necessarily lazy or unambitious. But the window for experimentation for a young person in China is much smaller than it is for Americans of a comparable age.

Dating, for example. With *gaokao* being a huge burden during the teenage years, they are all discouraged from distractions like the opposite sex — which isn't to say, of course, that there's no flirting or heartbreak. In 2007, a school in southern China even went so far as to ban hand-holding between male and female students. The top high school in Yizhou, a small town in southern China, issued rules stating boys and girls "should only talk together in well-lit places such as the classroom or hallway," and "exclusive talk between one boy and one girl is prohibited."

In China, the legal age for marriage for women is twenty (twenty-two for men). Women then have a window of about five to seven years before being considered officially too old for marriage, according to actual guidelines put out by the All-China Women's Federation, the organization established by the Communist Party to protect women's rights. After that, they're on the shelf, a condition charmingly termed *shengnu,* or "leftovers." With such a narrow window to make a life-changing decision, it's no wonder one in five Chinese marriages ends in divorce now, double the rate a decade ago.

Popular blogger Han Han, the Holden Caulfield of his generation, describes it thus: "Most parents won't allow their school-age children to date, and many are even opposed to their children dating when in college, but as soon as the kid graduates, the parents pray that all of a sudden, someone perfect in every respect — and if possible with an apartment of their own to boot — will drop out of heaven, and their child must marry them right away. Now, that's well thought out, isn't it?"

V

In 2012, Chen Hanbin sold the Beijing apartment his parents gave him, used the proceeds to buy two RVs, and embarked on a road trip around the world. Three years later he was still on the road, a modern-day Jack Kerouac chronicling his journey through short films and blogs.

Among his adventures: kickboxing in Thailand, scuba diving in Australia, picking watermelons in Iraq, and cuddling cobras in India. His group, called No Turning Back, have lost their passports in Cuba and narrowly escaped an avalanche in Norway and an earthquake in Chile. Original members have drifted away and been gradually replaced by new dreamers.

When Hanbin announced his intentions on Chinese social media, China's online community reacted predictably with encouragement, longing, and envy. But many commenters also voiced disapproval for his "unfilial" conduct and his abdication of parental responsibilities. One online user said, "If you have money to take care of your parents and use the leftover money to pursue your dream, then that's fine and I'm all for it. But if you selfishly sell the family home and hurt your parents' feelings, then that's another matter." I couldn't imagine this kind of reaction if an American thirty-something had decided to do something similar.

I met Hanbin in Los Angeles just after he had completed a cross-country leg that started in Miami. He'd managed to persuade his parents — who'd been lukewarm about his journey from the start — to spend a month on the road, a decision that had ended with his father breaking down in the parking lot at Universal Studios. His father started crying, begging him to come home, said Hanbin. "He said, 'Your life is too dangerous. Can you please not go on?'"

Hanbin couldn't do it. Referencing Tennessee Williams's "A Prayer for the Wild at Heart Kept in Cages," he said, "Everyone has cages but China in particular is a cage. Everyone follows one path, everyone measuring how expensive your apartment is, what school you went to, living up to your parental expectations. . . . I want to define my own life."

Was Hanbin selfish, or were his parents overly invested in their only child?

In 2012 Renmin University academic Du Benfeng coined the term *one-child family risk*. Wrote Du, "The one-child family has serious structural defects: injury and accident suffered by anyone in a family means disaster and even breakdown of this family, and the family is extraordinarily fragile." (Du's definition of fragile family structure contrasts with Western studies, where family fragility is mainly viewed through the lens of single-parent or unmarried households. These familial variations are relatively rare in China, in part because of the one-child policy's effects.)

Family fragility in China, says Du, is also exacerbated by the tendency of one single child to marry another. Only children also come under great pressure to sacrifice job mobility, career choices, and migration in order to please their parents, he said. To ameliorate this, Du suggested measures such as improving government compensation for the death of only children as well as the establishment of insurance for accidental deaths of only children. (So far, no commercial offerings of this nature appear to be available.)

These all seemed reasonable ideas. But in addition to advising tougher traffic laws and heightened safety standards in schools to protect only children, Du also suggested banning violent online games as "harmful to children's physical and mental health" and counseled that all government organizations take steps to "carry out activities being favorable to only children's safety." It was startling that Du seemed to advocate a coddled existence for only children.

VI

In 2013, I caught up with Liu again. He was still living at home, in the same small town. Among my circle of China acquaintances, this level of permanence was unusual. There were small changes, of course: He was no longer living in the glare of celebrity. There were no more rent-free apartments; he and his mother had moved to cheaper accommodation, a small five-hundred-square-foot apartment they had expanded through a series of built-in partitions. It looked like an elaborate system of bunk beds.

Liu had graduated in 2009. He'd managed to find a low-paying job in the university library. A few years later he found a graphic design job in Hangzhou but quit after less than a year. The high cost of living in a major city stretched his slender salary, he said, and long weekend trips home to see his mother also ate into his time. He was living on savings and writing his autobiography.

I found Liu unchanged, like a Chinese Dorian Gray. He was still thin, still dressed in shapeless large T-shirts and jeans, that long thumbnail, that sweet mien. Yong Min, on the other hand, looked younger than she had five years back. The lines of her face were smoother; her hair seemed glossier and had been cut into a fashionable bob. She was full of plans to make trendy air filter masks, modeled on Korean designs. Such things were becoming more popular in China's smog-filled cities, she said.

Liu, on the other hand, was drifting. In many ways, his situation seemed to confirm my assumptions: given the stifling demands of his parental obligations, he was not free to pursue his dreams, and indeed the cramped horizons had created a learned response of helplessness.

Liu reinforced my suspicions when he told me he'd auditioned for a reality TV show on Zhejiang TV. The show, called *Chinese Dream,* was modeled on BBC's *Tonight's the Night,* where ordinary people were assigned mentors to help them realize their dreams: starting their own business, or starring in a West End production, for example. Liu got an audition on the strength of his previous celebrity.

For his audition, he played the guitar and sang "Mother," the song that had been specially composed for him. But he didn't make the cut. "I told them my dream was to live happily and in peace with my mother, maybe write a book," he said. "They said my dream wasn't big enough."

When he saw me off at the bus station, I noticed he was wearing Converse-style rubber shoes with the label *Bu Xiang,* written in Romanized script. It's a cheap brand, very popular among youth from rural areas and factory workers. I'm not sure what the brand's name means — likely something positive — but the Pinyin script *Bu Xiang* could also be read to mean "Not thought of" or "Not dreamed": 不 想. I watched him walk away, his shoes rising and falling. *Bu Xiang. Bu Xiang. Bu Xiang.*

I felt sad.

I was wrong. In 2014, Liu finished his book, *We Will Be All Right.* Then he came out with a bombshell: he's transgender.

Liu had struggled with this secret the entire time he was being showered with accolades and called a national role model. Liu outed himself in a photo spread in *Southern Weekend,* a major newsmagazine, with startlingly intimate photos: putting on makeup, trying on a bra, debating whether to use the men's or women's toilets.

"Folks kept telling me not to be a sissy, to stand up, be worthy of my Moral Hero title," he said, "but deep inside I was torn because I knew I was in the wrong body."

All this time I had worried his horizons were too narrow, he had been nursing a dream of transformation.

Liu's mother had been devastated at first. The likelihood of grandchildren receded further into the distance. "People hope I can give birth to a child, which is the biggest sign of filial piety. I was conflicted," said Liu.

Eventually, he came to believe "when you can live well, you can have filial piety to your parents. I think it's time to give filial piety a new definition."

Soon, one of China's most famous Little Emperors will become an Empress.

Welcome to the Dollhouse

Sons shall be born to him:
They will be put to sleep
   on couches;
They will be clothed in robes;
They will have sceptres to
   play with . . .

Daughters shall be born to him:
They will be put to sleep on
   the ground;
They will be clothed with
   wrappers;
They will have tiles to play with.

—Book of Songs

You're going to have a gigantic mass of horny young men in China.

—Paul Ehrlich

I

In 2009 I was flipping through news items in search of a story when a headline caught my eye: "Runaway Brides Strike in Central China."

The story, a minor item, talked about how a small village called New Peace in Shaanxi Province had a rash of runaway brides. These women had decamped soon after their weddings, leaving bankrupt bridegrooms who'd paid substantial bride prices. It reminded me of the bride-buying story Liu had told me on our train journey the year before.

Despite my years in China, it was pretty much the first time I'd heard of *caili,* a kind of reverse dowry given by the groom's family to the bride's. In rural China, there is usually an exchange of money and gifts on both sides: dowries from the groom's family, and bride price from the bride's side. Usually, the balance tips in favor of *caili,* reflecting the economic value rural women brought as cooks, bedmates, and baby makers.

During the Mao era, such exchanges were modest — a set of clothes, or enamel washbasins. Wealthier families might, perhaps, rise to the heights of a Flying Pigeon bicycle or a suite of rosewood furniture. But starting from about 2001, *caili* values rose sharply when China's first one-child-policy generation started to reach marriageable age.

China's historical preference for sons predates the one-child policy, of course, but there's no question that the imposition of the one-child policy on this culture created the biggest gender imbalance in the world. By 2020, China will have 30 to 40 million surplus men. The country's population of single men will equal or surpass the number of Canadians or Saudi Arabians in the world. Ten years later, one in four men in China will be a low-skilled bachelor.

Son preference also exists in other cultures, but nowhere else is it as extreme as in China. Forced to limit their choices, many Chinese couples turned to infanticide, daughter abandonment, and, with technological advances, sex-selective abortion to ensure they had at least one son to carry on the family name. In India, where there is also son preference but never a one-child policy, there are 108 boys born for every 100 girls. In China at the time the policy shifted to a two-child rule, a staggering 119 boys were born for every 100 girls. (The global average is 105 boys to every 100 girls, seen as Nature's way of compensating for risky male behavior, which makes boys more likely to die earlier.)

The world has never seen such a huge national collection of bachelors, men who will not be able to find mates unless China opens its doors to massive immigration, a highly unlikely scenario. There is a name for these men: *guanggun,* or "bare branches," biological dead ends.

It seemed like New Peace might be a *guanggun* village. It is located in Shaanxi, which is one of the ten provinces in China with the dubious honor of having the most unequal gender ratios. If you look at a map of China, New Peace would be located somewhere squarely in the middle, geographically centered, culturally on the fringes. The nearest major city is Hanzhong, whose heyday was back in the Han dynasty, when the city was hailed as the birthplace of paper. Since then the city, population 3 million — about the size of Chicago, but small by China's standards — has bumped along with no national significance. Hanzhong didn't even merit a direct flight from the capital, Beijing.

I was curious about what a *guanggun* village might be like. I imagined groups of horny, sullen men lurking in village squares and Internet cafés, lust and violence as palpable as the polluted haze of Beijing skies.

To be on the safe side, I decided to travel to New Peace with our office's lone male researcher. The precaution turned out to be unnecessary. New Peace is like most villages in China, filled with old women and children. All the young people of working age — including the *guanggun* — were off earning money in the cities, as there was nothing but subsistence farming on the village's tiny rice plots. Since men stood to inherit family land, many retained their rural household registration status. The young women of New Peace, however, having nothing to inherit, hightailed it for bright lights and big factories as soon as they could. Few returned permanently.

In New Peace, Shufen, the mother of one of the duped bride-grooms, welcomed me into the family home. It was a comfortable dwelling, with a traditional sloping roof and big wooden doors, hos-pitably open to let in light and the occasional neighbor. The only thing out of place was a scarlet motorcyle parked in the living room, red rosettes drooping from the handles. It had been a present for the runaway bride.

While showing me wedding pictures, Shufen related the sad story of her son's aborted marriage. Zhou Pin, her son, had left New Peace as a teenager to work in southern China's factories. Long hours and regimented life on the line gave him little opportunity to meet women. Year after year, Zhou dutifully trudged home for Spring Fes-tival, only to meet his parents' increasingly agitated queries. In New Peace, a single son approaching his mid-twenties is a big source of shame, said Shufen.

A family friend told Shufen that her nephew had married a girl from Sichuan Province. The bride had three Sichuanese friends visit-ing her who might be interested in marriage, said the friend.

In the old days, marriage with outsiders would be frowned on by New Peace's insular villagers. Why, Sichuanese people didn't even speak the same dialect, said Shufen. But New Peace, with fourteen thousand inhabitants, had thirty bachelors on the books and no women of marriageable age. Clearly, they would have to adapt to changing times. Shufen took matters into her own hands and set up a meeting. She summoned her son home.

Zhou's wooing was swift and businesslike. He met the three women and proposed to the youngest and prettiest after the first meeting. The woman agreed, with a proviso: *caili* of a little over $5,500, which represented about a decade's worth of farm income for the Zhous.

Three days later, the couple registered their union. They posed for studio pictures, the bride's cheeks Photoshopped ivory to match her wedding dress. In another picture, the couple are resplendent in traditional embroidered Chinese outfits of red and gold. The bride pretends to light a string of firecrackers. Zhou mugs a grimace, hands to his ears.

At the wedding banquet a week later, Shufen formally handed over the *caili* — half of it cobbled together from family loans — to a woman she believed to be the bride's cousin.

Matrimony was catching. Soon, two neighbors sought the new bride out and asked her to introduce suitable friends to their sons. Two marriages happened in swift succession, with *caili* amounts similar to what the Zhous paid.

Within a month, all the brides had vanished.

There was something cinematic about this. I imagined the women sprinting across rice paddies, wedding gowns hiked to their knees, veils rippling in the wind. The truth was somewhat less picturesque. Zhou's wife escaped by pretending to have a diarrhea attack and climbed out of the outhouse.

When I arrived in New Peace four months later, most of the duped bridegrooms had left to seek jobs elsewhere. Only Zhou remained.

It turned out the marriage, formed so quickly and in such a pragmatic fashion, had touched his heart. Very early on he had suspected his bride was not the innocent country girl she'd claimed to be, he said. She'd understood some of his references to his factory work and asked a few questions that made him suspect she had worked in a city. Even so, Zhou hoped she would adjust to New Peace's quiet rhythms. She had seemed gentle and grateful for small attentions. He had planned to seek work closer to home and return often for feast days. He'd bought her the motorbike so she could blunt the dullness of village life with trips to Hanzhong. They made plans to see the terra-cotta warriors in Xian, a five-hour bus ride away.

I could see little to attract young women to New Peace and hold them there. It had a small shop, a one-stop outlet that sold things like washing powder and pesticide. (The latter is so commonly used in rural suicides, *New York Times* reporter Elisabeth Rosenthal called it "the Chinese equivalent of Valium in every bathroom cabinet.") Farming was still hard work. The fields were too small for machinery, and so a lot of field work was done the way it had been a hundred years before. Lots of houses didn't have running water. And while the young married women of New Peace worked extraordinarily hard in the fields and the home tending to children and in-laws, their husbands were free to roam outside for months on end. In this kind of situation, it's not difficult to see why, until the mid-2000s, China was the only country in the world where more women killed themselves than men, with the suicide rate highest among young rural women. This is changing now as villages empty of women; it's rural men who are increasingly the ones killing themselves.

Zhou's family feared he would take his own life in despair, and his parents forbade him to leave the village. In truth, Shufen said, all of them were in despair, worried about how to repay the heavy loans they had undertaken for the *caili*. Other New Peace families were worse off. One of the duped bridegrooms had a younger brother, also single, and the family didn't know how they could raise his bride price. His father moaned, "I wish I had daughters."

I had initially been drawn to the story of New Peace's runaway brides because of its tragicomic elements. I liked how this small band of women had somehow managed to strike a blow against China's patriarchal system. As a woman and despised daughter myself, I felt the problems of New Peace and other countless little hamlets seemed like poetic justice, payback for hundreds of years of systemic discrimination against women.

But Zhou's gallantry touched my heart. Even though his disastrous marriage had left him in debt and legal limbo, he refused to blame his wife. He didn't hate her for leaving, he said. "She must have her own troubles." He actually spoke to her a few times after she ran away—he said she'd called. "She said she was sorry, she had no choice."

Not all of China's bachelors would be as generous under similar circumstances, but they all face a bleak future that is not their doing.

II

There is no shortage of theories about how this male youth imbalance will shape China, and by extent the world. Undeniably, large groups of young males create situations ripe for social dissent and violence and are linked to developments such as the Arab Spring and the rise in rape in India. How, then, will it be for China, where the gender gap is by far the largest in the world?

In 2004, academics Valerie Hudson and Andrea den Boer's book *Bare Branches* argued that China's large population of single men could create a more warlike nation. The many periods in China's history that have seen a male surplus include two Qing-era rebellions in areas with extremely large numbers of single males. One, a rebellion of bandits in northeast China, called the Nien Rebellion, occurred in 1851 when famine and female infanticide had resulted in a ratio of roughly 129 men to every 100 women. One in four men was unable to marry at all, noted Hudson and den Boer. (Today, some provinces in China have between 26 and 38 percent more males than females, according to Yi Zhang, population researcher at the Chinese Academy of Social Sciences.) As Hudson and den Boer point out, a large population of single men is not, on its own, necessarily a recipe for violence. "The mere presence of dry bare branches cannot cause a fire, but when the sparks begin to fly, those branches can act as kindling, turning sparks into flames."

While intriguing, Hudson and den Boer's theories were considered by many social scientists as speculative and not necessarily predictive. Ten years later, their thesis gained slightly more credence, as China grew increasingly assertive in territorial spats with neighbors. In 2012, China's squabble with Japan over some barren uninhabited islands, called Senkaku by the Japanese and Diaoyu by the Chinese, heated up to such an extent that the *Economist*'s cover story raised the question "Could Asia Really Go to War over These?"

In 2014, ten years after the publication of *Bare Branches,* Hudson and den Boer argued in a *Washington Post* article that a "virile form of nationalism" has begun to creep into China's foreign policy rhetoric, which they believe has been deliberately stoked to keep the allegiance of "young adult bare branches."

Domestically, at least, it makes sense that more men equals more strife. In 2008, economists showed that a 1 percent increase in China's gender ratios increased violent and property crime rates between 5 and 6 percent. Researchers estimated that the "increasing maleness" of China's young adult population could account for as much as a third of the overall rise in crime. A 2013 study by Zhejiang University found that China's bachelors had lower self-esteem compared to married men, and much higher rates of depression and aggression.

While women in China do not experience the levels of public assault and molestation they face in places like the Middle East or India, they do experience a great deal of violence at home. One in four women in China confronts domestic violence, according to the All-China Women's Federation, and they have few legal protections. In 2011, Kim Lee, the American-born wife of a famous Chinese entrepreneur, tried fruitlessly to file a police report against her husband for battering her. When the police refused to recognize her beating as a crime, she went on Weibo and posted pictures of her bruises, sparking a media frenzy. Later she was awarded a divorce on the grounds of domestic violence — a landmark ruling — and emerged as a vocal advocate for women's rights. The Chinese government only drafted a national law against domestic violence in 2014.

Economically, the impact of China's gender imbalance appears mixed. Economists Wei Shang-Jin and Zhang Xiaobo argue the gender imbalance may stimulate economic growth by inducing more entrepreneurship. They found that regions with a higher gender imbalance have higher GDP growth and more vigorous growth of private companies. On the other hand, Wei and Zhang also think the imbalance has led to excessive saving, as parents with sons stockpile funds to increase their eligibility on the marriage market, and the researchers calculate that half the increase in China's savings in the past twenty-five years can be attributed to the increase in the gender ratio.

If this is the case, China's *guanggun* problem will make it harder for Beijing to transition from an export-led economy by stimulating domestic consumption. Wei and Zhang's theories are not mainstream — economists have many explanations for why China saves — but they do add to the growing body of evidence that the one-child policy, in many respects, created a demographic structure that will dampen future growth.

A 2014 Australian study also found that China's gender imbalance contributed to excessive savings and rising crime rates. Unfortunately, policies that seek to rebalance the gender imbalance will take decades and slow real per-capita income growth, though the study's writers concluded this slowed economic growth would be offset by gains made from reduced crime.

No one knows for sure yet if China's male surplus will decisively crimp China's economic growth or make it a more warlike nation. But it seems safe to say that it has hugely intensified marriage anxiety in a society where parents — particularly parents of only children — are extremely invested in their offspring's romantic choices.

Back in 2009, high *caili* prices were still an unfamiliar concept to many Chinese city folk. While prevalent in the countryside, *caili* was still "rare in urban Chinese environments," wrote Canadian scholar Siwan Anderson. Barely six years later, the real estate company Vanke had published a map showing *caili* rates across China. According to company data, cities with the most expensive *caili* were Shanghai and Tianjin at $16,000 and $9,600, respectively. These prices were just the tip of the iceberg, since desirable bridegrooms were also expected to own real estate.

Vanke's methodology was widely criticized. Some said it under-estimated bride prices — why was *caili* in Beijing, second-largest city in China, only $1,600 and two bottles of fiery Maotai, and zero in booming Chongqing? Still, almost no one disagreed with the dis-agreeable notion that *caili,* once a quaint custom of the countryside, was now a nationwide practice. More than ever since the 1949 launch of the People's Republic, marriage had become a matter of money, valuation, and investment.

It may be hard for Westerners to understand how marriages can be such stark dollars-and-cents transactions. But in China, parental participation is a given. Unions are never just between the bride and groom. Both parties are not just giving themselves, but potentially everything their parents have jointly accumulated.

With men vying for a limited number of brides, parents are chip-ping in to help them buy apartments and enhance their eligibility. This is called "building a nest to catch a phoenix," and the ones best feathering their nests are realtors. (Some economists estimate that the gender imbalance accounted for an increase of between 30 and 48 percent in housing prices in China between 2003 and 2009.) Cer-tainly, China's soaring real estate prices have created a colony of house slaves — literally, *fangnu* — hapless people on the hook for astronom-ical sums similar to America's subprime mortgage victims.

I met one such *fangnu* in Tian Qingeng, twenty-five, a good-natured lathe operator, in 2013. Tian lives in Ninghai, a pleasant lit-tle city a few hours from Shanghai. Tian works in a factory, making about $400 a month. That's not much even by Ninghai standards, where average incomes are about $3,000 monthly. To increase his eligibility, his parents emptied their savings — all $45,000 — and borrowed an additional $35,000 from relatives, to buy a two-bedroom apartment in central Ninghai.

Every month, mortgage payments take up roughly 80 percent of Tian and his parents' combined monthly income. That makes life a complicated dance of calculations and costs. Heat? Too much. Furniture? The bare minimum. Vegetables? Only what can be grown in the family plot at Tian's parents' country home. The only indulgences they allow themselves are lottery tickets.

Tian invited me to his apartment. The development itself was fairly new and boasted a pond, a topiary, and a rock garden designed to resemble Guilin's famous karst mountain scenery. As we walked through the courtyard, I heard the anthems of the middle class: the *blip-blip* of video games, somebody torturing John Thompson on the piano.

Tian may have staked his future on a nest to catch a phoenix bride, but it is a grievously bare one. Aside from built-in fixtures bought cheaply from the previous owners — a divorcing yuppie couple — the apartment is sparsely furnished and chilly. His mother made some attempt to soften the place with needlepoint pictures and handmade pillows. In Tian's bedroom, she's placed a three-foot-tall stuffed rabbit and bamboo plants. But the plastic sheathing on the bunny is covered with dust, and the bamboo is withering, for Tian never remembers to water it.

Tian has acquired the love nest but made few efforts to find someone to share it with. The trouble is, he doesn't quite know how to set about finding this person. Ninghai is not a major city like Beijing or Shanghai, with gyms and nightclubs and a rich singles life. People still wash their clothes at the river on fine days, and courting is still done the old-fashioned way, through introductions by someone you know. Horoscopes and auguries are still important. One of Tian's friends finally found a girlfriend, but they delayed the union to avoid marrying in the Year of the Horse. Astrologers see a Horse year as tumultuous and bad for marriage and counseled waiting for the more union-friendly Year of the Sheep, explained Tian. Of course, the couple must then take care not to conceive too soon, as Sheep babies are seen as too passive, too unlikely to succeed in life.

This whole clash of modern and traditional has proved too much for Tian. He'd rather retreat into his room and play computer games. There's another name his relatives freely call him: *zhai nan,* or geek. Literally "residence male," the term is derived from the Japanese *otaku,* "house male."

A few months before we met, Tian went on his one and only date, a fix-up arranged by his uncle. All he knew about her was that she was in her twenties and a fellow factory worker. After frugally working out a budget, Tian arranged to meet her at a café where $3.50 would buy him endless coffee refills, even though he dislikes caffeine. The conversation was turgid. He was disappointed. Her face, he complained, wasn't "harmonious." He said he didn't know what to say to her. In truth, he didn't know what to say to any woman his age, having no sisters and working in an all-male environment.

I asked him what he was looking for in a wife.

After a long silence, he ventured, "She must have a nice personality."

What does that *mean?* I pressed him.

"She must obey my parents." Pause. "And obey me."

Each weekend Tian's mother takes a bus from their countryside home to cook and clean for her son. In between bouts of floor wiping and slicing tomatoes, she drops hints: "Don't you think it's time?" and "I'm not too old to help with children." (I was amused to learn she works at a factory making horsewhips.)

It's imperative that Tian marry, not only to meet parental expectations. He calculates that his parents have about a decade of wage earning left in them. He needs to find a partner who can help him service the mortgage once they retire. Of course, this isn't necessarily fair to the future Mrs. Tian, who will be expected to help pay for Tian's flat but whose name isn't likely to end up on the property deed.

"Of course not," said Tian, when I asked if he would have the property jointly listed with the future Mrs. "My parents and I bought it," he said firmly.

Only 30 percent of marital home deeds in China's major cities include the wife's name, even though over 70 percent of women contribute to the purchase, according to sociologist Leta Hong Fincher. That becomes a huge problem when marriages sour and matrimonial assets are divided up in divorce court. In 2011, China issued a new interpretation of its Marriage Law specifying marital property as belonging to the person named on the property deed — almost always the husband. Given that much of the recent wealth creation in China has come from appreciating values in soaring property markets, Chinese women have therefore been left out of what is arguably the biggest accumulation of residential real estate wealth in history: some $27 trillion worth, estimates Hong Fincher.

The paucity of dating options in a little city like Ninghai contrasts with big-city offerings. There are high-tech choices, with matchmaking sites like Jiayuan and Lotus, and low-tech, such as parents placing ads in public parks on behalf of single children. This last method has been going on for over a decade and came about when retiree parents got together with peers to lament their children's single status. Soon, they started swapping information, and out of this were born the so-called marriage markets in China's public parks.

I first stumbled across one of these marriage markets by accident in 2006. It was cherry blossom season in Beijing's Yuyuantan Park, when I spotted a clutch of people gathered around a corner of the park. Curious, I wandered over and saw batches of handwritten notices, laid on the ground or clipped to lines strung between bushes.

I fell into conversation with a man who'd put out an ad for his son, who was in his mid-twenties and made his living as a painter reproducing famous artworks. The father had even brought photos of his son's work. "See? Isn't he talented?" he said, pointing to a copy of Van Gogh's *Irises*. Like most of the others advertised in the park, the son did not know his father was trolling for dates for him. "He would be very shy to know I'm introducing him to you," said the father. I quickly added I was married. His face fell. Carefully, he put away his son's pictures. Surely, I asked, it was a little soon to start worrying about his son's singlehood? He sighed. He knew China's marriage squeeze was on.

Over the years as I came across these marriage markets, I noticed a trend in the ads: the men tended to be in their mid-twenties, without a college education. The women advertised tended to be older and better educated. This is not just because China's legal age for marriage — again, twenty for women, twenty-two for men — creates a built-in expectation that men should seek younger (and presumably less established) mates. It is also of a piece with China's deep-seated hypergamous culture, where women marry up and men marry down. Naturally, this adds to an already tight marriage market. Hypergamy obviously disadvantages rural bachelors like the men of New Peace, but it also limits the choices of highly educated women, leading to a common joke: "There are three genders in China: male, female, and female with PhD."

I doubt many of these marriage market ads actually result in unions, but they do show the strong role parents play in China's dating scene. In her book *Who Will Marry My Daughter?* sociologist Sun Peidong found only three matches made at Shanghai's People's Park marriage mart, out of sixty-five postings. Despite this failure rate, Sun concluded that the marriage mart filled an important need, providing a forum for the parents of the one-child generation to share their fears about their children's future. It also reflected their anxieties about the growing frailty of China's family structure.

I wanted to know more about modern dating methods, in which

singles were active participants, not their parents. In 2013, I took part in a group matchmaking event organized by Jiayuan. The NAS-DAQ-listed company — ticker symbol DATE — is one of China's biggest matchmaking agencies with over 110 million registered users. The three-hour event targeted white-collar workers and cost about $16. About one hundred participants had registered for it, which was a relief, as some of these group-dating events had tens of thousands of participants.

Since I was decidedly on the older side and a foreigner to boot, my researcher, Shuang, and I came up with a cover story: I would introduce myself as her older cousin, an overseas Chinese, working in Beijing, who was accompanying her on her search for a mate.

It was a good thing we'd come prepared, for we were required to produce IDs at the registration desk. Nobody could creatively embellish his or her age, for we were furnished with tags indicating the decade when we were born. Shuang had a big red sticker saying "90s." Mine, of course, said "70s," which in Chinese dating circles classified me as 3S — Single, born in the Seventies, and Stuck. It felt like the scarlet letter. I asked the organizers how many of these "70s" stickers they gave out. "Not many," sniffed one, eyeing me dubiously.

We were then ushered into a ballroom, where chairs were arranged in squares, in groups of ten. In a corner were some refreshments: fruit, soft drinks, and sweet biscuits, no alcohol. I sidled over to a group, eyeing the other participants: a woman with the big "70s" sticker partially hidden under her hair and plastic Crocs on her feet, and a man in his thirties who never lifted his eyes from his phone. We were given small slips of pink paper on which we were supposed to write our details: name, hobbies, QQ number — QQ being a popular instant messaging service. The idea was that if we saw any potential suitors, we would exchange slips. Everybody gave furtive glances around before busying themselves with the pink slips.

When the MC bounded on stage, it was a relief, but not for long.

"Everyone! Stand up! Turn to your partner! Massage your partner!" I gingerly rubbed a skinny twenty-something's shoulder blades, before turning around so he could rub mine. Absently, I noticed I'd creased his beautifully ironed shirt. "That's it! Give it a good pounding!" roared the MC, and we dutifully thumped each other's shoulders.

We were told to pick a slogan as a group — something romantic — and then chant it together. The group that produced the loudest noise or the most creative slogan — I wasn't quite sure which — would win. Our group came up with the anemic-sounding "Eternal Love Warriors." We sounded as loud as newborn kittens when our turn came to chant, despite the energetic efforts of a forty-something I'll call Zhang, who had appointed himself the group's leader. "Come on! All together!" he screeched. "Eternal! Love! Warriors!"

We yelped again, feebly.

Then it came down to introductions. Everyone was dreadfully serious. All the women kept saying they were "looking for someone sincere." All the men enumerated their accomplishments: degree, job, car, and whether or not they had that all-important Beijing *hukou*. Nobody pretended they were just there for a good time, or to make friends, or to find a companion for walks on the beach. The desire was naked — to find a partner with a view to marriage — and it was about as romantic as someone spitting. Zhang, the self-appointed ringleader, introduced himself as someone who owned his own import-export business. He didn't go as far as some other men, who detailed salaries and apartment size, but said, with raised eyebrows, "Let me just say, I have what it takes." The woman in Crocs said she was a doctor whose busy schedule made it hard for her to meet people. She was the only female in the group who said she didn't mind dating someone younger.

When it came to my turn, I hastily trotted out my cover story: I was just there to accompany my cousin. Zhang eyed me sternly, "Yes, but let me ask you, are you *sincere?*"

And then we were asked to move on to the next group, to repeat the cycle: the massage, the slogan, the chanting, the introductions.

After we staggered out, I asked Shuang what she thought. She rolled her eyes. "It felt like I was back in school," she sniffed. "All those childish games."

The somberness of these dating events turns off many people besides Shuang. Sensing an opportunity, Alex Edmunds, a twenty-six-year-old Princeton graduate, launched a company called CaoCaoBa (the name means "Hey, Let's Get Together") that bills its mixers as "networking events" with built-in activities, such as hiking, badminton, or dinner. Many of Edmunds's clients are tech companies like GE, IBM, Microsoft, Sohu, and Baidu, which subsidize these events to the tune of $5,000 to $6,000 each time, through each company's Danshen Julebu — literally, "Singles Club."

"Nobody wants to go to a dating event — that's a big turnoff. We call it networking, but it's clear these things are held for people with the inclination to date," said Edmunds.

These companies aren't matchmaking for altruistic reasons but as a way to decrease staff turnover — married people are less likely to job-hop — and provide an increasingly valued company perk. These Singles Clubs not only attract workers themselves; they draw and reassure the parents, especially those whose only child is working away from home. Baidu, for example, sends an annual newsletter of its club activities to employees' families. Parents send back handwritten notes urging "more singles events," according to the *Financial Times*.

In any culture, the search for love involves work and, by extension, some hardship. But it seems like dating in China is particularly difficult because of the additional built-in pressures of heavy parental expectations and lopsided gender ratios. Not so long ago, most people in China resorted to matchmakers or moved in such narrow circles that a potential mate was relatively easy to find. Now there are more dating choices, but at the same time greater anxiety.

Although the one-child policy shrank family sizes and drastically reduced the extended family network, the basic contour of the nuclear family still holds true. Other definitions of family evolving in the West — gay families, multiethnic families, childless families, single-parent families, and unmarried and stepfamilies — are still rarities in China, partly because family-planning rules prevent some of these formations. There are few unmarried mothers in China, for example, since they would find it extremely difficult to get birth certificates and *hukou*s for any offspring without a marriage certificate.

Of course, some of this marriage anxiety is amplified and deliberately hyped up. Retailers, spotting a moneymaking opportunity, turned singlehood into a shopping event with Guanggun Jie, or "Singles' Day," each November 11. Started in the 1990s by a group of students at Nanjing University, who bought themselves small presents to console themselves for their single status, the event has now become the biggest online shopping event in the world, netting billions in sales and surpassing events like the US Cyber Monday. In 2012, online giant Alibaba went as far as trademarking the term Double 11 in China, threatening legal action against media outlets that took ads from competitors using the term. It was as if Amazon had trademarked "Valentine's Day."

The Communist Party also has a hand in ratcheting up marriage anxiety, especially among females. Given the male-female imbalance, you'd think women would feel more empowered and valued as a relatively scarce commodity. Not so. Marriage anxiety begins early for women in China because of the perception that their prospects fizzle when they are in their late twenties, a time when their counterparts in the West still consider themselves eligible.

Some of this was fostered by a 2007 government-backed campaign by the All-China Women's Federation, the Communist Party organ ironically tasked with promoting women's rights. Called the "Leftover Women" campaign, it coined the insulting term *leftover women,* or *sheng nü,* to describe over-twenty-five females as the stuff of kitchen scrapings and doggy bags. There was no such campaign to help single *men,* who are, after all, the group most in need of help.

Hong Fincher believes the "Leftover Women" campaign is designed to discourage educated women, specifically, from holding off marriage and childbirth as this is precisely the group the Communist Party wants breeding "quality" children.

One of the stated objectives of the one-child policy was reducing quantity in order to increase the quality of the population. A common slogan used by birth planners has been "Raise the Quality, Control the Size" (*Tigao renkou suzhi. Kongzhi renkou shuliang*). Evidently, authorities were not satisfied with the pace of this. In 2007 China's State Council announced that the country had a severe problem with the so-called low quality of the population that would render China uncompetitive in the global marketplace. Upgrading population quality became, once again, a high priority. Shortly after this the All-China Women's Federation launched the Leftover Women campaign.

China is not alone in its push to get educated women to marry and have children. Many Asian countries, faced with declining birthrates, have also struggled with a similar backlash against women's rights. In Japan, terms like *parasite* and *Christmas cake* ("goes bad after twenty-five") echo China's "Leftover Women."

In 1994, Lee Kuan Yew, founding prime minister of the tiny island nation of Singapore, lamented giving equal rights to women there because it made them less eligible in the hypergamous marriage system. "We thought we would open up the whole system, give equal opportunities for education and jobs, like the West," he said, "but we forgot that culture does not change rapidly. So you want to be the boss in your family. You don't want a wife who is smarter than you, and earning more than you."

This backlash has sparked a nostalgia for pre-liberation, pre-feminist times in China. About a year after the launch of the "Leftover Women" campaign, a number of adult education workshops promoting deference to men sprang up across the country. Known as "woman morality courses," or Confucius workshops, many are linked to local governments, schools, and educational foundations, with the express aim of teaching people in China "traditional values," as espoused by the philosopher Confucius. (These Confucius workshops are not to be mistaken for the Confucius Institute, the arm of the Ministry of Education tasked with promoting Chinese culture overseas.)

A researcher of mine attended one of these workshops and recorded the proceedings. The event was a once-monthly, one-day affair costing a little over $30 and organized by the Hebei Province Traditional Culture Research Association, which is linked to the province's literature federation. (Many of the association's leaders are senior government officials.)

Standing beside pictures of Confucius and Xi Jinping, teacher Ding Xuan told a packed classroom, "A husband is a wife's heaven. A wife should learn how to show respect to the heaven." Throughout the three-hour class, Ding constantly emphasized the need for women to take a back seat, with statements such as "Strong women will have different problems. They'll have cancer in the breast and other parts of the body. The gods are helping you, as you do not want to be a woman anymore."

Ding urged women to emulate President Xi Jinping's wife, Peng Liyuan, arguably China's most glamorous First Lady since Soong May-ling. Peng is a folksinger who was for many years more famous than her politician husband. For decades, the couple led separate lives as they pursued their careers in different parts of the country. But that, according to Ding, is not what made Peng a paragon of Chinese womanhood. "She can do noodles, *bing*, she can ride a bicycle and

buy vegetables by herself," leaving Xi Jinping free to focus on his career and "be the world-famous sage-king."

It seems incredible that such throwback messages exist in modern
China, yet these workshops appeal to a segment of society who feel
alienated in a fast-changing world. Women drawn to these workshops
typically have family problems, such as cheating spouses. Men — and
these workshops appear to appeal to both sexes — are drawn by messages that bolster their flagging egos at a time of crushing societal and
demographic pressures. In a September 2014 online poll with over
thirty thousand respondents, 51 percent said these courses had value.

There are Confucius workshops across the country in Shandong,
Hebei, Shanxi, Guangdong, and Henan. Some are free or subsidized;
others can be weeklong affairs costing a few hundred dollars. It's possible that some of the workshops have less inflammatory, less discrim-
inatory content. I heard, for example, of women's workshops that
focus on family counseling and teaching women domestic skills like
needlework.

At least one other Confucius workshop took a similar tone to
the one in Hebei. In Dongguan, a major manufacturing center with a
large young female population of factory workers, there was a wom-
en's workshop that upheld precepts such as "Don't fight back when
being beaten by your husband" and "Never divorce." In September
2014, authorities closed it down for operating without a license and
"violating social morality."

III

The one group that has substantially benefited from the one-child
policy is urban Chinese females. If you are a female born after 1980
in a major Chinese city, your chances of surviving past childhood,
getting enough nutrition, and attaining higher education are signifi-

cantly better than those of a Chinese daughter born in any earlier period this century or last.

Only-child females, especially, who didn't have brothers to compete with for parental resources, were the beneficiaries of the very pragmatic Chinese strategy of "raising a daughter as a son" (*guniang dang erzi yang*), notes anthropologist Vanessa Fong. As a result, record numbers of women in China are receiving a college education. In 2010, women made up half of the master's degree students in China. The country's female labor force participation is among the highest in Asia, with 70 percent of Chinese women either employed in some capacity or seeking employment, compared to just a quarter of their Indian sisters, according to Gallup.

But it's hard to make the case that the one-child policy advanced Chinese women's rights when, balanced against urban women's advancements, one considers the huge numbers of females killed at birth or abandoned, as well as aborted female fetuses. Nobel Prize–winning economist Amartya Sen estimates that infanticide and gendercide have contributed to a missing 100 million women in Asia. Roughly half of those would have been Chinese.

With the current gender imbalance, women are certainly more valuable, but not necessarily more valued. In addition to a rising anti-feminist backlash, the female shortage has resulted in increasing commodification of women. Prostitution and sex trafficking in China have been on the rise for the past decade, though nobody has precise figures, for enforcement is lax and transparency low. In 2007, the US State Department estimated that a minimum of ten to twenty thousand victims are trafficked domestically within China yearly, earning traffickers more than $7 billion annually, more than selling drugs or weapons.

While it's possible to argue that the one-child policy benefited *some* women in China, it's certainly been detrimental to women in bordering countries such as Vietnam, Cambodia, Myanmar, and North Korea, where trafficking and kidnapping of women for Chinese men have risen in recent years. Many are forced or tricked into being sold as wives for Chinese men. Unlike the runaway brides of New Peace, most are unable to run away or, having escaped, face worse treatment. Chinese law tends to treat victims of sex trafficking as offenders, and there is very little in the way of shelters and support for these victims. Some, like North Korean women, if caught, are deported, where they face internment or death. According to the human rights organization Durihana Association, the bulk of the estimated fifty to one hundred thousand North Korean refugees in China are women sold for about $1,500 per head.

Perhaps the creepiest example I witnessed of China's increasing commodification of women came when I visited a sex doll factory in Dongguan, the same city where authorities shut down the most extreme of the Confucius workshops. At least one manufacturer there had come up with a unique solution: If China is running out of women, why not make fake women?

In 2009, factory owner Vincent He (pronounced "her") and his partners were casting about for a new business after shuttering a company that made office furniture. What kind of high-value item could they make that would be in great demand? Their answer: sex dolls. Not inexpensive inflatables, but life-size, steel-jointed skeletons covered with pliable PVC flesh, made to look as realistic as possible, and retailing for $5,000 upward.

From 2009 to 2010, He and his partners experimented with different prototypes. They set up a test facility in Guangzhou's university district, seeking college students as testers. Feng Wengguang was one of those who responded, after seeing a flyer with the headline "Fake Dolls, Real Love."

Feng, an industrial design major, was curious — and not just for a taste of forbidden fruit. "I thought it could be a good business model," he said. After all, with the approaching avalanche of single men in China, fake women could be real business, he reckoned.

It took him a little while to find the test location in a dark, narrow alley not far from his college, Guangdong University of Technology. The storefront was covered with a piece of red cloth. A famous song, "Love Game," was playing. He hesitated outside, nervous and unsure, before pulling aside the red curtain. You can only go ahead of others by trying something new, he thought.

Thus Feng joined a strange club of single men. Calling themselves the Kawaii — Japanese slang for "cute" — Club, the group of eight undergraduates started meeting regularly for meals, karaoke sessions, and road-testing sex dolls for He, who named his company Hitdoll Inc. (Slogan: "Finest Love Doll from China.")

In the beginning it seemed like a twisted form of Goldilocks and the Three Bears: Feng and the other testers complained that the five-foot-long dolls were too stiff, too cold, or too unreal. Hitdoll's makers experimented with materials (silicone, rubber), breast size (C to EE), hair (synthetic, human), and ethnicity (African, Asian, Caucasian). "It was strange giving all this feedback because we didn't think of ourselves as the end customer," said Feng. With hefty price tags, Hitdoll was aiming the product squarely at the well-heeled and, most likely, married man.

Kawaii Club members "never consider we might one day need these things. We're sure we can find real women," said Feng, with the supreme confidence of a twenty-four-year-old. After graduation, he even joined the company as a designer.

In 2011, Hitdoll started production. Three years later, when I visited their workshop, they were selling ten to twelve units a month, with sales divided between domestic and international markets. Hitdoll's business is difficult to scale up. For one thing, the five-foot dolls are not easily transported, and they are shipped in huge wooden crates resembling coffins. They can't be folded up or stashed in a nightstand drawer. "They really are designed to take the place of real women," said He.

Nancy Cheng, manager of Buccone, a high-end sex toy shop in Guangzhou, told me a customer who'd bought a Hitdoll rang up a few days later to ask if there was any way the doll could be folded up. The customer explained that his mother lived with him and had taken a strong dislike to the doll. "Finally, he had to sit down with her and say, 'Look, I'm a bachelor and I have needs. Do you want me to visit prostitutes?' Then," said Ms. Cheng solemnly, "she consented to him having it."

In 2014, Feng helped design a lower-end line of sex dolls purely for China's domestic market, costing a more pocket-friendly $3,000. Features are scaled down: lashes and brows are painted, instead of made of real hair, and the dolls feel stiffer and less pliable. In dim light, they do look eerily like real women, in part because they have been designed to resemble specific East Asian soft-porn stars. Certain popular features from the higher-end model have been retained.

"The nipples — they are very tough," said He, tugging vigorously to demonstrate. "Normal ones," he said, "could never withstand such treatment."

Of course, Hitdoll represents an extremely niche market. But I believe it is part of a bigger trend in China resulting from the scarcity of women, which is manifesting itself in increasingly hostile attitudes toward women and feminism.

That's not likely to go away even as the pressures generated by the gender imbalance act to slowly decrease the bias against daughters. China's gender imbalance, while still high, has been slowly ebbing since its peak in 2004 of 121 boys to every 100 girls. Some social scientists believe it will move toward normal proportions, as has happened in other patriarchal societies like South Korea. Certainly, fewer people in China appear to be expressing a preference just for sons now. In

2013, a Zhejiang University survey showed that most people wanted both a son and a daughter. In cases where only one child was allowed, 21 percent preferred a daughter to 13 percent who wanted a son. Some of this is due to public campaigns such as the 2003 Care for Girls campaign initiated by the family-planning commission, which is designed to improve perceptions of the value of girls. Still, much more needs to be done.

It's worth remembering that the one-child policy accentuated a long-standing pernicious bias against females in China. The removal of the policy, on its own, isn't going to solve the country's gender inequalities. I was reminded of this when I visited my ancestral village after leaving Hitdoll's premises.

For many years, despite working in China, I'd resisted traveling to the Fong family village, Zili Village, just a two-hour drive from Dongguan.

My antipathy stemmed from my gender. My grandfather, Fang Wenxian, had come to what was then prewar Malaya and made his fortune. He also sired eighteen sons, of which my father was the sixteenth. Even though the family wealth vanished with grandfather's death and the Japanese invasion, the Fong/Fang family are proud of their lineage. When my mother married into this family and produced five daughters, no sons, it was a truth universally acknowledged among the Fongs that my father was in want of a better wife.

For a long time, I was too young to understand the great stress this placed on my parents' marriage, or the burdens this placed on my mother, particularly at great clan gatherings, like Lunar New Year. I simply rejoiced, in those times, at the chance to run wild with my male cousins. We pretended we were bandits, brandishing weapons and executing what we fondly imagined to be magnificent leaps and acrobatic kicks. In these games I was as loud and unmannerly as any boy and thought of myself as such. But at times my grandmother, Ah

Ma, would interrupt our play, cooing for her favorite grandchild of the moment — always one of my male cousins — so she could feed him a sweet, or wipe his sweat.

My sisters and I were never thus honored and took care to stay out of reach, for Ah Ma, a tiny woman with corpse-white skin, would occasionally reach out to viciously tweak our tummies, a pleasure she reserved exclusively for us girls.

My father never got over his sonless state and took it out on his children in beatings and apoplectic rages. The latter probably did him in, for he was felled by a stroke, at age fifty-seven, and never re-covered.

I was not, therefore, particularly eager to explore my Fong roots. In the ways of the clan, the female Fongs are just temporary members, to be married out to other families and thereafter lost to the family.

Still, over time I learned more about Zili Village from cousins who'd visited, and it piqued my interest. It turned out Zili was an enchanting landscape made up of thousands of towers that dotted southern China's flat green fields. It had even been made a UNESCO World Heritage Site.

These towers, *dialou,* are amazingly fanciful creations, inspired by what Chinese had seen working in far-flung places: a hodgepodge of Moorish arches, Corinithian columns, Byzantine domes, and crenel-lated walls. These McMansions of yesteryear ought to have looked garish and arriviste. In actuality, they are a startlingly romantic sight, reminiscent of something from Tolkien or Grimm.

As it turned out, Grandfather had built a tower, named Yunhoun Lou, or "The Tower of the Illusory Cloud." That last fact gave me the push I needed. I was a little unnerved after visiting a workshop of sex dolls. What could be a better antidote than a pilgrimage to the Tower of the Illusory Cloud?

The tower turned out to be a slim, boxy mass, opening up at the top to a broad terrace with sweeping views and Corinthian columns.

It looked very beautiful and peaceful, but tiny box-shaped slits on the balustrade — designed for rifles to fire through — reminded me that this tower had been built for defense. For returning Chinese who'd made their fortunes abroad, the towers were a sign of wealth and sophistication, as well as acknowledgment of the insecure times in which they lived. They were defense fortifications against the many bandits who roamed the area, the restive *guanggun* of their time. They were vertical panic rooms. Saddened by the turmoil, Grandfather had composed a poem carved on the tower:

> Flying dragon, dashing tiger: harboring great ambitions
> but unfulfilled;
> Only a life adrift overseas, years of void like an empty
> mountain.

After leaving the tower, I spoke to some Zili villagers and discovered I still had some relatives in the village, including a first cousin. We sat in his house, and he showed me family pictures. Idly, I asked him, "How many daughters did Grandfather have?"

The Fongs counted the sons, so my father was the sixteenth son, not sixteenth in birth order. I had never been too clear how many aunts I had.

"One," he said, instantly.

"Really? I remember at least two or three aunts."

He conferred with other relatives. They knew one daughter had been born to Grandfather's first wife, who'd remained in the village as the grand chatelaine. She had bound feet and refused to travel overseas. Grandfather's second wife had lived with him in Malaya and done the bulk of the childbearing. After she died, my grandfather took as his third wife my grandmother, who had been younger than some of his daughters. She had borne him four sons in his old age.

After a while, my cousin returned. "We only know of one. The others, they weren't counted. They were born overseas."

It was as I suspected. Zili's little family museum detailed the far-flung births of the Fong men, even those like my father in Malaya, but the women didn't count. It was a salutary reminder that gender discrimination was a poison in China long before the one-child policy.

But the Fongs, I discovered, could be selective. The museum traces the Fong lineage back to northern China in the 1300s. The first Fong ancestor, according to family historians, was a general who had married an emperor's daughter and moved down south to fight the Mongols. *That* female, they counted.

Better to Struggle to Live On, Than Die a Good Death

The study of dying is like gazing into a reflecting pool. The waters there reflect back to us the kinds of people we have become. More than ever before then, it is timely to ask the question: what kinds of people have we become?
—*Allan Kellehear,* A Social History of Dying

Two wasn't enough, that was the trouble. He's always thought that two was a good number, and that he'd hate to live in a family of three or four or five. But he could see the point of it now: if someone dropped off the edge, you weren't left on your own.
—*Nick Hornby,* About a Boy

I

In Kunming, the City of Eternal Spring, after breakfasting on his usual eggs and honey water one day in July, Ma Ke began hospital rounds punctually at 8:25 a.m.

Barely had he started, wrote Ma in his diary, when "a stir occurred. A nurse informed us that three patients were extremely unwell."

Thirty minutes later, all three were pronounced dead.

At the end of his first hour, the death toll rose to four.

Ma found himself comforting a patient crying "so hard, tears were flowing into her ears."

Lest you think Ma is an exceptionally bad or unlucky physician, allow me to explain that he heads China's most famous hospice, Kunming's No. 3 People's Hospital's Section on Palliative Care. Ma does not cure anyone. His job is to ease his patients' pain and make their last days tolerable, which can be difficult for a physician primed to heal and cure.

Partly, I suspect, as therapy, and partly because he finds the topic of how we face our last days deeply fascinating, Ma has made copious observations over the years, a Pepys of palliative care. His entries are whimsical, ironical, and sometimes tortured.

Over the years, he has evolved pet theories on the particular nature of China's aging and dying. One: China's recent wave of materialism has made dying especially hard. Two: those without children have it worst. Not so much for financial reasons — "People of my generation, we will have savings, pensions. But a country with so few young loses creativity," he said. "Loses hope."

It is this last point — unsurprising but most evident in the land of the one-child policy — that led me to him.

It is perhaps no surprise that China, as the world's most populous nation, also has a gargantuan share of the elderly. However, the peculiar element that singles China out from the global herd is not so much the *size* of its aging population, but the *speed* at which it is graying. I do not, of course, mean the Chinese are somehow growing old at a faster rate. It is a matter of proportion, as China's number of retirees is fast outstripping its number of workers.

Currently the Middle Kingdom has the kind of worker-to-retiree ratio that rejoices the heart of its economic planners, a five-to-one ratio. Lots of productive, taxpaying workers to pay for retirees. But in a little over two decades, China's attractive five-to-one ratio will shift to 1.6 to one, a ratio that is about as economically enviable as foot-and-mouth disease. It spells shrunken tax coffers, reduced consumer spending, and all-around diminished productivity. This kind of transition — more older people, fewer young — is happening almost everywhere in the world, for we now live longer and on balance have fewer children than people did a century ago.

Even so, this transition to a graying society took shape over more than fifty years in the West. Consequently, countries there have had more time to stock up for the gray years ahead economically and socially. (Many might argue that even these preparations are inadequate.) In China, the aging transition will happen in just one generation, and the cupboard is woefully bare.

This aging transition is the result of two things happening at once: people living longer, fewer being born. The former has nothing to do with the one-child policy; the latter, everything. Because of the one-child policy, China's aging transition will be a tsunami, its speed breaking with enormously forceful effect.

By the mid 2020s, China will be adding 10 million elders to its population each year but losing 7 million working adults. China's army of pensioners is already creating shortfalls: in 2013 pension shortfalls reached 18.3 trillion yuan, over 30 percent of GDP, and will continue to escalate. Half of China's thirty-one provinces cannot pay retiree costs and must get bailed out by the central government.

Of all the negative potential repercussions of the one-child policy, this is one we can see happening before our eyes. We don't know if China's gender imbalance could lead to a more warlike nation or greater domestic turmoil. We can't be sure if China's cohort of Little

Emperors could make for a nation of pessimistic, solipsistic, low risk takers. We can't even be certain of the extent to which the one-child policy will crimp China's future economic growth.

We *do* know that short of some cataclysmic plague or war, China's vast cohort of workers will grow older. And that means by 2050, one in every three people in China will be over sixty. Ted Fishman, author of *Shock of Gray,* notes, "If they were their own country, China's senior citizens would be the third largest country in the world, behind only India and China itself."

II

In our family home my mother kept three porcelain deities in our living room.

Fu, Lu, and Shou — the gods of Luck, Prosperity, and Longevity — were not of course as important as Guanyin, Gautama Buddha, and the ancestral tablets, which occupied the place of honor on a special five-foot-high rosewood altar.

When I was a child, this altar loomed above me, brimming with flowers, incense, and fruit. I associated this cornucopia with corporal punishment, for, after suitable chastising for my various misdeeds, I would be made to kneel before it, clutching my ears.

Naturally, I grew to hate it all: the incense, the ancestors, and even Guanyin's calm simper. More comforting to the eye were Fu, Lu, and Shou, little dolls the length of my forearm, a child's fingertip to elbow. The affable trio perched separately on a wooden cabinet, each with its own little plinth. I didn't have to kneel to *them.* No fresh flowers ever graced this trinity, but nonetheless, there they were, a visible manifestation of all that could be hoped for in this life.

Fu and Lu, both black-bearded gentlemen in flowing robes, were hard to tell apart. Shou — Longevity — was the easiest to recognize, a bald old man with a bulbous forehead. Put a red stocking cap on him and he could pass as a Sinified version of a benign Saint Nick.

If you look at modern China today, of these three, Fu, Lu, and Shou, probably the weakest is Shou.

Longevity, after all, is now easily achievable by all but an unlucky few. The average Chinese person can expect to live until seventy-four, a big jump from World War II, when the average life span in China was just thirty-nine.

Luck, the most ephemeral of beasts, is still hotly pursued. Prosperity is equally desirable, given there won't be much of a social safety net for China's huge elder cohort. Nobody wants Shou without Lu, and yet almost certainly China will have one without the other.

It's now an old saw, the saying that China will "grow old before it grows rich." I've heard this gloomy prognostication offered by economists, academics, politicians, and the average person on the street, said with an air of inevitability and submission. Nobody, it seems, is raging against the dying of this light. As the Chinese saying goes, it would be like playing a lute to a cow, an utter waste of effort. It feels irreversible, inevitable. Deng's economic reforms may have lifted 500 million above the poverty line, but that still leaves nearly a quarter of its 185 million retirees living on less than a dollar a day. China's graying transition is a first-world problem, but China hasn't achieved first-world prosperity yet. Despite becoming the world's second-largest economy, its per-capita GDP is just a sixth of South Korea's, and one-ninth the United States'.

Some, of course, see prosperity in China's longevity boom. Ninie Wang was an executive at Motorola when she came up with the idea of starting a company that would be a version of AARP, the American Association of Retired Persons, and the UK's Saga Group. It would offer a range of lifestyle services such as dancing, travel, and computer lessons to affluent middle-class retirees. She even envisioned classes for teaching modern child-rearing methods, geared toward doting grandparents.

Wang wrote up a business plan that won her the Roland Berger prize, awarded to the INSEAD student with the best entrepreneurial concept.

She christened her brainchild "Pinetree." "I wanted Pinetree as a name because the word for 'pine' in Chinese, *song,* sounds similar to the word for 'relax.' I didn't want traditional, depressing names, like 'Golden Sunset,'" said Wang.

Wang is in her mid-thirties but looks younger because of her clean-scrubbed look and honey-colored complexion. With her un-flappable air and commonsense pronouncements, Wang comes across as the girl who always gets voted class president, the one who seems older than her years, who ticks all the right boxes. And so she did: raised by a loving extended family, Wang studied economics, found a suitable marriage mate, and was a rising executive at Motorola before heading to business school. Her professors at INSEAD awarded her the Berger prize not because her business plan was flawless, but because they felt confident the capable Wang would execute it.

When I first met her at a vegetarian restaurant near her office in 2013, Wang appeared to have only a couple of items left unchecked on her bucket list: having a child and growing Pinetree.

Wang built Pinetree's original concept on what seemed like a sound premise. In China, the arc between retirement and terminal illness is probably longer than anywhere else in the world. Men retire at sixty, and women at the staggeringly early age of fifty, long before their contemporaries elsewhere.

Wang figured this herd of retirees would need something to do with all their leisure time, and she meant to fill it. In 2004, she launched Pinetree, with annual membership rates priced at about 10,000 RMB, or a little over $1,600. She forecast the company would hit $1 billion in revenue by 2008.

But Pinetree flopped. After two years, it had only two thousand members, and only after Wang slashed subscriptions several times.

"People loved it, but they didn't want to pay for it. It came under one of those 'nice to have' things, but it wasn't something they had to have," said Wang.

Wang, like other entrepreneurs eyeing China's vast retiree market, had come up against a dismal truth: the market was huge, but China's retirees simply weren't willing to spend. Unlike America's, who'd prospered during the postwar boom years and felt entitled to enjoy their golden years, people in China, who'd lurched from crisis to crisis following the Japanese Occupation, had fewer resources and also, said Wang, an inherently different mindset. "They want to save money to pass on to their children and grandchildren."

So she went back to the drawing board, asking herself, "What do old people in China want?"

The answer was surprisingly easy, and probably much the same as anywhere else. Old people in China want to live at home and maintain their lifestyle and independence as long as they can. More to the point: their *children* — many of whom pay the lion's share of bills — also want this, for putting your folks in a nursing home is still stigmatized in China's Confucian society.

Home health care is still largely a private concern in China, unlike in other countries where it is funded through a mixture of government services and insurance. China's insurers are currently rolling out some eldercare packages, but targeting people currently in their forties and fifties, so these products are still largely theoretical. China's current crop of people in need of home health care, people mostly in their mid-sixties upward, are generally paying out of pocket.

Wang relaunched Pinetree in 2010 as a provider for home nursing services. For modest per-visit fees ranging from as little as $16 to about $120 — laughably little by Western standards — Pinetree's personnel make house calls, monitor medications, and supervise physical rehabilitation. Unlike home health-care aides in the West, these are trained nurses, therapists — in some cases, even doctors — and they don't cook or clean.

Business grew quickly. In 2009, Pinetree had 20,000 subscribers. Two years after its relaunch, Pinetree had more than doubled its number of subscribers to 50,000. By 2015, this had jumped to 170,000, and Pinetree had expanded to Shanghai. Pinetree broke even in 2009 and is now profitable, says Wang, who aims to expand Pinetree into a nationwide franchise.

World domination it isn't, though. With such small costs per transaction, Wang depends on large volume. Handling a large, mobile staff requires good management skills to ensure consistent service. On the bonus side, Pinetree needs little capital infrastructure spending, so Wang is able to grow the business quickly.

"It's not rocket science," said Wang with a laugh. But for all her self-effacement, Wang is fiercely ambitious. She is lobbying for government funding and wants to expand Pinetree's services to suburban areas. She would like Pinetree to eventually cover 5 million senior citizens. "The whole world is aging. I'd like to think maybe China could offer some solutions for how to handle this gracefully," she said.

It's unclear yet what those solutions could be, for much of Pinetree's model — relatively cheap and abundant trained personnel, high population densities — seems unique to the Middle Kingdom. I learned a little of this through accompanying some of Pinetree's nurses on their in-home visits.

One summer day I met Nurse Gao at Chaoyangmen's subway station. To keep costs down, Pinetree's nurses take public transportation or bicycle to their various appointments. It's not easy in a place as sprawling and traffic choked as Beijing, requiring smart scheduling.

Nurse Gao, twenty-five, was a tanned native of rural Jiangxi Province. She'd been with Pinetree three years. We headed to a five-floor walkup nearby. The patient, let's call him Chen, was a seventy-three-year-old retired government official who suffered from early-onset Parkinson's and Type 2 diabetes. Two years previously, he broke his hip and had since been wheelchair bound. With no elevators in the building, he had scarcely been out of the apartment.

Before entering the apartment, Nurse Gao slipped on a mint-green overall with the Pinetree logo and pinned on a nurse's cap, also green. She put plastic covers over her shoes and handed me the same.

Chen and his wife lived in a spacious one-bedroom apartment with a sunny balcony. Their twelve-year-old grandson was playing computer games in the living room. Chen spoke slowly but was chatty. As Nurse Gao took his blood pressure, they chatted about his daughters and how city folk preferred girls to boys now. He told me about his niece, who had a good job and a flat in Singapore but was unmarried and a source of worry to her mother.

It was clear that Nurse Gao had a good bedside manner, chatting breezily as she helped Chen through a series of hand exercises. She massaged his upper torso while he remained in his wheelchair. Later, they moved to his bed, where she had him perform a series of leg and hand lifts. He was breathing heavily and sweating by the end of it. "Work harder, you can do this!" encouraged Nurse Gao.

It didn't look like a bad way to grow old. Chen's wife was still in good health and able to help take care of him. Their children and grandchildren lived nearby. The stairs were an inconvenience, but otherwise the apartment was handily located in central Beijing, near several hospitals, shops, and the subway. More importantly, the entire apartment block was assigned housing under Chen's previous work unit, so they knew all their neighbors. It was a village within a city. Everybody knew each other's business so well, when Nurse Gao entered the building, a passing neighbor hailed her. "Here for a massage again?"

We hopped on the bus to the next client. Along the way, Nurse Gao filled me in on her job. Before, she worked in a hospital, attending to hundreds of patients daily. "It was hard. I became a nurse because I wanted to help, but after a while, they just become so many bodies." (Long lines at China's big hospitals are so endemic, it's common practice to hire people to stand in line for you.)

Now she saw no more than six patients a day. Many, like Chen, whom she'd been treating for eight months, were regulars. She got to know their families, their little idiosyncrasies, and took pride in being able to see some heal and progress. They invited her to their grandchildren's weddings, gifted her with little red packets at Spring Festival. Night shifts and working during holidays were things of the past. She can't imagine returning to hospital work, she said. "I like being able to see my clients regularly. I can tell I make a difference," she said, beaming.

My initial forays with Nurse Gao appeared to reinforce the general feeling I had of retirement in urban China. Stroll through any park on any given weekday between the hours of 10:00 a.m. and noon, and you'll come away feeling like life post-retirement in China's cities is a pretty decent affair. With such early mandatory retirement comes plenty of leisure time, and so the parks are filled with pensioners engaged in picturesque activities: dancing, tai chi, sword fighting, kite flying, and, my particular favorite, a form of geriatric graffiti that involves tracing out Chinese calligraphy on pavements using brushes and water, which dries and leaves no trace.

A friend's father once took me to see him play Rouliqiu in the park, a favorite game among retirees using principles of tai chi and lacrosse. Using a paddle with a rubber center, he flipped a weighted ball to his partner, who caught the ball, twirled like a Sufi mystic, and tossed it back. More like a dance than a ball game, the sport was invented by a university professor in the 1990s and now has hundreds of thousands of adherents, not just in China.

So many retirees are practicing public dancing that municipal governments sought to place curbs on the noise emitted by their huge boom boxes. Affected residents have hurled abuse, water balloons, and in some cases excrement at these irrepressible "dancing grannies," as they are dubbed by local media, to little avail. "Granny square dancing" has even become a competitive sport. In Jiamusi, not far from the Korean peninsula, locals have created a style — lots of coordinated hand and hip movements, performed in white Minnie Mouse gloves — widely imitated in elderly cheerleading competitions across China.

Parks and IKEA cafeterias have also become a hot singles scene for retirees. At Beijing's Tiantan Park, not only are parents posting singles ads seeking mates for their grown children; now the elderly are doing it for themselves. Teng De'En, one of the organizers, shows me a fat folder of ads he brings to the park every Sunday. For 5 yuan — about 80 cents — subscribers between the ages of sixty and eighty-five place lonely-hearts ads. They typically list things like age, blood type (thought to predict personality), horoscope, and whether or not they have that all-important Beijing household registration.

This emphasis on what kind of household registration you have is quite common in the young singles scene. I hadn't thought it would be such a big deal for the elderly, who'd already raised their families. Of course, I hadn't thought it through: health benefits are tied to your registration status, and city dwellers get better coverage than those with rural residency permits.

Matchmaker Teng, a crusty divorcé, was himself in search of a new mate. His only daughter lived in the United States, and remarriage after sixty was becoming more socially acceptable, he said. "Who wants to die alone?"

This self-sufficient, vigorous vision of China aging is its most public, most engaging face. But there's a side to aging in China that is easily hidden. On one of my forays with Pinetree's Nurse Gao, we visited a woman in her eighties, living alone with severe diabetes and early-onset dementia. Almost all of Nurse Gao's clients paid for treatment, but this woman's once-weekly Pinetree tab was paid for by the local municipality.

We heard the TV blasting as soon as we entered the building. Nurse Gao banged on the door, yelling, "Granny, Granny, it's me, Little Gao!"

There was no answer.

Nurse Gao then fished out her phone and called her, whispering, "She's a little deaf." Finally the door opened. An old lady, her bleached face emerging from the darkness, eyed me incuriously. She turned around and shuffled back to the TV set. For the rest of the time, her eyes never left the set.

It was playing a Thai soap opera, her favorite, said Nurse Gao. A miscarriage, an awakening coma patient, and a bankruptcy erupted in swift succession across the screen. Nurse Gao kneaded the old lady's arms and legs, keeping up a patter that petered out. Questions on her diet, her daily habits, her exercise patterns, her bowel movements all died on the vine.

In between, the commercials that flittered across appeared aimed at a younger set: milk powder, candy, cell phones, cars. Sadly, the aged appear to be a dead demographic for China's marketers; I didn't see so much as an adult diaper ad, although China is on track to overtake Japan and the United States as the world's largest adult diaper market.

The apartment was on the ground floor. It looked like a cavern, the TV its campfire, light bouncing off this woman's immobile face. The air reeked of stale cigarette smoke, and the walls were brown and water stained. There was no artwork, only a calendar that was two years out of date and a framed studio portrait. It was one of those glossy jobs with an artificial blue sky and airbrushed expressions. Two middle-aged women, a man, all neat hair and neutral smiles. I thought it must be her family. In a whisper, Nurse Gao told me not to ask. "They don't visit," she said.

There were the remains of a meal on the kitchen table, biscuits and oranges. The orange peel was neatly quartered. The biscuit packet had been folded into a Rubik's Cube of squares, as small as it could go, each fold as sharp as if she'd ironed it. I pictured this woman sitting, folding and refolding for hours in the dark.

The visit was an hour, but it seemed an eon. When we emerged from the building, I felt like Plato's caveman, blinded by an unaccustomed sun.

Even Nurse Gao's cheery demeanor was dimmed.

"Do you think you're the only person she sees all week?" I ventured.

"No, but it's the only time she gets touched," she said sadly.

III

In his book *Being Mortal,* American physician Atul Gawande writes about end-of-life care in America. Most want to avoid the indignities and loss of control that come with institutionalized care, he says. Despite the portraits of sprightly independent life we've seen in sitcoms like *The Golden Girls,* despite the plethora of eldercare services from retirement communities to assisted living, Gawande concludes, "Your chances of avoiding the nursing home are directly related to the number of children you have." Which is bad news for China.

One of the biggest ravages committed by the Communists was its assault on China's family structure. Mao realized revolution was impossible until he could get people to put the interests of the state above family. Over fifty years, Communism sawed away at the underpinnings of the famously clannish Chinese society, encouraging the young to turn on their parents during the Cultural Revolution and stifling ancestor worship. When the Communists rolled out the one-child policy in the 1980s, it was the coup de grâce.

Now, faced with rising divorce rates and the coming explosion in retiree ranks, China's leaders realize it must rebuild some of the familial institutions it tried to tear down. In 1996, the National People's Congress passed a law requiring children to support their aged parents. In 2013, Beijing followed up with a law requiring children of elderly parents to visit frequently. Such laws are difficult to enforce, but passing them sent a clear message: what the state cannot do, the family must.

Unfortunately, some of the damage may be difficult to repair. Take nursing homes. In Gawande's America, having children may help you stay out of the nursing home. In China, *not* having children could shut you out, a double pain that *shidu* couples — those who lose their only child — are discovering. Many nursing homes will not admit *shidu* couples because they have no progeny to authorize treatments or act as payment guarantors. This form of discrimination appears to extend beyond the grave: some *shidu* parents complain that cemeteries won't sell them burial plots — not for them, not even for their deceased children — concerned there will be nobody to pay for future upkeep.

Shidu parents — and there are currently a million of them, and growing — petitioned Beijing with a laundry list of demands: higher compensation, priority in adoptions, as well as plans that reflect their pension, medical, and burial requirements. They argued — with some justification — that since Beijing has made money off fines from one-child violators, it should compensate families who observed the laws, only to lose significant financial security with the death of their sole progeny. The argument is Solomonic and heartbreaking in its logic.

Beijing responded by raising compensation slightly, but other requests haven't gotten much traction. (The *shidu* compensation scheme was started relatively late, in 2007. Currently, *shidu* parents receive reimbursement of between $16 and $50 monthly.)

Shidu parents, for example, have requested nursing homes that cater to their specialized needs. One reason: visiting days. "Seeing other people with their families . . . it's just unbearable," said one *shidu* parent.

A 2014 proposal by a local Guangzhou legislator to use social compensation fees, collected from one-child fines, for this purpose went nowhere. Authorities said the fees were needed for existing government expenses.

IV

People like Matchmaker Teng and Nurse Gao gave me some idea of what aging in urban China is like. But that is only half the story. Strictly speaking, 60 percent of the story. The rest of China lives in rural areas where the picture is decidedly more depressing, for the gap between rural and urban China is like the gulf between London and Lhasa.

On every measure, elderly rural folk in China are less well educated and less financially well-off. What's more, they are also more likely to be cut off from family support, for at no other time in China has there been such a form of age apartheid, where the old are immured in villages and the able-bodied in cities.

It is in the countryside that you are most likely to hear woeful tales of elder abuse, such as the case of farmer Chen Shoutian, who kept his hundred-year-old mother in a pigpen. Chen, who lives in a six-bedroom house, told a local TV station that his mother preferred living in a separate cinder-block structure, sharing her quarters with a huge sow. Then there's Zhang Zhefang, the ninety-four-year-old who made history by suing her children for abuse. The villager claimed she was locked in a dark room, pinched, and slapped and forced to empty her own slops. What makes her story sad is how unremarkable it is for rural China: she was undernourished, married at a young age, with offspring who are senior citizens themselves and in similar dire situations, depending in turn on their children's largess.

It is perhaps not surprising, then, that incidences of suicide among rural elders are rising, at a time when China's overall suicide rate is falling sharply.

While most city residents are covered by pension plans, only about a quarter of rural residents are covered. Many must work until they can't. Medical treatment is scarce and rudimentary. Nobody knows this better than Xiao Hebi, a "barefoot doctor" in her late sixties. Barefoot doctors were a 1970s phenomenon — semitrained medics in rural areas who played a significant role in reducing infant mortality and the spread of contagious diseases. They helped China become one of the first countries to eradicate smallpox and polio. But when China launched its market reforms in the 1980s, many public health services were defunded — including barefoot doctors. Health costs soared, and many village medics quit. Xiao is the last of a dying breed, and she plans to stay in the harness until she drops.

Xiao's reasoning is straightforward: despite serving her community for over four decades, she is not eligible for a pension. More importantly, she knows if she quits, her small community in the mountainous Sichuan area is unlikely to get a replacement.

"After me, I don't know if anyone else will come," she said.

I met Xiao in her clinic in Panshi, which means "Circle of Stone." It is near a quarry full of cliffs teetering down to paddy fields. For the past forty years, Xiao has trudged up and down these steep areas in the dark, making night house calls for less than a dollar per visit.

In the day she is usually found at her clinic. The day I met her, dressed in a silver-sprinkled floral blouse and polished leather shoes, Xiao was hooking up a flu patient to an IV. On the walls, the pictures of two Chinese medicine sages looked on: Sun Simiao, author of the first encyclopedia of Chinese medicine, and Li Shizhen, who wrote the first definitive work on Chinese medicinal herbs.

Xiao, however, had little truck with traditional Chinese medicine. In a corner of her dispensary, empty and dusty from disuse, was an antique-looking cabinet with over a hundred small drawers used to store Chinese herbs. It was too complicated, costly, and ineffective for modern-day needs, said Xiao. Instead, she dispensed vitamin C injections, paracetamol, penicillin, and amoxicillin from a glass-fronted cabinet. She did so with a new patient who wandered in, waving her straw hat and complaining of the heat.

"It's too hot here! At least get a fan!" she exclaimed.

She sat on the end of the couch. "What's the matter with you?" she cozily asked the patient hooked up to the IV.

The flu patient opened her eyes. "Flu," she mumbled.

Xiao gave the second patient two days' worth of painkillers, neatly wrapping each pill in white paper. The woman handed her a 5 kwai note, about 80 cents. Xiao made change.

In her heyday Xiao delivered babies, set bones, and gave vaccinations. But Xiao hadn't done an inoculation in over a decade, and the only babies she delivered now were livestock. Almost all her human clientele were over sixty, with typical ailments such as hypertension, diabetes, and dementia. She had little in the way of training or medication to help such ailments.

In 2008, one of Xiao's relatives contracted cancer. He was admitted to the hospital, stayed a week, and didn't die as expected. When medical expenses grew too high for his family to cover, he came home. With her oil-covered paper umbrella in one hand and flashlight in the other, Xiao climbed a steep mountain path twice daily to visit him, slithering up paths made slick by the summer rains. She kept him on a regimen of IV drips that included a mixture of painkillers and antibiotics. To hydrate him, she dabbed moist cotton balls on his lips. This patient, she said proudly, was still alive.

Rural residents have in recent years been able to get medical coverage, though it is still very limited. China was slow to adopt universal medical coverage, but it has been growing by leaps and bounds. *Yibao,* its version of Medicare, was rolled out in 2008, as well as an equivalent medical insurance scheme for rural dwellers. Every individual in Panshi pays 70 yuan — a little over $10 — yearly under the plan. Many Panshi dwellers complain, however, that reimbursement rates are low, and out-of-pocket expenses high.

Still, it's a vast improvement after the past twenty years, when the dismantling of socialist infrastructure led to a rampantly capitalistic, for-profit health-care system. Now, Panshi's residents have coverage for major health-care crises, but it's tied to their household registration, making it difficult for elders to move in with their children in distant cities and still retain coverage. Also, there are simple logistical issues that become insurmountable when you are old, and poor, and live in a remote area. For example, doctors won't prescribe more than a week or two's worth of pain medication at a time. So Panshi's sick elderly have to make frequent trips to the nearest big city, Dazhou, two hours away by bus, a costly and tiring business, said Xiao.

Xiao opens her clinic doors every day at 5:00 a.m. She starts making her house calls at nightfall. Midnight is reserved for paperwork, and she goes to bed at 2:00 a.m., in a room attached to the clinic. Her three children have asked her to retire, or at least ease up on her punishing schedule. "But what is there left for me to do?" she said matter-of-factly, perched on a table. She swung her legs, drawing attention to her shiny leather shoes, as if to say, "What, me, barefoot?"

You might imagine that concepts such as filial piety, the backbone of old-age security, would be stronger among supposedly more traditional rural dwellers. But anthropologist Yan Yunxiang says filial piety has essentially collapsed.

Yan spent more than a decade doing fieldwork in a small village in northern China. As he explains it, the basis for parental power was the concept of *enqing* — that children owe their parents a debt that can never be repaid because their parents gave them life. Parenthood also had an elevated status because of village kinship systems and religious rituals like ancestor worship. Communism and 1980s materialism basically eroded these beliefs, leading to what Yan calls the "demystification of parenthood."

"The idea that human reproduction is sacred is no longer accepted by younger villagers," he wrote.

Probably the strongest reason for today's erosion of parental power is economic. The prospect of inheritance has always been powerful protection against elder mistreatment. But land reform and collectivization mean rural elders today have little to pass on to their children economically.

Xiao said the elders in Panshi who felt the most secure were those caring for grandchildren. "That's how they feel useful. They know as long as they're doing that, their children will continue to send money home," she said. She's also known cases where grandparents have been summoned to cities to take care of their grandchildren. "Those people have an awful time. They don't know anyone and the cities are so dirty," she said. "Nowadays our children have become rulers; we just don't dare say anything to make them angry. Not like the past, when your children obeyed you until you died."

Suddenly, a bell rang. A young boy dashed into the clinic.

"*Popo, popo,* open the cupboard," he gasped.

Xiao opened a padlocked drawer.

I wondered why this sense of urgency. A cut? Diarrhea?

Rummaging inside, he pulled out a lollipop. He handed her a grubby note. Other children followed, and Xiao was soon kept busy collecting money. Unlike the medicine cabinet, the candy cupboard, I noticed, was locked.

"Wow, you do so many things, treating sick people *and* running a sweetshop, too," I exclaimed. I meant it as praise, but Xiao glanced away, embarrassed.

"I heal people," she said softly.

V

Why do I see such a bleak picture of aging in China? After all, aside from loosening the one-child policy, there are other steps that China can take to ameliorate a graying transition, including raising the retirement age and reforming a clunky pension system. Some of these measures have already happened, or are likely to happen soon.

There's also no doubt that China's social safety net is growing quickly. In 2011, rural pension schemes covered only a quarter of the rural population. In 2013, this expanded to half, then three-quarters in 2015. China began health-care reforms in earnest only in 2009, but *yibao* has swiftly evolved; premiums have risen quickly in the past five years, significantly reducing out-of-pocket expenses.

Despite this, there's little to celebrate. There are two things that help make old age more tolerable: money to pay for comforts, medical treatments, and necessities at a time when you can no longer work; and family, or family substitutes, for emotional support and care. Neither resource is solid in today's rural China.

For China's elderly to have a secure and pleasant old age, its economic engine must continue to chug on, making enough to service eldercare and pension demands. But China's economy is slowing down, and an aging demographic will add significant headwinds. This situation is likened to a "speeding bicycle that has to keep going just to keep from falling over," according to a report by the Center for Strategic and International Studies. China's aging issue makes economic growth more essential but more difficult to achieve. In over three decades of China's economic reform era, the expansion of its working-age population has on average added 1.8 percentage points per year to its GDP growth rate, CSIS reported. By the 2030s, the contraction of its working-age population will be *subtracting* 0.7 percentage points per year.

As for family, China has done too little, too late. The one-child policy has been loosened to a two-child policy. But babies take time to mature and become workers. Even that major shift will do nothing to smooth over the problems of the next two decades in this area.

The one-child policy significantly reduced the number of caregivers for China's elderly, not just in quantity alone, but also in quality. There are fewer women in China now — and by extension, fewer daughters-in-law, and they're the ones who really take care of the elderly.

VI

The city of Kunming is possibly one of the most pleasant places in China in which to live and die. It is located in the south near Vietnam and Myanmar but lacks the muggy heat of those places, for it is on an elevated plain six thousand feet above sea level, similar to Tahoe. That height also serves to keep away the pollution that clogs almost every other provincial capital in China. Kunming is the only major city in China I've been in recent years where blue skies are the norm.

Ma Ke's No. 3 People's Hospital's Section on Palliative Care in Kunming is renowned by nature of its age — it is the oldest — and size — it is one of the biggest. China's most famous hospice opened in 1986 with just six beds, two doctors, and a nurse. Now it has seventy beds and will more than quadruple that in 2015 with a new wing. Those are pretty outsize numbers even by China's standards, where ten beds for palliative care is more the norm.

Still, to be the top hospice provider in China is to be a giant among pygmies. In an index created by the Economist Intelligence Unit that ranked the quality of care for the dying, China came in close to the bottom on almost every metric: quality, affordability, availability.

The hospice is a unit inconspicuously tucked within a general hospital, which is handy camouflage. In a culture that venerates luck and fortune — good old Lu and Fu — talk of death has the opposite effect, leading to Chinese abhorrence of things that even hint at this: the number 4, for instance, whose name sounds like the word for "death." Neighborhoods around hospices have been known to raise vehement protests. In the late 1990s, for example, residents living near Beijing's Songtang hospice smashed its windows and forced nearly a hundred dying patients into the streets in the middle of the night.

Ma is slight and energetic, a member of the Hui minority. (The Huis, one of China's largest ethnic minorities, are Muslims. Kunming, being on the old Silk Road, has a sizable number of Hui folk. Most are no longer strict Muslim practitioners, which may be just as well, since practices like observing Ramadan have been recently banned by Xi Jinping's government.) Ma originally trained as a neurosurgeon, but "China has so many surgeons, it's hard to distinguish yourself." Sensing a pioneering opportunity, he turned to hospice care. Having made a name for himself, he intends to publish the diary he keeps, with the title "At the Gate of Heaven."

One room in Ma's hospice comes closest to representing this putative gate, the room where they lay out the dead. Prominently located in a highly trafficked section of the building, the room is christened "Mount Penglai," after a mountain that holds a place in Chinese mythology roughly equivalent to Olympus. Penglai is a fabled dwelling place of the immortals with no pain, no disease, and bountiful food, wine, and peach blossoms.

The hospice's Penglai, however, holds little suggestion of the divine. There is an altarlike niche with a picture of an unidentified deity that could represent almost any religion. It is flanked on each side by a lugubrious couplet:

Where is the moon and the spring breeze? I don't know.
The peach blossom falls in the river and is gone.

I peer in and see a body in white. Staffers tell me the deceased is Muslim and is being wrapped in a ceremonial white shroud. On other occasions, Mount Penglai might be used for Taoist rituals, or Buddhist prayers.

There is no real reason for this room to exist. The hospital already has a mortuary, where dead bodies can be laid out before being claimed by relatives. Ma says the Penglai room fulfills a need. "Sometimes, we have a death a day, and relatives don't know what to do," said Ma. "We don't have systematic religion in our country, but we do have many burial customs which bring peace to the living."

There is also, of course, another, more prosaic reason for the room's existence: it is leased to a local funeral home and is an important revenue source for the department. Most hospital departments—oncology, pediatrics, and so forth—in China are run as profit-making entities, whose revenue in part depends on the number of treatments prescribed. Staff are paid a bonus on this, which can frequently match or surpass their base pay. Such avenues are, of course, limited for hospice staff, who can prescribe little in the way of curative treatments for the terminally ill. This is one reason why they have difficulty luring medical personnel, said an administrator. The Penglai room therefore helps replenish coffers.

But the Penglai room also has another effect. Death, instead of being tucked away and hushed out of sight, is given a prominent space.

One of the things I discovered while talking to Ma, other doctors, and patients was how small a part the elderly play in making decisions about their own health care. Doctors usually relay news of the patient's conditions to the family, leaving them to disseminate the news to the patient. Or not. In cases where the patient's family wishes to hide or conceal details, doctors usually comply, sometimes reluctantly. "We only tell white lies," one doctor told me.

Offspring can and often do induce doctors to perform futile medical procedures and surgeries that the patient doesn't want or need. UK-based public health scholar Chen Hong found in her study of end-of-life China cancer patients that doctors are "overly aggressive" in their treatments, with measures that tend to prolong the suffering of patients.

"I had a patient with rectal cancer," Ma told me once. "He himself was aware there was blood in his bowel movements. The daughter wouldn't let us tell him he had cancer. She would rather her father remain unaware, and she told us to tell her father it was simply hemorrhoids.

"Months passed, but the patient did not feel he was getting better. He still found blood in his stool. He was not happy with me. He thought he wasn't getting proper treatment and refused to cooperate anymore."

Ma finally persuaded the daughter to allow him to let the patient know the truth of his condition. According to Ma, he tried to break it gently.

"I tried talking to the patient, to see if he was strong enough to accept the truth. I told him, 'Look, you're already seventy, at this age lots of people get sickness, like cancer. My previous diagnosis might be wrong. It is possible you might have cancer. Have you thought about that?' He replied, 'It's all right. I have two children; one of them is in Hong Kong, the other in Kunming. They both have jobs and families, they're very happy. I am well prepared for this.'

"I did not believe he was prepared. So the second day, I came to his room and said I would reexamine him. I waited until the third day to tell him it was actually cancer. I thought he might be able to accept it. But after half an hour, he passed out. He only awoke fifteen days later. A week later, he died."

I asked Ma if this really happened in such a dramatic fashion. He insisted it was so. It is not one of his proudest moments, he said.

"We failed in this case," he said.

There are several reasons for this peculiar state of affairs in China, where family takes precedence over patient. Economics is one: doctors defer to the adult children of patients, because they're the ones paying the bills. This generation of Chinese elderly are relatively impoverished next to their children, who've been able to enjoy the fruits of China's economic boom.

The more unfortunate explanation is that the deathbed is where the all-but-gone filial piety rears its head. "It's all about *mianzi*, 'face,'" said a Beijing hospital administrator. "Children have to show that they really tried, and so they insist on doctors doing everything at the end, even if it means a whole lot of unnecessary and painful treatments."

Ma has another theory: the past thirty-plus years of China's experiments in capitalism have created a culture of materialism. "In recent China, we have turned into materialists; not me, but the other people. Thereafter we didn't have an education about death. Materialists only believe in what they see with their eyes and deny what could not be observed with eyes. They are not religious."

I'm not sure I agree with Ma. Chinese culture does abhor anything close to talk of death. We don't have fourth floors, or fourteenth floors — and sometimes, as a nod to Western superstition, thirteenth floors either — which can make elevator rides bewildering. We don't like vintage clothes, white flowers, or giving clocks, all things that are associated with death and bad luck. These practices do impede our "education about death," as Ma put it. In my family, any talk of death would always be punctuated with a pithy *"Choi!"* — the Cantonese equivalent of "Bite your tongue."

But I think the reason for this abhorrence stretches beyond materialistic culture and has its roots in the Chinese system of beliefs around what happens after death. Broadly speaking, most Han Chinese hold beliefs that are an amalgamation of Taoism, Buddhism, and Confucianism, with a good dollop of folk religion and ancestor worship sprinkled in. In general, it results in a vision of the afterlife similar to this one: you still need money and creature comforts, you still have bureaucracy and hierarchy, and you must slog on in a more-or-less eternal cycle of rebirth. Unlike the Muslim and Christian creed, there is very little vision of a soothing Eternal Rest.

One of the best places in Beijing to glimpse the Taoist view of the afterlife is at the Dongyue Miao. Dongyue has stood in the same location for over eight hundred years, even as *hutong* alleys around it have crumbled before the onslaught of skyscrapers.

In Dongyue, there are various chambers, each holding plaster-of-Paris tableaux depicting the afterlife. Each chamber represents an office in the afterlife, and overall they add up to a grim vision of unending bureaucracy, where the dead are judged for past deeds and have to appease numerous supernatural deities.

In the underworld, there is a department of signatures, as well as a department of signing documents. There is a department of recording merits, of determining individual destiny; departments for confiscation of property, examining false accusations, controlling theft, wilderness preservation — who knew *that* would be important in the afterlife? — and, my personal favorite, the department for implementing "fifteen kinds of violent death" (though the finer points of postmortem death elude me), all laid out in as much gory detail as red paint and plaster will permit.

With this less-than-enchanting view of what is to come, no wonder Chinese abhor talk of death and take heroic measures to prolong life. As a popular Chinese saying goes, *Hao si buru tousheng.* "Better to struggle to live on, than die a good death."

When my father died, we laid him out in state on the veranda, his coffin packed in dry ice. The visitors' first stop was the reception desk, where relatives sat with a giant book, recording contributions of "white gold" — gifts of money in white envelopes to help pay for the funeral. We, the daughters and wife of the deceased, pinned scratchy sackcloth hoods on our heads and burned joss paper to pay for his comforts in the afterworld.

Every year at Qingming and Double Nine Festivals, we would visit the columbarium where we kept his ashes. There, we'd make more ashes, burning "Hell Money" — sheets of paper purchased at religious stores. These literally had the words "Bank of Hell" and "Legal Tender" printed on them, as well as a picture of the Jade Emperor, the emperor of heaven in Taoist mythology.

Aside from festivals to honor ancestors, we also celebrated Ghost Month, where offerings were made not just for our own clan, but for all spirits. During this month, it is believed that the gates of hell open and ghosts are free to roam the Earth seeking food. These unfortunate ghosts are ones who no longer have people paying tribute to them.

Ghost Month is therefore rife with superstition, a month when nobody gets married or starts a business. As a child, I loved to wander with my mother into the religious shops in the weeks ahead of Ghost Month, for they had paper models of houses, cars, and people, looking exactly like toys. I longed to touch and play with them but was never allowed to, of course, for this would have been extremely bad luck.

These offerings have kept up with the times: I've seen paper Louis Vuitton handbags, paper iPhones, and, of course, the all-purpose afterlife accessory, a paper Amex Black card. In 2006, China's Ministry of Civil Affairs even went to the trouble of imposing a ban on the burning of "messy sacrificial items" such as paper replicas of Viagra, luxury villas, and karaoke hostesses.

All this shows that, while most religious and cultural systems stress that you can't take it with you, the Chinese eminently believe you can, as long as you have descendants, the more the better. To die without issue is to *duanzi, juesun* — one of the worst curses you can visit upon someone Chinese, for it means an eternity as a Hungry Ghost.

VII

The Kunming hospice has a smell I've come to associate with institutional life in China: pork bone soup and instant noodles mingled with the occasional waft of urine from the toilets and a fug of cigarette smoke.

Patients sleep two to a room. There are no showers, so residents have to make do with sponge baths or, if they are able-bodied, go home to bathe. There is just a narrow space between beds, enough for a person to sidle through sideways. To compensate for the rooms' lack of space, large communal seating areas dot the floor, with raft-like wooden chairs and couches in peeling vinyl. Small food tins, scrubbed clean of their labels, serve as ashtrays. Here, residents and visitors linger, smoking, sewing, chatting on the phone.

In one of the sitting rooms, I met Li Jiayi placidly embroidering flowers on shoe soles. Li's mother had been an inmate for the past seven months, hit with both Alzheimer's and Parkinson's.

Jiayi was thirty-five, with a cloud of long, dark hair and a serene face without a speck of makeup. With her was her five-year-old daughter, Qingxue — "Little Stream" — an engaging sprite with a gappy smile. A tiny tiara was perched on her braids. They were the hospice's youngest regulars.

Jiayi was four months pregnant with her second child, taking advantage of the recent *dandu* reforms, the relaxation of the one-child policy that allowed couples to have a second child, provided one of the parents was an only child.

"Sometimes, my friends ask me, 'You're so old, why do you want another child?' But I think to take care of the old is very stressful. There isn't enough community support. Neighbors don't get along like when I was growing up. This one," she said, motioning gently to her chattering daughter, "will have a hard time alone."

Jiayi's mother was diagnosed eight years previously with Parkinson's, the chronic movement disorder that has no cure. China already has more than 40 percent of the world's Parkinson's sufferers, but by 2030 this will grow to almost 60 percent, a huge amount for an affliction so new the Chinese haven't had time to come up with their own nomenclature for it. To Jiayi, it's *Pa Jin Sen* — three Chinese characters that individually mean "handkerchief," "gold," and "forest."

At first, the disease was manageable. Her parents helped Jiayi with child care, picking up Little Stream from daycare every evening and making dinner. The child learned to hold on to her grandmother's hand and support her as her balance worsened. Then Jiayi's mother started falling down. They lived on the third floor of a seventh-floor walkup, with no elevator. For safety, she started staying in bed all day, listening to Shanghai opera and watching soap operas.

In the winter of 2013, her mother could no longer move her legs and needed someone to carry her to the toilet. She developed bedsores. Jiayi's seventy-eight-year-old father couldn't cope anymore. They looked at several nursing homes and hospitals, finally ending up at Kunming No. 3 as the most economical. Monthly costs are about $3,000, out of which 90 percent is covered by *yibao,* China's equivalent of Medicare. Other options, such as private nursing homes, cost thrice that and were not covered by insurance. Each place had a waitlist several months long.

Her hands flashing among the threads, Jiayi said, "I feel I was lucky. So many people have sick parents, and they don't have access to these facilities, or even know about them."

Jiayi's parents raised her in what she remembers as an idyllic environment, a communal housing compound for their work unit. She was aware that world no longer existed. In talking over her reasons for having a second child, she made constant reference to how urbanization and modernization had shredded ties between neighbors. She also lamented how family sizes had shrunk so drastically. Both her parents had six siblings. Her husband, Guobao, whose name means "National Treasure," had five.

Now, the Chinese language is very precise in its definition of family ties, with numerous words to define kinship. An uncle is never just "uncle," for example: he could be *bobo* if he was your father's older brother, *shushu* if younger, *jiujiu* if he was your mother's brother, and so on. Little Stream would never just be "sister" to Jiayi's unborn child, for there is no plain-vanilla Chinese equivalent of that word. She would always be *jiejie* — "older sister" — her status locked in, never *meimei,* "younger sister."

The Chinese language, with its emphasis on placing you firmly in the family pecking order, shows how much China values seniority and structure. But this elaborate taxonomy is collapsing. By the time Little Stream has her own children, many of these terms will be as archaic as Latin.

Over the weekend, I saw Jiayi again. She had brought her mother some steamed egg custard. The food at the hospice — mostly soups and rice congee — wasn't nutritious enough, she felt. She spooned the trembling yellow curds into her mother's unresponsive mouth.

Her mother was a tiny mound underneath a mass of blankets, her gaze hovering somewhere near the spot where a television once stood. When she first moved in, Jiayi installed a TV at the foot of the bed so that she could continue to watch her favorite soap operas. But soon after moving in, Jiayi's mother stopped responding to stimuli.

"So, no more TV." Jiayi shrugged.

She was dressed that day in black jeans. Her pregnancy hardly showed.

These past few years with her mother had been hard, she said. "My father is too old. There is no one but me," said Jiayi. "I don't want this for my daughter. Her sister or brother will live longer than we will. Probably, it will be her longest-lasting family relationship."

Over the past year, the constant back-and-forth to the hospice, combined with child care, taxed her strength. Her hair dropped out. She started snapping at Little Stream. In the end, she decided to quit her job. With savings, and her husband's salary, she calculated they could get by for two years without her needing to work. After that? She shrugged.

Despite this, Jiayi believed family planning in China was necessary. "The large number of people — it makes social benefits hard to implement." Then she added the phrase almost every Chinese person brings up when I ask about family planning: "*Ren tai duo.* Too many people."

Jiayi's attitude might seem strange to people outside China, but in reality, a great many urban Chinese do support its family-planning policies, a fact that is probably easier to understand if you've lived there and had to fight for spots everywhere from the crowded subways to elite schools.

When I asked Jiayi, however, if she supported methods employed by family-planning officials, like forced abortions, her hand fluttered protectively to her stomach. "Of course not," she said. "Force is never justified. Those people were really evil."

In Jiayi's high school class of thirty people, only four or five had a second child, she said. Most classmates were civil servants, who risked losing their jobs if they broke the rules.

"Now I feel a lot of my friends are envious of me," she said.

Little Stream climbed onto her lap and started taking loving nips at her mother's arm.

Jiayi tussled with her gently, speaking in a singsong voice. "Who's going to take care of Ma-ma? Will you take care of Ma-ma?"

Perched heroically above her unborn sibling, Little Stream nodded.

The Red Thread Is Broken

China promised stability and certainty. At the end of the process, however long and demanding it might prove to be, we would have a child. And no one could take her back.
— *Jeff Gammage,* China Ghosts

I

If you've adopted a child from China, how do you trace that child's roots?

Brian Stuy thinks he knows how. In his mid-fifties, with a shock of white hair and a showman's sense of timing, Stuy congratulated the small group of parents who filed into a St. Paul, Minnesota, auditorium one Saturday morning. "You are a small minority of the US adoptive community," he said. "Most families don't care, so thank you for at least coming."

Stuy is a controversial figure among the adoptive community. Many dislike the ex-Mormon's crusading message about corruption within China's adoption system. For the many parents who believe they've done a good deed, this is an inconvenient claim that makes Stuy about as popular as Al Gore at an OPEC convention. "Be very careful of Brian Stuy," a journalist acquaintance and adoptive mother of a Chinese child told me. "He is a lightning rod."

Some accuse Stuy of hypocrisy. He adopted three daughters from China, so why is he criticizing the program now? Others accuse him of profiting from his accusations, which, to some extent, he is. Since 2002, Stuy's small outfit, Research-China, which he runs with his China-born wife, Lan, has specialized in doing background research on China adoptees.

Sweeping the room with his eyes, Stuy announced he would unveil a list of what he believed were orphanages that engaged in child trafficking. "I already know some in this room will see their orphanage mentioned," he warned. "Don't take it personally."

The screen flickered. Next to me, Heather Ball bit her lip. Her daughter's orphanage was on the list. She took a moment to absorb the shock. Shrugged. Then came ruefulness. "What can you do?"

Is the wave of Chinese adoptions, as many believe, an altruistic act that rescues thousands of unwanted, mostly female children from a life of penury and institutionalization — or is it really baby buying on an international scale, sanctioned and even facilitated by the Chinese government? For two decades, over 120,000 children from China have been adopted internationally. This byproduct of the one-child policy is its most international aspect, and it has significantly shaped global attitudes toward race, family, and the ethics of inter-country adoption.

In the adoptive world, where demand for healthy young children far exceeds supply, Chinese adoptions are, or were considered, the gold standard. China had almost everything adoptive parents were seeking: healthy young infants in large quantities, and an adoption process that was government run, streamlined, and relatively expansive. When China's overseas adoption program first began, singles, retirees, and gay couples were considered eligible to adopt, which was rare elsewhere.

The one-child policy imbued the whole process with virtue: the outside world believed these girls to be unwanted and voluntarily abandoned. China's orphanages were overflowing, and conditions were abysmal. Adoptive parents believed China was the most ethical choice among an array of suspect options. Unlike adoption in Guatemala or Ethiopia, they weren't going to be accused of buying babies, or exploiting the poverty of birth parents.

After Beijing opened its orphanages to intercountry adoption in 1992, numbers started rising vertiginously. By 2005, its peak, Americans were adopting almost eight thousand China babies yearly. Even now, when the supply of adoptable infants has fallen sharply, China continues to be by far the largest source country for adoptions, with Americans adopting over two thousand children from China in 2014. That's almost three times the number of adoptions from Ethiopia, the next-largest source of adoptions.

That sunny scenario changed in 2005, when six orphanages in Hunan — some of the biggest suppliers to Western adoption agencies — were accused of baby buying. Chinese authorities initially denied the reports but eventually jailed laborer Duan Yuaneng and family members for trafficking eighty-five infants. Duan's mother, a children's home aide, said she was initially reimbursed a few dollars for finding abandoned babies. But demand swiftly rose, for orphanages gained $3,000 for each overseas placement, not to mention donations from grateful parents.

"The orphanage asked for more babies. It started paying $120 each. Then $250. Then $500 by 2005," said the Duan matriach. The family smuggled infants in milk powder boxes, four at a time, on the train for a six-hundred-mile journey from Guangdong to Hunan, a distance roughly equivalent to that between New York and Charlotte, North Carolina.

After serving out his prison term, Duan told *Marketplace* reporter Scott Tong that his trafficking operation was far broader in scope than media reports had indicated.

Showing Tong records that indicated he trafficked over a thousand infants, Duan said the orphanages falsified foreign adoption papers for each of those trafficked babies. "The documents I saw indicate at least one went to American parents," Tong told me.

Chinese authorities said the Hunan incident was an isolated case, but in 2009, another scandal erupted. This time, family-planning officials in Guizhou Province were discovered to have seized children born in violation of the one-child policy and sold them to orphanages, according to the *Los Angeles Times*. In 2011, the newsmagazine *Caixin* reported a similar case. Some of these children ended up in American and Dutch homes, according to the magazine.

Other trafficking cases in Guizhou and Shaanxi provinces have also added question marks to the whole adoption process.

There is no reliable way to ascertain how widespread the wrongdoing is. Parties with the most to gain in the process, from Beijing to adoption agencies to adoptive parents, maintain these cases are isolated.

Melody Zhang, who runs the China operations of the St. Louis–based adoption agency Children's Hope, acknowledges flaws in China's international adoption system but points out it has saved the lives of many children who would otherwise have perished in China's institutions. "Truly, conditions were bad in the early days," said Zhang. Opening up China to the adoption market also brought increased Western support and substantially improved orphanage conditions. For example, the Berkeley-based foundation Half the Sky spent over $56 million improving orphanage conditions in China over fifteen years.

But not everyone who runs an adoption agency is as sanguine. In 2009, Ina Hut, director of World Children, the Netherlands' biggest adoption agency, resigned in protest over the Hunan scandal. Troubled by the stories, Hut fruitlessly pressed both Chinese and Dutch authorities for answers. In 2007, she traveled to China to conduct a month-long investigation.

Hut came away with the conviction that the practice of buying babies "is much more widespread than we know." Contacts in the adoption industry told her midwives were paid fees to spot out-of-plan babies and annex them before birth. Also, orphanages often had more information on adopted children than they disclosed to China's Central Adoption Agency and adoptive parents, she said. Chinese authorities privately told her at least two children from the Hunan trafficking scandal had ended up in Dutch homes, she said, but Hut was unable to get either the Netherlands or Beijing to pursue this further. "As far as they were concerned, it was over and done."

Hut does not come across like a crusader. Blond and soft-spoken, with a sunburst of smile lines on her tanned face, Hut was a successful software entrepreneur and a university administrator before she joined World Children in 2002. It was soon after her first child died at birth, a traumatic experience that made Hut decide "the next step was to make the world a little better," she said.

Hut had initially planned to adopt herself but took her name off the waiting list after discovering firsthand the inner workings of adoption. "When I looked behind the scenes, I was shocked. I came to discover that a lot of adoptions are done in the interest of the parents, not the children. Everybody has the right to want children, but you don't have the right *to* children. *Children* have the right to parents."

Hut went public with her convictions and paid a price for her candor. After her 2009 resignation, she didn't work again for five years. Employers were scared off by her reputation as a whistleblower, she thinks. Finally, in 2014 she was appointed head of CoMensha, a Dutch nonprofit that helps trafficking victims.

In the world of adoptions, domestic adoptions theoretically have priority. Called the subsidiarity principle, this is one of the best practices enshrined in the Hague Adoption Convention to which China is a signatory. The one-child policy made a mockery of this principle. To prevent families from passing off their over-quota offspring as adopted children, China's adoption laws explicitly discriminated against local adoptive parents. For them, the bar to adopt was far higher. In 1992, the minimum age for foreigners adopting was thirty, for example, compared to thirty-five for locals. Also, adopted children were counted against the parents' quota of children, meaning many Chinese who adopted were barred from having their own biological offspring.

Ethicists like Samford University law professor David Smolin say the high ideals espoused in the Hague Adoption Convention are constantly violated. Kay Ann Johnson, head of Asian Studies at Hampshire College, is more blunt.

Johnson and I had been discussing child trafficking in China when she abruptly said, "What is a buyer? Everyone who has adopted a child from China," including herself in that definition. Johnson had adopted a daughter from China in the early 1990s, when she knew little about the situation there and believed domestic adoptions could not keep up with the increasing overflow in orphanages. Since then, she has come to believe that many domestic adoptions in China have been unfairly classified as child trafficking since prospective parents must pay middlemen in an unregulated system, the only way most can adopt. By contrast, Western adoptive parents like herself have paid much more, albeit through the government-regulated system. "Why are we seen as 'adopters' while they are denigrated as 'buyers'?" she challenged. (While the Ministry of Civil Affairs' China Center for Adoption Affairs [CCA] governs adoptions out of China, there appears to be no equivalent body handling domestic adoptions;

many adoptive parents in China I spoke to said their adoptions were mainly handled through private connections and networks.)

Johnson is now a strong critic of the system, arguing that China's discrimination against domestic adoption perpetuated the myth that girls were not valued in China. In reality, many of those girls could have found loving homes within the country, she maintains.

Almost all the harshest critics of transnational adoption I spoke to are adoptive parents and beneficiaries of what they say is a broken system. Stuy acknowledges the disconnect. "You have to go down the rabbit hole before you find out," he said. "I would say 95 percent of adoptive parents don't want to know, and even if they know, don't care to do anything about it. Why rock the boat?"

II

In 1995, Stuy was a thirty-six-year-old from a devout Mormon family living in Lehi, Utah, a small town that was used to represent the conservative, dance-hating community in the 1984 movie *Footloose*. Like many young Mormons, he spent two years on an overseas mission, in Germany. After graduating with a business degree from Brigham Young University, he began a series of office jobs that quenched his youthful idealism. "I didn't like being a cog in a wheel. All you do is work until you retire with a gold watch. The next day, business goes on without you," he said. "You don't make a blind bit of difference."

Stuy was ripe for a new purpose and mission in life when his then-wife, Jeannine, came back from church and suggested they adopt a Chinese orphan. This was a time when the airwaves were filled with stories of numerous abandoned girls in China resulting from the one-child policy. Two years before, BBC's controversial documentary *The Dying Rooms* had come out, detailing inhumane and cruel practices in Chinese orphanages. A Human Rights Watch report following that characterized China's orphanages as little more than places where children were sent to die.

A firm believer in the zero population growth movement, Stuy jumped at his wife's suggestion. In 1997, they returned from China with an eight-month-old infant girl they named Meikina — *Mei* for "beautiful" and *kina,* the Hawaiian word for "from China." Three years later a group of adoptive parents raised money for a new refrigerator for Meikina's orphanage. Stuy volunteered to deliver the money.

While in China, he met one of two women listed on the record as having found Meikina. The woman, according to Stuy, gave him an extremely detailed account of her experience.

"She had been walking to work with her coworker one morning, had heard a baby's cry over the noise of the crowd, had investigated and found a cardboard box containing a small, two-day-old baby girl. As she described it, the baby was dressed in 'countryside clothes,' had an empty bottle lying next to her, and some cash with a red birth note."

Stuy was electrified by the wealth of details he'd unearthed. To him, it suggested Meikina had been abandoned on the side of the road by her birth mother, who had cared enough to leave cash and clothing for the baby. He went repeatedly to Meikina's finding place near the Ministry of Civil Affairs and tried to visualize the scene: the crying infant, the incredulous passerby, the silent, grieving mother watching from the shadows. It was, he said, a "miraculous" experience, and he wrote about it enthusiastically to other parents in his adoptive group.

Most parents of China adoptees are given scanty information on their children's origins. Stuy's experience tapped a longing to know more that many shared. Several wrote back asking him for help. Some thirty families contributed $135 each so Stuy could make a return trip to China. That was the genesis of his company, Research-China.

Looking back on the story of Meikina's discovery, Stuy laughed. "I can't believe I swallowed that."

Ten years later Lan Stuy tracked down the other woman listed as Meikina's finder. She reluctantly confessed she had made up the whole thing, said Lan. "She was really apologetic. She said she'd just agreed to have her name on record to help the adoption. She hadn't actually found any babies," she said.

It's a moment of revelation that Stuy talks about constantly. In St. Paul, he wryly told the audience, "I realized she was probably prepped by the orphanage. They probably told her, 'Make him feel good,'" he said, pausing. The audience chuckled. "And that's what she did. For ten years, she made me feel *great.*"

In 2000, Brian and Jeannine Stuy's marriage broke up while they were in the process of adopting a second child. Part of the reason for the breakup was his departure from the Mormon faith, said Stuy. He went ahead with the adoption as a single father, naming his second child Meigon (pronounced "Megan").

Like most American adopters, Stuy's first port of call was Guangzhou, where the American consulate processed adoption visas on Shamian Island. Shamian is a historic sandbank filled with stately Art Deco buildings, an expat ghetto during the days of the Opium Wars.

Later on, Shamian Island would acquire a different sort of fame as the launch point for American adoptions. Shamian's five-star White Swan Hotel, a glass tower with lavish views of the muddy Pearl River, was nicknamed the White Stork Hotel. The hotel did so much business from adopting families, it devoted three floors purely to this group of travelers and gifted each family with a limited-edition Mattel doll called "Going Home Barbie," a blond hausfrau clutching a tiny Chinese baby. (These days, those Barbies have $300 asking prices on eBay.)

The new father took little Meigon to one of the numerous shops on Shamian that offered T-shirts and silky costumes, many of them in pink. There, he met the woman who would eventually become his second wife, Lan.

Lan, a deeply tanned woman with delicate features and long, graceful fingers, sold tourist tchotchkes and did pen-and-ink sketches of America's newest little citizens. Stuy commissioned one of his two daughters, a process that took several months. During the period, the couple struck up an e-mail correspondence.

Later that year Stuy flew back to Guangzhou, partly to see Lan and partly to find out more information on Meigon. During Meigon's adoption, while paying the various fees and donations, he noticed he had been billed 420 yuan, about $55 at the time, for a "finding notice."

He learned that finding notices are newspaper ads Chinese orphanages are required to place for children they are submitting for international adoption. On his return to Guangzhou, he tried to find out more. After visiting many area newspapers, he and Lan found a small newspaper that ran those ads. The paper had a roomful of old print copies, and Stuy eventually located Meigon's finding ad. It listed where she had been found and, most importantly, had a picture of a four-month-old Meigon he had never seen before.

Those finding ads became Research-China's bread and butter. The Stuys — he and Lan married in 2004 — started buying up old newspaper copies across China, usually for pennies. They sold the finding ads to adoptive families in America and Europe for a huge markup: $75 each. "The first few years were gravy," he said. The couple adopted a third daughter, Meilon.

By 2004 Research-China had diversified, offering customized reports on individual orphanages and analysis reports. For this, the Stuys continued to rely on information culled from the finding ads, using the information listed — finding ages, genders, health data, finding locations — to draw conclusions and discover patterns.

In St. Paul, Stuy provided a sample of his findings, lavishly illustrated with charts and graphs. A normal Chinese orphanage, Stuy argued — one not engaged in baby buying — receives a wide spectrum of orphans of different ages, genders, and abilities, found abandoned at a variety of places.

Retroactively analyzing data from six Hunan orphanages implicated in the baby-buying scandal, Stuy found they all showed abnormal traits: they all claimed to have found mostly girls, mostly very young infants, at only a few locations. The first two qualities suggested market demand rather than random chance. The latter suggested orphanage directors too lazy to properly cover their tracks. According to Stuy, in five years, these six orphanages claimed to have found only 17 male children out of a total of 2,202. One of the orphanages, Changning, claimed to have found almost 40 percent of its children abandoned in just two locations. From studying these ads, Stuy believes more than half of China's orphanages are buying babies. That's not a message any adoptive parent wants to hear.

Not even special-needs children are exempt from suspicion, claimed Stuy, responding to a question from the audience. A woman in a brown shirt was in line to adopt a special-needs child from China. Surely, these children were really unwanted and abandoned? she asked. Stuy hesitated. "I can't say special kids, no problem. We've learned the tiger changes its stripes constantly."

According to his data, China orphanages claimed to have found very few children with special needs abandoned between 2000 and 2005. Now they make up almost half of the findings. The year 2005 is the inflection year for Chinese adoptions, when numbers adopted fell sharply following the Hunan scandal.

"Did it mean that before 2005, children with special needs simply didn't survive long enough," asked Stuy, "or that after 2005, orphanages realized these kids are adoptable, so let's invest?"

Then he qualified his answer, giving the woman a kind of absolution. Special-needs children, considered unlucky in China, face a very bleak future. He found it hard to condemn the practice of adopting these children, even if they had been bought, he said.

It's difficult to verify Stuy's claims. I don't know anyone else who is independently analyzing orphanage population data across China. Much of his data comes from these "finding notices" published in newspapers, and it's quite possible they are incomplete. Stuy's data does not cover children in orphanages who are not placed for adoption overseas, since they do not have finding ads. Stuy acknowledges these flaws. "I'd love for someone else to independently look into this. I'm just providing a starting point. But time and time again our assessments have been validated by trafficking stories from inside China."

Stuy's research is "an unsettling postmortem of the dead dream of China as an ethical source of unlimited numbers of adoptions of healthy young and older children," says law professor David Smolin. "Even if no one believes Stuy, the facts are there to see, in the numbers, and in the narratives."

III

Western families who adopted Chinese babies worried about how these children would adapt to mostly Caucasian environments. How would their daughters deal with the knowledge that they were abandoned because of their gender? Would all this create alienation and dislocation?

For answers, they looked to the first major wave of Asian adoptees. Starting in the 1960s, some two hundred thousand Korean children — again, mostly girls — were adopted into American households. Some Korean adoptees reported strong feelings of anger at being raised with little to no cultural knowledge of their land of origin. They resented their adoptive families' using a "colorblind" approach to raising them, little preparing them for racist encounters.

A 1996 *Boston Globe* article entitled "The Riddle of Julia Ming Gale" hinted at the kinds of issues China-adoptive families would face. The article profiled twenty-four-year-old Julia Ming Gale, who had been adopted from Taiwan into a white family. Though her Caucasian parents were Chinese-speaking academics, Julia grew up speaking next to no Mandarin and identifying strongly with her white siblings. She visualized herself as a redhead with freckles. "I think I was always hoping I would just become white," she was quoted as saying.

China-adoptive families tried to inoculate their children against suffering these same issues by incorporating Chinese elements into their upbringing. It would be a sort of cultural Band-Aid. The group Families with Children from China, or FCC, became a powerful entity with over a thousand chapters across the United States. Every year, FCCs across the country planned activities around Chinese cultural events like the Lunar New Year celebrations, Mid-Autumn Festival, and Chinese language lessons.

It helped, of course, that China was in ascendance as a global power and anxious to increase its "soft" power. Many of these events were sponsored by the Confucius Institute, the arm of China's Ministry of Education tasked with promoting Chinese culture overseas. Cannily spotting a public diplomacy opportunity, Beijing also began sponsoring "Going Home" tours for adoptees and their families.

Did it work? Few adoptees learned to speak Mandarin fluently or were truly comfortable in a cross-cultural environment. Some experts say the main benefits were psychological, designed to reassure the adoptees that their differences were embraced and accepted.

Not all adoptees feel this. "People say, 'You're so lucky you have two cultures open to you.' But a lot of us feel the opposite of that, not completely here nor there," said adoptee Grace Newton. "A huge part of cultural loss feels physically grafted to my skin."

Many adoptees I spoke to expressed conflict. They know they are beneficiaries of a system that gave them, for the most part, loving and affluent homes. But many also want acknowledgment of the losses involved in their adoption, a desire that can cause strife with their adoptive parents.

Newton first became aware of the troubling issues with Chinese adoption when she took a college class on transnational adoption. Her mother said she hoped Newton wouldn't return from class "thinking we're 'white colonial imperialists.' It was kind of joking, kind of not."

After hearing about incidences of kidnapping and trafficking, she would call her mother, crying. It created a rift. "My parents had gone in [to adoption] thinking it was good, ethical. They had good intentions," said Newton. Toward the end of the course, she mended relations with her mother, but "it was hard for her to see my ideas change and my questioning of the system that had brought our family together." Toward the end of the course, Newton said her mother "realized that my critiques of adoption weren't a critique of them."

Echoing the sentiments of many adoptees, she said, "When a loved one dies, it's horrible, but there is an ability to honor that person's memory. With adoption there is a sense of ambiguous loss since most adoptees' first families are out there somewhere. There's always the wondering — *Do they think of me? What are they doing now? What would have my life been like?*"

Like their Korean counterparts, it is likely that more China adoptees will probe their history as they grow older. Possibly, they may even become a political or social force like Korean adoptees, who successfully lobbied the South Korean government to give them dual citizenship and open up access to sealed adoption records.

At present, the number of China adoptees who've shown interest in locating their birth parents is small. Most of the oldest are only in their late teens, still wrestling with school, college, and dating issues. (Experts say that adoptees' interest in discovering their origins usually peaks in two phases, in their early twenties and when they become parents themselves.) What's different today is they have a powerful new tool: DNA testing, a double-edged sword with an explosive potential for finding biological needles in China's billon-strong haystack.

I saw firsthand some of the interesting possibilities with the Stuys. While they were in St. Paul, they met a woman whom I'll call Jane. (She did not want her name or too many details of her story disclosed.) A few weeks earlier, Jane had received a letter from China. The letter writer claimed to be writing on behalf of a man saying he is the biological father of Jane's adopted daughter. This man had put his daughter into foster care to avoid being punished for violating family-planning policies. In the letter, which I saw, he wrote, "My uncle and his wife have spent 14 years looking for her ever since." They obtained Jane's address from "a government contact."

Jane sent a DNA kit to China. She agonized over whether to tell her daughter or not. In the end she decided against it, as her daughter was undergoing a volatile teenage phase and had "zero interest" in knowing anything of her Chinese roots. Jane concocted an elaborate subterfuge, collecting the entire family's DNA, including her unsuspecting daughter's, under the guise of celebrating World DNA Day. "Who knew there was even such a day?" she said, laughing. It turned out later the samples were not a match.

Two years ago, the Stuys began conducting birth parent searches using DNA testing. First, they identify a "hot spot," where an orphanage is reportedly trafficking children. The Stuys contact cluster groups of adoptive parents who have children from that orphanage. If they get a group together, the Stuys conduct a localized search, interviewing foster parents and orphanage workers in the area and collecting DNA samples. Adoptive parents pay $275 initially, and an additional $200 if the Stuys locate the birth parents. The Stuys say they have conducted five or six such searches and located twelve birth parents this way. To her knowledge, said Lan Stuy, only three or four adoptive families have initiated contact with these birth parents. The others presumably saved this Pandora's box of information for the future.

Now the Stuys are creating a small DNA bank by sending Chinese samples to a major US-based DNA research facility. "We used to just collect swabs from all these parents, and if it didn't turn out to be a match, it was such a waste," said Stuy. "Then I started thinking, 'Why not bank it?' Somewhere, sometime, some girl in the US could be searching. Maybe she will find a match." Each sample costs under $100, and the Stuys pay for the collection and kits through donations.

While it's true the Stuys' business benefits from growing concerns over the irregularities in China's adoption system, they do not appear to be making much. Records show Research-China's blog has about one thousand subscribers paying an annual $20 fee. The company also markets small services like Lan's sketches, DVDs and photos of orphanages, and translation services. Aside from Lan, Research-China has no full-time employees. Stuy himself went back to full-time work last year so that he could get better insurance coverage for the family. "I'm tired of beating the drum," said Stuy.

IV

In 2011, the investigative magazine *Caixin* ran a story about family-planning officials in Hunan who had kidnapped children born in violation of the one-child policy. These children ended up in the Shaoyang Orphanage. Some were adopted overseas. Four years later, I met up with some parents of these stolen children.

The abductions all had certain similarities. All the parents had been away, consigning their children to the care of their grandparents while they toiled long hours in distant towns. All the children seized had irregularities in their birth registration. Mostly, they were out-of-plan babies, or babies born out of wedlock, which made them fair game. Indeed, it isn't even certain that the seizure of these children is considered a crime under Chinese law. Certainly, none of the officials were criminally charged, though some were demoted or transferred. Family-planning officials I spoke to in other parts of the country said it was widely understood that they could act with impunity in such matters.

Yang Libing's child, a chubby girl named Ling, had been born out of wedlock. In 2004, Yang had been a forty-year-old who'd returned home with his pregnant teenage girlfriend, Chen Zhimei. They couldn't marry because Chen was below the legal age of marriage.

Besides, Chen's mother opposed the match. "She complained, 'He's one year older than I am!'" recalled Yang, a man with tired eyes and cheeks that resemble steep cliffs, high and caved in.

After Ling was born, they left her in Yang's parents' care and went to seek work in the industrial south. Before leaving, they scraped together enough money for a studio portrait. Looking twenty years younger, Yang sat against a backdrop of blood-red spring blossoms. On his lap, baby Ling is a tiny Michelin man in a down jacket so thick her chubby arms stick out. On her feet, handmade shoes blaze a motley riot of color: pink, yellow, blue, brown. Dressed in a padded jacket, her mother hovers protectively.

It was their first and only photo as a family. While the parents were gone, officials seized the child. They convinced Ling's grandparents, who are illiterate, to affix their thumbprints to documents putting the child up for adoption. Officials later claimed Yang signed papers giving her up. Yang was able to prove he was physically in southern China at the time and could not have signed the documents. But the damage was done. Ling disappeared into Shaoyang Orphanage.

"They told me, 'Forget about her. We'll give you approval for a second child,'" said Yang.

When Brian Stuy read the story, he sent a note to his network of adoptive parents. He asked those who had adopted from Shaoyang to respond. A couple in Illinois replied. Looking at the timing and circumstances of when they adopted, and after comparing photos they'd sent, Stuy became convinced the Illinois girl was baby Ling. She had a birthmark that corresponded to one Ling had, said Stuy.

He exchanged e-mails and telephone conversations with the Illinois parents, who were understandably shocked. At first, said Stuy, the adoptive mother was very cooperative. But when Stuy suggested a DNA test, the frightened couple cut off contact.

Stuy refused to divulge the identity of these parents but agreed to forward a letter I composed to them. In it, I offered to pass on any messages they might have to their daughter's possible biological parents, whom I was meeting in China. There was no reply.

In 2009, Lan Stuy met Yang. She showed him pictures of the child they believed to be Ling. She also took a sample of his DNA. "I was overjoyed. She looked just like the picture I have of her, only older," he said. The pictures showed a four-year-old in what looked to him like a "big villa," said Yang. "Everyone must live like that in America," he said, daintily spitting out flecks of tobacco from between his teeth.

Things had not gone well for him. He and Chen had a son, Chengjie, but she left them three years later. "She couldn't stand the poor life. She stopped believing I could find our daughter."

I asked him what he would do if he discovered, and could prove, that this was his child.

"I'd want her back," he said instantly.

"But she'd be already ten years old. She wouldn't be used to the lifestyle in China. She wouldn't even speak your language," I suggested.

"Then I'd like her to at least visit me once a year. Or I could visit her. And I'd like her to learn a little Chinese so we could talk," he said.

I tried to envision this scenario: Yang, with his thick accent and tobacco-spitting habits, not, from his own account, a hands-on parent. Chengjie was being raised by his grandparents, and Yang lightly sketched out what appeared to be a tough upbringing of his own: heavy farm chores after school, a father he didn't see often and who had not had a steady job in years. I tried to imagine how a ten-year-old American girl with a roomful of Barbies would fit in.

None of the Shaoyang mothers and fathers I spoke to seemed like ideal parents. They barely saw their kids, for they were forced to work in faraway cities. China's household registration system created a them-and-us caste system, and without city household registrations, they couldn't bring their kids along, not if they wanted to educate them, or get health care.

I was angry when Yuan Mingsan told me how his third child was seized from her grandmother. Family-planning officials detained Yuan's mother as she was taking her grandchild home from the clinic. They said she was "too old" to care for a baby and asked her to sign papers saying she was giving up the child. When Yuan's mother refused, "they had her do airplane arms. They threatened to punch her if she put her arms down," said Yuan. Finally, she agreed.

"What was your daughter's name?"

She didn't have one, he said. She was over a year old.

"When did you find out about this?"

Six months later, when he called home. I thought I'd heard wrong and asked again. Yes, six months later, he said. It was 2003 and cell phones were still beyond the reach of most migrant workers.

Once he heard, Yuan rushed home and tried to get his daughter back. He was told to pay a fine of 16,000 RMB ($2,000) for violating family-planning policies. Yuan refused. Later, he went back to work outside the village. Family-planning officials kept harassing his family. Worried that they might seize his other grandchildren, Yuan's father pleaded with him to pay at least part of the fine. After he reluctantly paid 5,000 RMB (about $550), the harassment stopped.

I felt conflicted. Part of me burned with anger at the way these people's children were so coolly whisked away, with no recourse. I hate bullies, and these family-planning officials seemed like some of the biggest thugs in the countryside.

But the other part of me — the part that had spoken to adoptive parents and seen adoptees on the other end of the globe — couldn't help wondering if the adoptees were better off.

Indeed, this is the justification some adoptive parents use. A midwestern news executive I spoke to adopted two daughters from China in the early 1990s. Her daughters' origins are a mystery, she acknowledged. But two years ago, during a rare Christmas decorating fit, "I couldn't help looking at my daughter and thinking, 'If she hadn't been adopted, she might be making those decorations in the factory, not hanging them.'"

To adopt a child is almost like embracing a religion, with a particular set of beliefs and constructs, and articles of faith. A common one in the China-adoptive community is the red thread, drawn from a Chinese fable that says when a child is born, invisible red threads stretch out to connect the child to everyone who will be important in her life. It's a message that appeals to adoptive parents, conveying a sense of destiny and inevitability. It was *meant to be.*

I read many accounts by adoptive parents that use religious overtones to describe the process. It demands certain leaps of faith. In her book *The Lost Daughters of China,* Karin Evans quotes adoptive mother Carole Sopp as saying, "If I start to disbelieve what they [China authorities] told me, I'm just perpetuating the myth that she doesn't have a past that we can rely on, and that's even more disconnective for the future."

Jeff Gammage, a hard-nosed reporter for the *Philadelphia Inquirer,* says he does not believe the choice to match him and his adoptive Chinese daughter was random. In his book *China Ghosts,* Gammage, who is white, speculates that some faceless Chinese bureaucrat spotted a facial resemblance between him and his daughter. "If you were to take Jin Yu's referral photo and place it beside a picture of me as a toddler — me in a crew cut, she with her head shaved — you would see a resemblance that borders on identical. Same mouth, same cheek, same ears."

The flip side of saying some adoptions are meant to be, however, is saying some children are fated to be abandoned.

In her blog *The Red Thread Is Broken,* Grace Newton cuttingly observes, "It is also saying birthmothers are equally destined to be in situations in which they have to relinquish their children, and that these children are destined to lose their first families, countries, cultures, and everything they know."

There has to be a line. And it has to be this: it's *wrong* to steal children.

Yang Libing's story developed a strange twist. Chen, his erstwhile girlfriend, confessed to Lan Stuy that Yang was not the father of her child. She had followed him back to his village for protection after getting pregnant.

Yang had known this when we met but had not said so. Later, I asked him why he lied by omission. "She is my daughter," he stubbornly insisted. "I took care of her and her mother even before she was born. You don't have to give birth to be a parent."

In 2013, the Stuys sent Chen's DNA sample to a US data bank. They don't have the Illinois child's DNA sample, so the entire exercise is a nod to a possible future when this girl may seek the truth of her origins. "It will be there, waiting," said Stuy.

I think of those DNA samples as so many unexploded bombs, with the potential to fragment lives, stories, beliefs.

Babies Beyond Borders

There's nothing surer,
The rich get rich and the poor get children.
— *Richard A. Whiting, Raymond B. Egan, and*
Gus Kahn, "Ain't We Got Fun"

I

After my eggs were removed, I woke with a desperate need to pee.

The nurse wouldn't let me. "No standing. Forty minutes."

I tried to lie still and think fertile thoughts. I visualized dozens of plump eggs, like frog spawn or caviar, slowly suctioned out, ripe with possibilities. I should have been feeling empty but replete. Instead I had the burning conviction that years of toilet training would rapidly be undone.

"Please, I really have to go," I pleaded. Reluctantly, the nurse fetched a bedpan. Holding the kidney-shaped dish aloft, she demanded, "Twenty kwai."

Incredulous, I looked at her, then my hospital-gowned self. Where did she think I kept my spare cash? But that was Chinese health care for you. Cash up front or you didn't get served — even, apparently, for something as small as a $3 bedpan.

Up to that point, every visit, every scan and injection I underwent, had been paid for up front, cash only. Since China's largest denomination is only a 100-yuan note — about $15 at the time — I carried around brick-size chunks of currency in a shabby tote, slinking like a bagman in a bad crime movie.

That wasn't even the biggest absurdity, of course. Here I was, having fertility treatments in the land of the one-child policy. People *left* China to have more babies; they didn't go to the world's most populous nation looking to add to it.

Nine months after my miscarriage, I was in a private hospital in Beijing undergoing IVF. I never thought I would agree to such an invasive procedure, let alone in China, with all the attendant difficulties, but the miscarriage had changed everything. I was no longer uncertain or ambivalent about motherhood. I wanted a child, I was fertility challenged, and since I lived in China, this was where I would have to seek treatment. (Given what I knew of Chinese adoptions, I was wary of taking that route, and besides, waiting times for a child had stretched to five years at that point. Trying to conceive still seemed the easier option.)

For a country with such a large population, there were surprisingly few infertility treatment choices. I lived in Beijing, where the most famous center was the Peking University Third Hospital. In 1988, China's first test-tube baby had been born there, a decade after the world's first test-tube baby. But the waitlist was long. Between 1983 and today, China's infertility rate had risen threefold to 10 percent, on par with that of most developed nations. For a nation of 1.3 billion people, that translated into a lot of patients, and there weren't enough fertility clinics to meet demand.

A friend told me about the private Jiaen Hospital. Started by a US-trained Chinese doctor, the Jiaen Hospital didn't look very impressive. It was a small white building tucked away in Haidian, Beijing's university district. The front entrance was dominated by the cashier's counter, which sat behind a barrier that looked like the bulletproof counters I used to see in Bronx gas stations. The toilets were traditional squat ones, which made giving a spatter-free urine sample as easy as threading a needle in a moving vehicle. They burned sticks of incense in the toilet to mask the ammonia stench. But the driveway had a number of black Audis — the preferred ride for China's top bureaucrats and elite.

Seeking fertility treatment in one-child-policy China had its own special issues. I showed up at Jiaen with a wad of papers: my work visa, passport, a letter from my employer, and, most important of all, my marriage certificate. My husband and I had gotten married in his hometown in Maryland, and our marriage certificate looked impressively authentic, with its shiny gold stamp. I suspect I could have gotten something similar from the local color printers, with nobody in China the wiser. But that was part of the process: you couldn't get IVF treatment as a single unmarried woman. Under the one-child policy, advanced reproductive technologies were strictly for married couples.

The one-child policy also skewed Jiaen's clientele: some were women like me, who'd spent their twenties and thirties focused on their careers and were nearing the end of their reproductive years. But quite a few of the women I met at the hospital were younger, without age-related fertility problems. They were looking specifically to have twins or triplets as a way to get around the one-child policy. Multiples counted as a single birth, providing a loophole to those who wanted larger families but couldn't risk endangering their careers. I talked to a Tianjin middle-school teacher who said she'd lose her job if she had the two children she wanted in separate births. She was pregnant with twins and fervently hoped they would be a lucky "phoenix-dragon" combo, a girl and a boy.

It seemed like a lot of my time at Jiaen was spent at the cashier's desk, pushing large wads of cash across. Some of the sums seemed ridiculously low. A consultation with a doctor — provided you didn't request the august Dr. Liu Jiaen himself — was just 20 RMB, the same price as the bedpan I ended up needing so desperately.

After the bedpan incident, I lay in a fuzzy post-op stupor. (My hastily summoned husband coughed up the fee.) There were two other couples in the room with me, also recovering from egg retrieval. One woman was an event planner. Her husband produced music for CCTV, China's largest broadcaster.

Sleepily, I heard him recounting a documentary he'd seen in America. It was on Mao's disastrous Great Leap Forward movement, when he had tried to galvanize the country into leapfrogging from an agrarian to an industrial society by turning farms into backyard steel furnaces. Over 20 million people starved to death, but not many in China are aware of some of the Great Leap's more drastic effects.

"People were eating babies," said the CCTV producer, dramatically. Silence. I sensed skepticism in the room. He continued, "It's true. I saw it on Discovery Channel!"

I drifted off, drowsily thinking of cannibals, families, and the fate of baby-devouring nations.

II

In the land of the one-child policy, the fertility wizards became kings. The number of officially licensed clinics in China offering IVF and other fertility treatments mushroomed to over two hundred, from just five in 2001, and unlicensed clinics are numerous. Sales of clomiphene — a fertility drug that causes superovulation — soared, with online prices dipping as low as $1.50 a packet.

The number of twin births in China more than doubled over the past decade to the point where one out of eighty-nine babies born would be a twin. That's still below the rate in the United States, where it's about one in thirty. But while rising twin rates in America are mainly due to women having children later in life, in China the one-child policy accounted for at least a third of the increase in twins, according to a study by a group of economists from Harvard and Peking University. That means many women were deliberately having "twins" as a way of getting around the one-child policy, either by using fertility drugs or by registering non-twin children as twins.

In 2000, for example, officials in Yunnan found seven hundred pairs of such "fake twins" in over three hundred villages. Provinces with higher birth fines had significantly higher incidences of twins than places with more liberal rules, researchers found. In Shanghai, by at least one estimate, one in every fifty babies born was a twin, according to one news report.

In 2010, a successful Guangzhou businesswoman tested the limits of fertility, and the family-planning commission's tolerance, by having eight babies within a month. She did this through the use of fertility treatments and the help of two surrogate mothers, while carrying several fetuses to full term herself. The press nicknamed her *babaotai muqin,* or China's Octomom. Local news reports said the mother spent close to $160,000 in fertility treatments, surrogacy, and medical fees and hired eleven nannies. The news was leaked when the photo studio the family visited splashed the pictures online. The initial public reaction was disbelief.

"Heavens. To have one family with eight kids . . . in an era of family planning where most people have just one, the contrast is just too much," said a CCTV commentator. "It doesn't sound like news. It sounds more like a fairy tale."

The family went into hiding to escape media attention. Two years later, the Guangdong Family Planning Commission said investigations into the issue had been completed and the couple would be heavily fined an unspecified sum.

Surrogacy itself is a gray area in China. The Ministry of Health bans the medical institutions and staff under its aegis from performing any surrogacy procedures. Of course, this allows intermediary agents to flourish, unregulated.

There are no official statistics available on the number of surrogate pregnancy agencies in China, but the well-respected Guangzhou-based *Southern Metropolis Weekly* newspaper estimated that around twenty-five thousand children had been birthed by surrogate mothers in China over the past three decades. Current compensation for surrogate mothers ranges from $3,000 to $6,000, about a tenth of US costs.

With the one-child policy stifling regulatory oversight of the reproductive services industry, the result was a veritable Wild West of baby making. Some surrogate agencies in China unabashedly offered services guaranteeing a boy, which involved making surrogate mothers abort female fetuses. A mediator quoted in a local news report said one client tried five surrogate mothers in a quest for a son. "It is quite embarrassing. Every time we find it's a she, we have to change a surrogate mother."

Surrogate mothers and birth parents were also vulnerable to crackdowns by family-planning authorities. In 2009, three surrogate mothers living in a communal flat in Guangzhou were hauled away by family-planning authorities and given abortions. "I was crying, 'I don't want to do this,'" a young woman called Xiao Hong, pregnant with four-month-old twins, told Reuters. "But they still dragged me in and injected my belly with a needle."

Not only did advances in reproductive medicine give affluent Chinese an out from the one-child policy, they also deepened income inequality. Elsewhere it may be a truism that the rich get richer and the poor get children. In China, the rich found it easier to get the whole package: wealth *and* extra progeny. Increasingly, the well-to-do, or well connected, were willing and able to pay the fines or engineer ingenious ways around the policy, including using fertility treatments both in and out of the country. It's not that poorer people in China couldn't have more than one child. But the laws of the one-child policy were structured such that the greatest flexibility was afforded at opposite ends of the income spectrum: the poorest, who live in rural areas where one-child exemptions tended to be more easily obtained, and the richest, for whom such laws increasingly commanded only lip service. China's middle classes were the ones to whom the rules most applied; China's poor, the ones who faced the most brutal enforcement.

After the Octomom incident, a user on the Sina microblog service commented, "If you have money, what does the law mean?" Another Sina user commented, "Chinese law is the law of the rich. The rich can have as many babies as they want, because they have the money to pay the penalty." That message also carried graphic photographs of factory hand Feng Jianmei, she of the forced late-term abortion. Perhaps the most apt representation of where China found itself is, in fact, a dystopian fantasy, Margaret Atwood's *The Handmaid's Tale*. A futuristic story set in a loosely disguised Harvard University, the novel depicts a population rendered infertile by pollution. Women are commodities, and the custom of concubinage has been revived to foster the creation of children.

China is facing a severe pollution problem, which is increasingly being linked to infertility, though scientists have yet to fully understand how. Or, perhaps more to the point, *who*. In 2013, for example, the government think tank Chinese Academy of Sciences announced the launch of a five-year study of the relationship between air pollution and female infertility. Other scientists, however, argue that the pollution crisis affects men, not women. In 2013, newspapers announced Shanghai was facing a "semen crisis," with only a third of semen at its main sperm bank meeting World Health Organization standards. Several studies were published linking worsening environmental conditions to the falling quality of Chinese men's sperm.

It's not difficult to do the math. With over 60 million females who were never born, killed in infancy, or given away, and another 40 million females experiencing infertility, women who can easily conceive are increasingly scarce commodities in China, just like in Atwood's book.

We see this not just with surrogates, but with the return of the mistress culture in China. The custom died down with the start of Communist rule but revived with capitalism. The image of officials with mistresses and multiple offspring has become a trope in China, and these women are valued not just for their beauty but for their fecundity, a byproduct of youth. These stories are a refrain in exposés of corrupt officials. Zhong Bifeng, the ex-director of the city construction bureau in Deshan, Hunan Province, was exposed by his mistress. She wrote on Rednet, Hunan's official bulletin board, that Zhong, desperate for a son, found her through a marriage agency and promised to give her 500,000 RMB, or about $80,000, if she gave him a son. If she had a daughter, she would have an abortion and be given $16,000 as compensation. "When I went to his house to find him on February 2014, I was beaten by his wife," she wrote. Zhong was expelled from the Communist Party.

Lei Yuanli, vice mayor of Chenzhou City, had relationships with nine lovers and was caught embezzling funds to support them, including establishing a trust fund for an illegitimate son. For embezzling and bribe taking, Lei was sentenced to death, which was later commuted to a twenty-year prison term.

These experiments in reproduction aren't limited to Chinese shores, nor are they solely China's concerns. For increasingly, some of these babies are American born.

III

In 2010, Shanghai native Tony Jiang and his wife, quoted as "Jennifer" according to the couple's request, had a daughter by an American surrogate. Then, twins. All three of their children are US citizens, as the United States is one of the few countries that grant automatic citizenship to children born on its soil. But that's not why they chose this unusual conception method, said Jiang. For affluent folks like the Jiangs, there are easier ways of getting foreign citizenship. "It would take years," said Jiang. American-born children can sponsor their foreign-born parents for green cards only when they reach twenty-one. Also, the United States is one of the few countries that require its citizens to pay taxes even when they're living elsewhere. "A Canadian passport can avoid lots of tax levy. To be honest, a US citizenship to Chinese at this moment is not worth that much money."

To them, the main draws offered by America, or more specifically the state of California, were top-flight reproductive services and solid legal protection for parents of children born to surrogates, all of which are unavailable in China.

When they got married, Tony and Jennifer were quintessential yuppies, both with marketing jobs with multinationals that paid well and demanded lots of travel. Both came from small families. Tony, thirty-six, was born slightly before the onset of the one-child policy and has an older sister. Jennifer, from the first one-child generation, has no siblings. Family pressure for the couple to have children early was strong, but in 2008, Jennifer was diagnosed with a smaller-than-normal uterus. It meant she would almost certainly not be able to carry a child to full term.

"I was a little bit disappointed but at that time was not that ready to be a father," said Jiang. "But my wife was so frustrated. She thinks it's her problem, she blames everything on herself."

I met Tony Jiang in Shanghai years after his gynecological odyssey. He was modishly dressed in a snug red sweater, leather pants, and a chunky, expensive-looking watch, the kind that supposedly works equally well when deep-sea diving or Alpine climbing. Not that the busy Jiang has the time or inclination.

Jiang now runs a fertility consultancy business, DiYi Consulting. He is the middleman for a fast-growing market of Chinese clients seeking egg donors, sperm donors, surrogates, and IVF services in America. The genesis of this, of course, was his own experience, which he recounted in a cool analytical fashion, not mincing words.

The Jiangs tried surrogacy repeatedly in China. It cost them two years and close to $30,000. Nothing happened. One surrogate simply vanished, returning home without notice. The other two didn't get pregnant. Jiang had initially thought, "As long as you pay, you get your babies; it's easy because basically there is another way to get around it. But in China we tried and realized it is not so simple."

There are huge differences between Chinese and US IVF services, he said. Chinese fertility clinics are overcrowded, doctor-patient relationships impersonal, and infrastructure rudimentary and not always sterile. ("You have to masturbate in the male toilet," said Jiang.)

He started exploring overseas options. He considered Ukraine, India, and Bangkok in addition to America. In the United States, a package of IVF, surrogacy, and delivery services would run about $120,000, he calculated, three times what it would cost in India. But American states like California have well-established legal protections for the rights of biological parents. Horror stories abounded of stateless infants born to surrogate mothers in India and Thailand, stranded in legal limbo. Jiang also decided against Ukraine, where "they charge foreigners two or three times more, just like thirty years ago in China."

So America it was. It was their last chance. "We could not emotionally and financially afford another loss. We would rather try the best place, the most sophisticated solution and process." Jiang's parents even quietly suggested that he consider divorce because of his wife's fertility problems. He didn't mention the suggestion, he said, but "she could feel it."

Jiang was referred to three potential surrogates by an American agency. Even though the other two surrogates lived in Southern California, nearer to the Santa Monica clinic Jiang had chosen, he selected Amanda Krywokulsky, who lived a short plane flight away in the San Francisco Bay area. She appealed to Jiang because she was white and married to a police officer, all of which suggested stability. "I think it is a felony to impersonate a police officer," he said, and "culture-wise, I tend to believe in a white family."

It felt odd to hear Jiang dissect his decisions so openly. An American, I felt, might have made similar decisions but would likely not have openly expressed a preference for a white surrogate. In China, an overwhelming Han ethnic majority has made the population deaf to the nuances of racial political correctness. Lisa Chiya, who runs a Beverly Hills surrogacy agency, said, "Other clientele don't care so much for demographics, but the Chinese care about education and ethnicity. They ask for college degrees, they want Caucasian or Latina, but they don't want African American. Always, they say, 'Anything but an African American surrogate.'"

I was familiar with this bias, which stems in part from a cultural preference for fair skin. For the Chinese, prettier means paler. For a people striving to get out of the fields into cubicles, paler skins also symbolize success. An African American friend once indignantly stormed out of a Beijing spa because they tried to push skin-whitening treatments on her. The proprietor simply couldn't understand why anyone would be offended. To her, everyone wants to be *bai, fu, mei:* "white, lucky, beautiful."

The Jiangs were lucky not to encounter a similar racial bias in their search for a surrogate mother. Three couples had also been referred to Krywokulsky for her consideration, and the Jiangs were the only Chinese couple. She was most drawn to them, she said. "I think it was just the way they talked about wanting their own child, and the failed attempts. This was a last-ditch attempt. It touched my heart."

She was trying surrogacy at the suggestion of a friend, who'd done it twice before. Krywokulsky had had an easy pregnancy with her son, at that time a toddler, and had enjoyed being pregnant.

"I think one of the biggest questions people ask is, 'How do you dis-attach?' I tell them you have to keep in mind, the baby's not genetically yours. It's not going to come out looking like you. For me, the big thing was helping people."

Around Christmas 2009, the Jiangs flew out to visit Krywokulsky in her home in a suburb some two hours from San Francisco. Krywokulsky showed them around and introduced them openly as the couple for whom she would be a surrogate. "She was so nice," said Jiang.

He was reassured by the family's solid middle-class credentials. "She lives in a nice house, so I don't think she would purely do this for money," he said, "but nobody is really pregnant for fun, you know."

For her services, Krywokulsky would be paid $30,000, a standard rate on the market. Given the effort and time spent, it isn't a huge sum, and many surrogates I spoke to say financial incentives are only a part of their motivation. Sometimes, even this financial incentive can be reduced. Krywokulsky and her husband had expected her medical bills during pregnancy to be covered under her husband's work-provided plan. But the insurance company later billed Krywokulsky for half the costs of her checkups — to the tune of some $15,000 — stating they would not fully cover pregnancy for compensation. A friend of Krywokulsky's received a similar insurance bill. Some fertility consultants now advise surrogate mothers to get insurance under the

Affordable Care Act, which does not explicitly preclude coverage for surrogate pregnancies, though this may change.

After the visit, the Jiangs began fertility treatments. In April 2010, they were in Santa Monica for the retrieval and implantation process. By mid-April, Krywokulsky was pregnant. Two weeks later, they were told it was a single pregnancy, which was a slight disappointment — "I was hoping for twins because I didn't want to do it again," Jiang said. Two more weeks later, another slight disappointment: scans showed a female fetus. Jiang's father had hoped for a boy to carry on the family name. "I told myself I would have to do it again," he said.

The relationships among three busy individuals across several continents deepened as the pregnancy progressed. An Icelandic volcano exploded in the spring, stranding Jennifer for weeks in Switzerland, where she had been working. Isolated and depressed, she waited to hear if Krywokulsky was pregnant. Early in the pregnancy, Krywokulsky had a fender-bender. Jiang said, "When I read those e-mails I had a lot of sweat on my hands. I thought about making an irrational call to the agency requesting Amanda stay away from cars, but I realized it was stupid. Nobody's on public transportation. She was a housewife, how could I forbid her from driving?" He learned to trust Krywokulsky.

In the fall, a kink in their plans. The state of California initiated drastic budget cuts, and Krywokulsky's husband was laid off. Jiang, in France on a two-month work stint, offered to fly to San Francisco to comfort Krywokulsky. She had lost her insurance, so Jiang paid for coverage under COBRA, the pricey program that allows the recently unemployed to continue receiving health coverage. It cost over $600 monthly. At this point, Krywokulsky was five months pregnant.

The baby was born in December 2010, on the first day of sunshine after a week of rain. Jennifer held Krywokulsky's hand during the vaginal birth, which went easily and quickly. "I think I pushed three times," said Krywokulsky.

Everybody cried: the Jiangs, Krywokulsky, her mother, "even the nurse was tearing up," said Krywokulsky.

One year later, the Jiangs began to think about trying for another baby. "You look at the one-baby family in China. A lot of kids don't know how to share, they get extremely bored and indulged by grandparents," said Jiang. They still had several frozen embryos in storage. They approached Krywokulsky again, and she agreed.

This time, things were different. Krywokulsky's son was now old enough to ask questions. "I told him, 'Mommy's having a baby for someone else,'" said Krywokulsky. As it turned out, she was having two. The twins were born prematurely, one month ahead of schedule. Jiang's insurance coverage didn't kick in so early. Uninsured, he was billed about $10,000 for every day the twins spent in intensive care. In the end, the hospital bill came to a stunning $280,000, though Jiang was able to negotiate it down to $220,000 for an immediate cash settlement. Now Jiang advises his clients who are expecting twins to purchase coverage for premature births. The premium is pricey — $50,000 — but worth it, he said.

These are high sums indeed, but fertility consultants in America tell me that's fairly common with their Chinese clientele. "I've never gone back and forth in negotiations with them, which is not typical of US and other countries," said Wendie Wilson-Miller, coauthor of *The Insider's Guide to Egg Donation,* who also runs an egg donor agency.

The two families regularly communicate by Skype or e-mail once a week. "I play a pretty big part in their family, like a sister who lives farther away," said Krywokulsky.

In late 2012, Jiang quit his job to set up DiYi. "In my previous job, out of fifty-two weeks I'd spend thirty-two traveling. With three kids, I needed a better work balance." He puts his clientele into four categories: people suffering from infertility; single men or women who need third-party help to have children; gay people ("It's not that rare;

I believe in this country there are 50 to 60 million highly discriminated against gay people"); and, until recently, people trying to evade the one-child policy.

The last category included people whose jobs were at risk if they have more than one child, such as government officials or executives at state-owned companies. "People who fall into this category are rare, less than 10 percent. Most people I see are infertile; that's about 75 percent of the business."

Recently, Jiang consulted with some clients and learned the intended father was a high-ranking government official who was very afraid of exposure, he said. They ultimately backed out. "Basically people are coming to me for family building. They're eager for the child, that's the ultimate essence. They are *so* eager for a child."

IV

Jiang's clients are part of a bigger group who come to America to have babies. It's a surprising reversal of the tide that began with Americans going to China for babies a decade ago. While there are no reliable figures on how big this phenomenon is, there is ample evidence that the numbers have risen sharply in recent years. The Washington, DC–based Center for Immigration Studies estimates that there are forty thousand so-called birth tourists annually but does not break down the figure by nationality. Several news reports say at least ten thousand Chinese "anchor babies" were born in America in 2012, citing an estimate by the Maternal Management Organization, a little-known online platform dedicated to monitoring and rating confinement centers for Chinese women giving birth in the States.

Confinement centers are establishments that cater to the Chinese tradition of a one-month postnatal "confinement period," called *zuoyuezi* "sitting the month," which some consider essential to the future health and well-being of child and mother. These kinds of places have mushroomed in Southern California in recent years, to cater to Chinese nationals giving birth in America. They typically charge $30,000 and upward for an all-inclusive six-week stay. They have also made an easy, centralized target for the anti-immigration movement, amid growing calls from extremists for a repeal of the Fourteenth Amendment, which grants citizenship to all persons born or naturalized in the United States. Since 2010 the number of raids on confinement centers has increased, and a major 2013 operation involving federal agents is "likely to culminate in the biggest federal criminal case ever against the booming 'anchor baby' industry," said the *Wall Street Journal.*

As a result, the *zuoyuezi* business will likely go underground or be stamped out. Next on the list may be fertility services that cater to the China market, where, at the high end, consumers spend between $120,000 and $150,000. Some using fertility services may not have infertility issues but use reproductive technologies to have the kind of children they want. This usually means choosing the sex and the number — twins are favored — and screening out genetic diseases. In cases where an egg donor is desired — and where genetic material is passed on — Chinese parents are also trying to select traits like intelligence, height, looks, blood type, even double eyelids.

"Everybody comes in wanting bright, but every culture will choose pretty over bright no matter what they say," said Wilson-Miller. "But the Chinese almost always want taller, at least five foot five. And they have questions about eyelids; they want to see baby pictures to see if the donor's had eyelid surgery."

Since there aren't many egg donors of East Asian descent, they usually command a premium, but the incursion of Chinese parents over the past years has driven demand through the roof, say providers. Typically, egg donors get about $6,000 in compensation, but East

Asian donors can get twice or even triple that amount. "Every single Chinese donor I get, I could match her for ten cycles," said Wilson-Miller. (To avoid health risks, donors should not donate more than six cycles, say experts.)

Almost all of Wilson-Miller's East Asian egg donors are college students in the United States on student visas. There still aren't enough to meet demand, which is increasingly leading to a bizarre circularity: egg donors from Taiwan and China are flown to America to help make babies that will be brought back to China.

When I spoke to Jiang, he was on the verge of arranging for just such a transaction with a Taiwanese donor. Taiwanese donors are favored because they have visa-free entrée into the United States, although recently loosened US visa requirements for Chinese nationals are changing this scenario. "We have to figure out ways to meet demand," said Wilson-Miller. "We're not getting enough Chinese donors."

Chinese nationals are not the only folks availing themselves of these so-called designer baby techniques. But of all nationalities they are probably the most enthusiastic, and their numbers and economic clout will significantly shape this developing market.

Due to the one-child policy, Chinese nationals have already been conditioned to think of reproduction as a tool for bettering society and spurring social mobility. The habit of making hard choices in childbearing has become ingrained, and they are already accustomed to controlling for the number and gender of their offspring, while some are even selecting for intelligence, height, and looks via egg donors. From there to "designer babies" is not such a great leap. In a 2012 survey conducted in Changsha City, southwest China, almost four hundred respondents were asked what kind of genetic screening they would prefer. Over 50 percent of respondents said they would be interested in health-related genetic screening; 23 percent chose "eugenics," meaning screening for brighter kids.

What happens if genetic screening for intelligence really becomes available? Research in this area is already happening. In 2013, researchers at BGI Shenzhen, the largest gene-sequencing facility in the world, began a project to explore the genetic basis for human intelligence. It's far from clear if such a thing is possible. Many scientists argue that intelligence is too complex to be isolated to a pure genetic component. BGI Shenzhen certainly has put huge resources and brought together bright minds on this project, including behavioral geneticist Robert Plomin and University of Michigan physicist Steve Hsu. Perhaps the most intriguing member of the group is project head Zhao Bowen, a prodigy who dropped out of high school and coauthored a research paper on the genetic sequencing of cucumbers at the tender age of fifteen. Zhao believes, "People ought to be free to manipulate their children's IQ. It's their own choice."

The BGI team predicts it will be possible in their lifetimes for people using IVF to select embryos that have better genetic markers for intelligence, thus enabling parents to boost their offspring's IQs prenatally by up to twenty points.

Although this scenario is still in the realm of speculation, it makes me uneasy. The one-child policy already widened inequalities in China. If you're rich, you're likely to have had more children, with less impunity. What if those children can be smarter, less disease prone, and taller? Then China will draw even closer to the dystopian society envisioned by Aldous Huxley in *Brave New World,* where the population is created in the lab and classified. Alphas are rulers, and worker bees like the Epsilons are cognitively stunted and programmed never to aspire above their station.

In 1995, China passed the National Maternal and Infant Health Law, forbidding couples who had "genetic diseases of a serious nature" to procreate. The conditions listed include mental retardation, mental illness, and seizures. These couples were required to undergo a mandatory premarital medical exam. It was hugely controversial, reviving international criticism that China practices eugenics.

Actually, the wording of the national law was considered mild. Some provinces had more explicit regulations. In 1988, Gansu Province passed local regulations prohibiting "reproduction of the dull-witted, idiots, or blockheads." Gansu abolished that law in 2002. Similarly, the National Maternal and Infant Health Law was de-fanged when requirements for the premarital medical examination were quietly dropped in 2003.

V

What happens when the world's most populous nation has a baby shortage?

For the past twenty years, China has seen below-replacement birthrates. In the meantime, the problems of a huge elderly population, a labor shortage, and a shortage of women would best be ameliorated by an uptick in births, which isn't happening and may never happen.

After over three decades of the one-child policy, the Communist Party has finally taken steps to end it, only to find to its dismay that many middle-class Chinese don't want more than one child.

As we saw, in 2013, China allowed more couples to have second children through the *dandu* exclusion — where at least one half of the couple is a single child — but the take-up has been far below even the most pessimistic projections. Only a tenth of eligible couples applied for permission to have a second child. Even though polls show many couples would like to have two children, many say in practice it's un-affordable, too stressful, and will impinge on their personal goals too much. Many also view fertility as a strategy for social mobility: by having one child, they can better concentrate their resources and have a more successful child. "It's actually seen as selfish and bad parenting to have another child," demographer Ma Xiaohong told the *Washington Post.*

In that sense, the one-child policy can be judged a huge success, for it changed the mindset of Chinese people. A young friend said, "For years, the government has been educating its people that birth planning is the best family style. It means wealth, happiness, and a less crowded society. I think such propaganda is very successful. And this one-child policy does improve a lot of families' life standards. For me, brought up in a one-child family, it seems natural to bear only one child."

Perhaps proof of the one-child policy's effectiveness is obsolescence: in demographer Ma's survey on why Chinese parents have just one child, 60 percent said the one-child policy had nothing to do with their decision.

Harvard University professor Susan Greenhalgh has argued that China's rapid fertility decline has less to do with the physical coercive tactics employed by officials, and more to do with Chinese society's view that controlling fertility could lead to upward mobility. In terms of reproduction, "the Chinese represent a case of extreme economic rationalism," wrote Greenhalgh.

In Huxley's *Brave New World,* the dictator Mustapha Mond argues that the world is better run when children are hatched in labs. "The world's stable now. People are happy, they get what they want, and they never want what they can't get. They're well off; they're safe; they're never ill; they're not afraid of death; they're blissfully ignorant of passion and old age; they're plagued with no mothers or fathers."

In a paean to human irrationality, the hero, the Savage, defiantly replies, "But I don't want comfort. I want God. I want poetry. I want real danger, I want freedom, I want goodness, I want sin."

In time, China's problem will become that of every other major East Asian economy: a dwindling population. It's a problem almost all developed countries are facing. Countries that switched from anti-natalist to pro-natalist policies have so far found that turning *on* the baby tap is far more difficult than turning it off.

By 2025, India will overtake China as the world's most populous nation, a crown China is only too happy to relinquish. Somewhere in the decade between 2020 and 2030 China's absolute population will hit its peak and start to decline. By 2100, China's population could have declined back to 1950 levels of about 500 million, according to academic Chen Youhua's projections.

Perhaps the Communist Party can turn the tide. It did, after all, launch the most successful campaign against childbearing in modern history. But I suspect it will be hard, if not impossible. The idea of approaching childbearing with a mindset that is three parts calculation has become ingrained in China's psyche. In the end, perhaps the greatest damage inflicted by the one-child policy is how it forced people to think rationally — perhaps *too* rationally — about parenthood, a great leap into the unknown with an infinite capacity to stretch our understanding of what it means to live and love.

EPILOGUE

The IVF treatment in China didn't work. I didn't get pregnant.

In essence, IVF boils down to putting the best egg and the best sperm together in a lab. Theoretically, this makes conception a bit of a slam dunk, like giving a footrace competitor a bicycle. However, the next stage, implanting the embryo and waiting to see if a healthy pregnancy results, is something science still cannot control.

Sometimes it takes, sometimes it doesn't. I wasn't "taking," or catching fire, or sparking, and the reason why I couldn't was as much a mystery to my doctors as it was to me.

So I made the radical decision to leave my job and leave China. I had hoped I could continue my work and still be a mother, but it wasn't happening. Deep down, I had half-acknowledged fears that a deadline-driven lifestyle and life in polluted Beijing were to blame. I had to stop, learn how to stand still.

In late 2009, we traded China's landlocked capital for Venice Beach. There couldn't be a more stark contrast. Instead of Beijing smog, we had fog rolling off the Pacific coast. Instead of a sea of commuting brunets, I saw blonds and Rastafarians ambling in the California sunshine, smelling of weed.

I missed Beijing, which, for all its inconveniences, was enormously exciting, with surprising pockets of tranquillity. I yearned to ride my bike around the moat surrounding the Forbidden City, watching open-air barbers plying their trade under the shadow of weeping willows. Living in Beijing, you could never take things for granted. Every blue-sky day was a benediction. It tightened the sinews but also sharpened the senses. Now I was cocooned in cotton wool.

Echoes from my old life lingered. I would freeze at crosswalks, surprised that cars actually stopped for pedestrians. At a checkup, my doctor detected a rattle in my lungs and told me to stop smoking. (I don't, never have.) I could drink tap water again, and the fluoride helped my teeth shed the yellow sheen they had acquired after years of drinking bottled water.

I started prenatal yoga classes with women who wanted at-home water births and didn't believe in the measles vaccine. When I told my Mommy N' Me group that my birth plan involved drugs, "and lots of them," the women looked at me pityingly as they composed themselves in graceful asanas.

I stopped reflexively checking the news and tried to will myself into a state of Buddha-like calm. I started IVF again.

I like to think I nobly refrained from making the sort of cool, calculated choices that made me so uneasy: prescreening for genetic diseases, choosing for gender, choosing multiples. Truth is, it didn't occur to me. I had such a hard time getting pregnant, it never entered my mind to pick at the salad bar of reproductive choices. So I didn't go in saying I wanted twins, or boys, but that's what I ended up with.

In 2010, my twin boys were born. First came little Eternal Virtue, followed one minute later by Steadfast Virtue.

Ever dramatic, Steadfast lifted his little arms high, a graceful pirouette as the surgeon lifted him out of me. It was a perfect photo op. They looked like plucked chickens, and they were beautiful.

I observed the confinement month, with baths and outdoor

walks, reveling in an orgy of baby worship. I watched Steadfast and Eternal plump up, developing chunky thighs I loved to squeeze. Those long summer afternoons under the ceiling fan, two drowsy babies at my side, will live on in my mind as one of the most peaceful periods of my life.

When I look at the turn my life has taken, I hardly recognize who I've become. There are no more sudden jaunts to trouble spots, no quickening of the pulse for a fast-breaking story. I must stay rooted, I must give of myself, I must lose myself.

As the youngest in my family, I had nieces and nephews long before I had children of my own. To my family, I was the exciting aunt, the one who went to exotic places and brought them unusual souvenirs, the one who scuba-dived in oil spills and talked her way into places she wasn't supposed to go. A nephew once told me, "Don't have children, Auntie Mei. Then you'll be *boring*." Well, I have children now, and I *am* boring. What was it that P. J. O'Rourke said? "Don't try and come on like Jean-Paul Belmondo/Aspire instead to two kids and a condo."

At bedtime, I tell my children stories. Some are Chinese folktales, like the tale of the archer who shoots nine suns from the sky, or Chang-O, the lady on the moon. There are the old chestnuts from Grimm or Andersen. For Eternal and Steadfast, the most successful tales are frequently the most bloodthirsty. There is something that seizes their imagination when I say, "And then, he slew him," even though they have yet to understand what this means. In this magic landscape, mothers exit, stepmothers appear, children are cast out, eternally hungry wolves prowl.

One day, I will tell them about a country once so poor, an emperor ruled that each family could have only one child. Of how a great sadness came over the land, and how people gave away their children, or stole other people's, or sought the help of magicians to make their single precious child the strongest and brightest they could. And how it came to pass that there were fewer and fewer babies born to the land, and it became a country of the old.

I don't know the ending to this story.

And then I lie awake as they sleep, the steady rhythm of their breathing the most peaceful and frightening sound in the world.

ACKNOWLEDGMENTS

This book is the culmination of two decades of reporting in Asia and a lifetime as a Chinese daughter.

When I started off as a reporter in tiny Singapore, I found to my dismay that people were invariably afraid to be quoted. In an island with a population of 5 million and tough libel laws, there was justifiable fear of giving offense. So first and foremost I give thanks to the many who shared their stories with me. This book could not have been written without their candor and generosity.

In writing this book I had to learn about topics as diverse as demographics and hospice care, and I am extremely grateful to the folks who shared their expertise: Wang Feng, Cao Yu, Dan Goodkind, Nicholas Eberstadt, Bill Lavely, Wu Youshui, Liang Zhongtang, Zhang Erli, Joshua Kurtzig, Zhao Yaohui, Lena Edlund, Lisa Cameron, Vanessa Fong, Arthur Kroeber, Joan Kaufman, Matthew Connelly, Chen Hong, Jennifer Lee, Changfu Chang, Jamie Metzl, Tex Cox, Harry Wu, Steve Mosher, and Clayton Dube. I am also much indebted to the works of Susan Greenhalgh and Thomas Scharping in researching the history of China's population policies.

I owe much gratitude as well to friends and fellow writers and reporters who offered valuable critiques of early drafts: Evelyn Iritani, Andrew Batson, Matt Richards, Sebastian Tong, Peter Herford, Liu

Shuang, Ron Orol, Kathleen McLaughlin, Lucy Hornby, Kathy Chen, Geoff Fowler, Kevin Voigt, Doug Young, Amanda Whitfort, Alison DeSouza, Carla Sapsford, Ian Johnson, Scott Tong, Rob Schmitz, Eva Woo, Joy Chen, Isaac Stone Fish, Gary Okihiro, Marina Henriquez, Carol Quinn, Hessie Nguyen, and Barry Newman. Many thanks as well to various friends for their warm hospitality on reporting trips, including Marsha Cooke, Gu Qiao, Robin and Jasmine Lewis, and Sue Ward.

Thank you as well to Will Schwalbe, Matthew Pang, Peter Ford, Evan Osnos, Martin Roessingh, Tiff Roberts, Deb and Jim Fallows, Jes Randrup Nielsen, Mara Hvistandahl, Ching-Ching Ni, Leta Hong Fincher, Anthony Kuhn, Peh Shing Huei, Li Yuan, Jonathan Kaufman, Hao Wu, Emily Rauhala, Duncan Clark, Richard Burger, Jerome Cohen, Patrick Radden Keefe, Peter Cohn, Sara Dorow, Patty Meier, Patti Smith, Jena Martinberg, Didi Kirsten Tatlow, Mitchell Zuckoff, and FB groups APA Media Mavens and Asian/Pacific Islander Women Writers for valuable advice, contacts, and insight.

To my former boss, Rebecca Blumenstein, heartfelt thanks for guiding a Malaysian to an unhoped-for prize, the Pulitzer; huzzahs to all my Hong Kong and China bureau colleagues, a dream team so fantastic they basically ruined me for any other journalism gig. And to the foreign press corps in China, my fervent hope that Beijing will loosen visa restrictions so you can continue your valuable work.

This book could not have been written without the company of and valuable input from researchers: Kersten Zhang, Ellen Zhu, Sue Feng, Gao Sen, Helena Yu, Yan Shuang, Hu Pan, Violet Tian, Echo Xie, Brandon Yu, Janet Lundblad, Fu Tao, Shako Liu, and Cecilia Xie; special thanks to those of you who uncomplainingly accompanied me on travel that was frequently uncomfortable, and sometimes hazardous.

I would probably have languished as an indifferent piano instructor in Kuala Lumpur without crucial early encouragement from teachers, editors, and mentors such as Constance Singam, Yeap Gaik Koon, Laura Abraham, Junie Simon, Lee Ching Pei, Charlie Letts, Gopal Baratham, Tan Wang Joo, 8 Days' Michael Chiang, Rahul Pathak, NUS's Robbie Goh and Susan Ang, and Bill Berkeley and Dave Fondiller at Columbia, as well as the aid of scholarships from Singapore Press Holdings and the Lee Foundation.

Students, too, are teachers, and I am very grateful to mine at USC's Annenberg School and Shantou University for innumerable lessons. As well, thanks to the *Wall Street Journal*'s Cathy Panagoulias and Laurie Hays for giving me my first shot at the paper and having confidence in me when I didn't.

Special thanks to my agents, John and Max Brockman, editor Ben Hyman, and copy editor Barbara Wood, who helped bring this book to reality in ways that I could not envision. As well, much gratitude to New America Foundation for providing support and stimulating intellectual companionship. Writing would be a lonelier business without such company.

Last, this book is ultimately about families, and I am grateful every day for mine. My mother and sisters taught me to value strength in womanhood; my in-laws, June and Marshall, read drafts, translated, and made sure my children were fed while I was in a writing vortex; my children, whose presence reminds me of what matters most; and — I know it's almost grounds for divorce not to mention your spouse in a writer's acknowledgments, but I really truly, do give thanks to my husband, Andrew, who has been my shield and support in a hundred million ways.

There are those who say too much family hinders, but it is only with such ballast that we can fly.

NOTES AND REFERENCES

Author's Note

page

ix *GDP figures are "man-made":* Tom Orlik, "Lies, Damned Lies, and Chinese Statistics," *Foreign Policy,* September 20, 2013, http://foreignpolicy.com/2013 /03/20/lies-damned-lies-and-chinese-statistics/.

Prologue

x *Thus began the one-child policy:* There is some debate over the start of the policy, as some pilot projects were initiated in 1979; however September 25, 1980 is widely seen as the start of a nationwide plan.

xi *"I would be surprised if more than 0.1% of this":* Interview with the author, June 13, 2014.
    one out of every four people in China will be over sixty-five: Xin Dingding, "One in Four Chinese 'Aged Above 65 by 2050,'" *China Daily,* May 20, 2010, http:// www.chinadaily.com.cn/china/2010-05/20/content_9870078.htm.

xii *China's massive 800-million-person work force:* James Tulloch, "How China's Demographics Affect Its Workforce," *Open Knowledge,* Allianz.com, April 24, 2010, http://knowledge.allianz.com/demography/population/?369/how -chinas-demographics-affect-its-workforce.
    started to contract in 2012: According to China's National Bureau of Statistics, cited in numerous publications including "China's One-Child Policy Backfires as Labor Pool Shrinks Again," *Bloomberg Business,* January 20, 2015, http:// www.bloomberg.com/news/articles/2015-01-20/china-s-one-child-policy -backfire-deepens-as-labor-pool-shrinks.

a tenth of eligible couples applied to have a second child: "Only 1/10th Chinese Couples Had 2nd Child After Policy Relaxed," *Press Trust of India,* March 10, 2015, http://www.business-standard.com/article/pti-stories/only-1-10th -chinese-couples-had-2nd-child-after-policy-relaxed-115031001049_1.html.

By 2100, China's population may have declined to 1950 levels: Anthony Kuhn, "One County Provides Preview of China's Looming Aging Crisis," National Public Radio website, January 14, 2015, http://www.npr.org/blogs/parallels /2015/01/14/377190697/one-county-provides-preview-of-chinas-looming -aging-crisis.

xiii   *"Even an extra 50 to 100 million people wouldn't have made a huge difference":* E-mail correspondence with the author, June 29, 2015.

xiv   *the real number of births averted was probably 100 to 200 million at most:* Wang Feng, Cai Yong, and Gu Baochang, "Population, Policy and Politics: How Will History Judge the One-Child Policy?," *Population and Development Review* 38, Issue Supplement s1 (February 2013): 115–29.

ranked the one-child policy as one of the most important stratagems: "The Deepest Cuts," *Economist,* September 20, 2014, http://www.economist.com/news /briefing/21618680-our-guide-actions-have-done-most-slow-global-warming -deepest-cuts.

the United States has less than 5 percent of the world's population: United States Department of Energy, Carbon Dioxide Information Analysis Center, 2010 CO_2 Emission Data, http://cdiac.ornl.gov/trends/emis/top2010.tot.

xv   *all governments should "adopt a one-child policy":* Charles R. Clement, "Is the World Ready for a One-Child Policy?," *Science,* November 12, 2010.

"a planetary law": Diane Francis, "The Real Inconvenient Truth," *Financial Post,* December 14, 2009, http://www.financialpost.com/story.html?id=2314438.

"one of the most important social policies ever": Interview with the author, November 5, 2013. Potts later expanded on his viewpoint, saying the policy was "motivated by a sincere if mistaken belief that, difficult as it would be to imple- ment, the one-child policy was the only way to lift people out of poverty" (e-mail correspondence with the author, August 13, 2015).

1. After the Quake

3   *95 percent of couples there had pledged to have only one child:* Susan Greenhalgh, *Just One Child: Science and Policy in Deng's China* (Oakland: University of California Press, 2008), 202.

where over two-thirds of families are single-child families: Jianmin Wen, "Shifang, China's First City, Exercises Family Planning, Becoming an Aging Society in Advance with Reduced Population of 400,000 in 30 Years," *Sichuan Online,* January 6, 2014, http://sichuan.scol.com.cn/dwzw/content/2014-01/06 /content_6713125.htm.

4   *a license plate with the number 18:* Bettina Wassener, "Vanity Plates a Perfect
    Match for Flashy Hong Kong," *New York Times,* September 24, 2012, http://
    www.nytimes.com/2012/09/25/business/global/vanity-plates-a-perfect-match
    -for-flashy-hong-kong.html?_r=0.

6   *about a third of the population faced strict one-child limitations:* Avraham
    Ebenstein, "The Missing Girls of China and the Unintended Consequences
    of the One Child Policy," *Journal of Human Resources* 45, no. 1 (2010), https:
    //scholars.huji.ac.il/sites/default/files/avrahamebenstein/files/ebenstein
    _onechildpolicy_2010.pdf.
    "slipping into irrelevance": Leslie T. Chang, "For Many in China, the One-Child
    Policy Is Already Irrelevant," *Chinafile,* March 19, 2013, http://www.chinafile
    .com/many-china-one-child-policy-already-irrelevant.

7   *pension funding shortfalls could be as much as:* "China Pension Fund Gap to Top
    80 Pct of 2011 GDP by 2050," Reuters, December 13, 2012, http://www.reuters
    .com/article/2012/12/13/china-economy-pension-idUSL4N09N2QH20121213.

10 *The number arrived at was 338 million:* Wang Feng, Cai Yong, and Gu Baochang,
    "Population, Policy and Politics: How Will History Judge the One-Child Policy?"
    *people's reproductive habits would roughly trend the same from the 1950s to the
    1990s:* Martin King Whyte, Wang Feng, and Cai Yong, "Challenging Myths
    About China's One-Child Policy," *The China Journal* no. 74 (2015), 1324-9347
    /2015/7401-0009, Australian National University.

11 *An estimated 13 million people share her predicament:* Stephanie Gordon,
    "China's Hidden Children," *The Diplomat,* March 12, 2015, http://thediplomat
    .com/2015/03/chinas-hidden-children/.

13 *"like black butterflies flying low":* Zhang Qingzhou, *Revelations from the
    Tangshan Earthquake* (Shanghai: Shanghai People's Publishing House, 2006).

2.   And the Clock Struck 8/8/08

24 *Dr. Li pioneered a surgical technique for vasectomies:* "History of No-Scalpel
    Vasectomy (NSV)," Weill Cornell Medical College, Department of Urology,
    https://www.cornellurology.com/clinical-conditions/no-scalpel-vasectomy
    /history/.

25 *wide use of this sterilization technique:* Bing Xu and Jinbo Zhu, "An Analysis of
    Sichuan Province's Success in Promoting Male Sterilization Operation," *Chinese
    Journal of Family Planning,* no. 5 (1993).
    Fewer than 1 percent of China's schools provide sex education: Jeremy Blum,
    "Babies Do Not Come from Rubbish Dumps, Chinese Sex Education Video
    Says," *South China Morning Post,* November 7, 2013, http://www.scmp.com
    /lifestyle/family-education/article/1350056/babies-do-not-come-rubbish
    -dumps-sex-education-video-says.

29 *Huang Qi, a Chinese cyber-dissident:* Michael Bristow, "China Activist Huang

Qi Sentenced to Three Years," BBC News, November 23, 2009, http://news
.bbc.co.uk/2/hi/asia-pacific/8373573.stm.

Liu Shaokun, a schoolteacher, was sentenced: Tania Branigan, "Chinese Teacher
Sent to Labour Camp for Earthquake Photos," *The Guardian,* July 30, 2008,
http://www.theguardian.com/world/2008/jul/30/chinaearthquake.china.

Environmentalist Tan Zuoren, who coined the phrase "tofu dreg project": "Chinese
Earthquake Activist Tan Zuoren Released After Five-Year Prison Term," *The
Guardian,* March 27, 2014, http://www.theguardian.com/world/2014/mar/27
/chinese-activist-tan-zouren-released-five-year-prison-term.

30 *been a prizewinning entry in a competition:* Mei Fong, "A Deformed Doughnut?
No, China's TV Tower!," *Wall Street Journal,* November 7, 2007, http://www
.buro-os.com/a-deformed-doughnut-no-chinas-tv-tower/.

31 *"how small you are, and how big the state":* Mei Fong, "CCTV Tower Mirrors
Beijing's Rising Ambitions," *Wall Street Journal,* November 7, 2007, http://
www.wsj.com/articles/SB119438152241184281.

   A multitude of mistranslated English signs: Mei Fong, "Tired of Laughter,
Beijing Gets Rid of Bad Translations," *Wall Street Journal,* February 5, 2007,
http://www.wsj.com/articles/SB117063961235897853.

32 *The mascots were collectively dubbed* fuwa: Haishan Zhang, "Lucky Dolls
Become Witch Dolls, Olympic Mascot Blocked on Opening Ceremony,"
Dajiyuan website, August 10, 2008, http://www.epochtimes.com/b5/8/8/11
/n2224032.htm.

34 *The Weather Modification Bureau had deployed:* Zheng Yu, "Beijing Uses High-
Tech to Prevent Rain from Dampening Olympic Opening," *Xinhua* website,
July 28, 2008, http://news.xinhuanet.com/english/2008-07/28/content_8787
101.htm.

   They'd wanted more Yao champions: Brook Larmer, *Operation Yao Ming: The
Chinese Sports Empire, American Big Business and the Making of an NBA
Superstar* (New York: Gotham Books, 2005).

35 *the one-child policy fostered selfishness:* Klaus Brinkbäumer and Bernhard Zand,
"Basketball Great Yao Ming: 'Never Underestimate Strength of Character,'" *Spiegel
Online,* January 23, 2014, http://www.spiegel.de/international/world/spiegel
-interview-with-former-chinese-basketball-star-yao-ming-a-944567.html.

37 *"Olympics marked a beginning":* Peh Shing Huei, *When the Party Ends: China's
Leaps and Stumbles After the Beijing Olympics* (Singapore: Straits Times Press,
2013).

38 *The quantities of water conduits and power lines:* "China: 5,335 Students Killed
or Missing After 2008 Quake," CNN website, May 10, 2009, http://edition.cnn
.com/2009/WORLD/asiapcf/05/07/china.quake.deaths/index.html?$NMW
_TRANS$=ext.

41 *an estimated 1 million* shidu *parents:* Beibei Bao, "Shidu: When Chinese Parents
Forced to Have One Child Lose That Child," *Atlantic,* May 9, 2013, http://www

.theatlantic.com/china/archive/2013/05/shidu-when-chinese-parents-forced-to
-have-one-child-lose-that-child/275691/.

shidu *parents have trouble:* Yuanfei Niu, "Shidu Parents Facing Problems When
Getting into Nursing Home," *Dazhong Web,* February 21, 2013, http://paper
.dzwww.com/dzrb/content/20130221/Article11002MT.htm; and Ke Ji and
Qiong Wu, "Afraid of No Progeny to Pay Tribute at Tomb, Shidu Parents
Refuse to Buy Burial Plot," *Mingzhu News,* May 23, 2012, http://news.thmz
.com/col89/2012/05/2012-05-231124828_2.html.

more prone to depression: Yuanfei Niu, "China Will Have 10 Million Shidu
Families in Future," *Tencent Web,* April 10, 2013, http://news.qq.com/a/20130410
/000084.htm.

3.   *Cassandra and the Rocketmen*

44   *"We could hold our heads high":* Interview with the author, August 2013.
     Liang warned that the policy would be a "terrible tragedy": Greenhalgh, *Just
     One Child,* 181.

45   *Susan Greenhalgh:* Ibid., 182.

46   *the Chinese Association for Population Studies was founded only in 1981:*
     Thomas Scharping, *Birth Control in China, 1949–2000: Population Policy
     and Demographic Development* (Oxford: Routledge, 2003), 51.
     "only rather crude numbers": Ibid.
     "a legless man teaching running": Saying attributed to Channing Pollock.

47   *dazzled the Italian traveler Marco Polo:* Mike Edwards, "Marco Polo, Part II:
     In China," *National Geographic,* June 2001, http://ngm.nationalgeographic
     .com/print/features/world/asia/china/marco-polo-ii-text.
     "There's nine hundred million of them in the world today": Monty Python,
     "I Like Chinese," 1980.
     "three are too much": Scharping, *Birth Control in China, 1949–2000,* 49.
     *In that decade, the average woman in China went from having six children to
     three:* According to World Bank figures.

48   *"Economic development is like a cake":* Ted Alcorn and Bao Beibei, "China's
     Fertility Policy Persists, Despite Debate," *The Lancet* 378 (October 29, 2011),
     http://www.thelancet.com/pdfs/journals/lancet/PIIS0140-6736%2811%29
     61661-9.pdf.

49   *"adjust women's average fertility rate in advance":* Song Jian, "Natural Science
     and Social Science Scholar's Population Study First Predicts the Domestic
     Population Development in the Coming One Hundred Years," *Xinhua,*
     February 13, 1980.
     aging and fertility dialed up or down, like levers on a machine: A similar analogy
     was employed by Susan Greenhalgh in *Just One Child,* 228.

"In thirty years, when our current": Malcolm Moore, "Thirty Years of China's One-Child Policy," *The Telegraph,* September 25, 2010, http://www.telegraph .co.uk/news/worldnews/asia/china/8024862/Thirty-years-of-Chinas-one-child-policy.html.

bestseller, The Population Bomb: Paul R. Ehrlich, *The Population Bomb: Population Control or Race to Oblivion?* (Rivercity, MA: Rivercity Press, 1975, republished from the 1968 version by special arrangement with Ballantine Books), prologue.

50 *published* The Limits to Growth: Donella H. Meadows, Dennis L. Meadows, Jørgen Randers, and William W. Behrens III, *The Limits to Growth* (New York: Signet Books, 1972).

many hands reaching for one loaf of bread: Ironically, Singapore today is desperately trying to raise its birthrate, which is one of the lowest in the world, through pro-natalist policies and setting up of government-sponsored matchmaking agencies. One was initially named Social Development Unit, or SDU, an unfortunate acronym that soon earned the label "Single, Desperate, and Ugly."

rationing children: Tyrene White, *China's Longest Campaign: Birth Planning in the People's Republic, 1949–2005* (Ithaca: Cornell University Press, 2006).

51 *"He seemed like a regular guy":* Interview with the author, August 4, 2014.

52 *Song was given access:* Evan Feigenbaum, *China's Techno-Warriors: National Security and Strategic Competition from the Nuclear to the Information Age* (Stanford, CA: Stanford University Press, 2003).

controlling China's birthrate: Mara Hvistendahl, *Unnatural Selection: Choosing Boys over Girls, and the Consequences for a World Full of Men* (New York: PublicAffairs Press, 2011).

the paper disappeared from view: Greenhalgh, *Just One Child,* 228.

53 *It would be twenty long years before he was politically rehabilitated:* Ma Yinchu did not live long to enjoy his new status as Father of the One-Child Policy. He died three years after the launch.

would continue to balloon: Greenhalgh, *Just One Child,* 218.

54 *"How did you calculate":* From interviews and collected writings of Liang Zhongtang.

"it's absolutely correct!": Zhongtang Liang, "My Autobiography," *Netease* (blog), August 23, 2009, http://liangzhongtang.blog.163.com/blog/static/109426508 20097230340812/.

"using science as a disguise": Ibid.

55 *"we have been the victors, we have mastered the world":* Song Jian and Yu Jingyuan, *Population System Control* (New York: China Academic Publishers, Springer-Verlag, 1988), 1.

a variety of questionable assumptions: Greenhalgh, *Just One Child,* 159.

"countless heroic assumptions": Ibid.

56 *half the rate of the previous decade:* "The Most Surprising Demographic Crisis," *Economist,* May 5, 2011, http://www.economist.com/node/18651512.
"no good theory to explain": Matthew Connelly, *Fatal Misconception: The Struggle to Control World Population* (Cambridge, MA: Harvard Belknap Press, 2010).
between 8 billion: Margaret Besheer, "UN: Global Population Expected to Top 8 Billion by 2025," Voice of America, June 13, 2013, http://www.voanews.com/content/un-africa-to-drive-rise-in-world-population-in-2050/1681300.html.
13 billion: Sarah Williams, "Experts Be Damned: World Population Will Continue to Rise," *Science,* September 18, 2014, http://news.sciencemag.org/economics/2014/09/experts-be-damned-world-population-will-continue-rise.
as many people as there were on Earth in the 1950s: Floyd Norris, "Population Growth Forecast from the U.N. May Be Too High," *New York Times,* September 20, 2013, http://www.nytimes.com/2013/09/21/business/uns-forecast-of-population-growth-may-be-too-high.html.
"science fiction": E-mail exchange with the author, June 29, 2015.
"social, economic aspects were not factored in": Interview with the author, August 4, 2014.

57 *Song had risen:* http://www.chinavitae.com/biography/Song_Jian/career.
"the kindness of humanity is limited": Song and Yu, *Population System Control,* 2.

58 *Yicheng and its sisters:* Gu Baochang and Wang Feng, *An Experiment of Eight Million People* (Beijing: Social Sciences Academic Press, 2009).

59 *weren't really representative of China:* Gu Baochang, Song Jian, Liu Shuang, Wang Jinying, and Jiang Lihua, "Practice and Inspirations of Two Child Fertility Policy Areas," *Journal of Population Research* 32, no. 4 (July 2008).
"it was still the same reaction": Interview with the author, September 10, 2014.

60 *"He was treated like a god":* Interview with the author, September 10, 2014.
Too Many People in China?: Liang Jianzhang and Li Jiangxin, *Too Many People in China?* (Beijing: Social Science Academic Press, 2012).
China had become "like an armored car": Interview with the author, August 20, 2013.

61 *officials caught her:* Hannah Beech, "China: Forced-Abortion Victim Promised $11,200, but Family Fears for Life," *Time,* July 13, 2012, http://world.time.com/2012/07/13/china-forced-abortion-victim-awarded-11200-fears-for-life/.
"I could feel the baby jumping around inside me": Malcolm Moore, "China 'Forced Abortion' Photograph Causes Outrage," *The Telegraph,* June 14, 2013, http://www.telegraph.co.uk/news/worldnews/asia/china/9331232/China-forced-abortion-photograph-causes-outrage.html.
Stanford anthropology student Steve Mosher personally witnessed several: Steven W. Mosher, *Broken Earth: The Rural Chinese* (New York: Free Press, 1984).

62 *"Chinese women have made huge sacrifices":* Frank Langfitt, "After a Forced Abortion, a Roaring Debate in China," National Public Radio website, July 5,

2012, http://www.npr.org/2012/07/05/156211106/after-a-forced-abortion-a
-roaring-debate-in-china.

a new baby boom: Sui-Lee Wee, "Investors Look to Nappies, Pianos as China
Drops One Child Policy," *Independent,* November 20, 2013, http://www.inde
pendent.ie/business/world/investors-look-to-nappies-pianos-as-china-drops
-one-child-policy-29768127.html.

Shares at Japanese diaper maker: Danielle Demetriou, "Japanese Companies
Relish China's One-Child Policy Reform," *The National,* January 14, 2014,
http://www.thenational.ae/business/industry-insights/economics/japanese
-companies-relish-chinas-one-child-policy-reform.

64   *the baby boom's been a bust:* Shan Juan, "Fewer Couples Want Second Child,"
China Daily, October 30, 2014, http://www.chinadaily.com.cn/china/2014
-10/30/content_18825388.htm?utm_source=The+Sinocism+China+News
letter&utm_campaign=1d33689d9e-Sinocism10_30_1410_30_2014&utm
_medium=email&utm_term=0_171f237867-1d33689d9e-29619965&mc_cid
=1d33689d9e&mc_eid=a85f130e96.

4. The Population Police

66   *a bloated behemoth:* Scharping, *Birth Control in China, 1949–2000,* 164.

67   *births must be spaced at least five years apart:* Ma Shipeng, "Despite Two-Child
Policy in Yicheng, Villagers Prefer to Have Second Child, Financially Better
Off," *Dong Fang Zao Bao,* November 12, 2013, http://epaper.dfdaily.com/dfzb
/html/2013-11/12/content_834806.htm.

68   *Nonpermanent barrier methods like condoms, the Pill, and IUDs:* Betsy
Hartmann, *Reproductive Rights and Wrongs: The Global Politics of Population
Control* (Boston: South End Press, 1999), 164.
China sterilized over 20 million people: China Health Statistics Yearbook (Beijing:
Peking Union Medical College Press, 2010).

70   *marched off in handcuffs:* Scharping, *Birth Control in China, 1949–2000,* 55.

72   *"just a piece of meat":* Cheng Xiaowei and Zhao Yejiao, "Fine Determined by
Personal Discretion, Said Wenzhou Family Planning Official," *China News,*
April 8, 2010, http://www.chinanews.com/sh/news/2010/04-08/2213437.shtml.
a "crisis in birth planning": Scharping, *Birth Control in China, 1949–2000,* 72.

73   *had already breached population targets:* Ibid., 73.
publicly pee in cups: Ibid., 176.

74   *"The doctor injected poison":* "Forced Abortion and Sterilization in China:
The View from Inside," hearing before the Subcommittee on International
Operations and Human Rights of the Committee on International Relations,
US House of Representatives, 105th Cong. (June 10, 1998), http://commdocs
.house.gov/committees/intlrel/hfa49740.000/hfa49740_0f.htm.
wanted for suspected fraud: Daniel Kwan, "Birth Control Couple Accused

of Swindles," *South China Morning Post,* July 1, 1998, http://www.scmp.com
/article/246563/birth-control-couple-accused-swindles.

77 *harsh enforcement of the one-child policy to be rare:* "Flap over 1-Child Policy
Stirs," *Washington Times,* February 18, 2009, http://www.washingtontimes
.com/news/2009/feb/18/revival-of-us-aid-stirs-unease-on-beijings-one-chi
/?page=all.
turn enforcers into parenting counselors: "Enforcing with a Smile," *Economist,*
January 10, 2015, http://www.economist.com/news/china/21638131-enforcers
-chinas-one-child-policy-are-trying-new-gentler-approach-enforcing-smile.

78 *a mass sterilization campaign:* Amnesty International, "China: Thousands
at Risk of Forced Sterilization," April 20, 2010, https://www.amnesty.org/en
/documents/asa17/016/2010/en/.
"Big cities depend on land"': Pang Jiaoming, *The Orphans of Shao: A True
Account of the Blood and Tears of the One-Child Policy in China* (New York:
Women's Rights in China Organization Publishers, 2014), 60.

80 *an estimated 13 million people:* Gao Haoliang, Wang Haiying, and Wu Shuguang,
"Illegally Born Children Could Register Without Fine," *Banyuetan Magazine,*
June 3, 2014, http://www.banyuetan.org/chcontent/jrt/2014531/102874.html.

81 *Beijing began a crackdown on human rights lawyers:* Andrew Jacobs and Chris
Buckley, "China Targeting Rights Lawyers in a Crackdown," *New York Times,*
July 22, 2015, http://www.nytimes.com/2015/07/23/world/asia/china-crack
down-human-rights-lawyers.html?_r=0.

84 *fifteen out of a hundred students recognized the photo:* Robin Young and Jeremy
Hudson, "How the Tiananmen Square Massacre Has Been Largely Forgotten,"
National Public Radio website, June 4, 2014, http://hereandnow.wbur.org/2014
/06/04/tiananmen-louisa-lim.

5. Little Emperors, Grown Up

86 *100 million only children:* "Single-Child Population Tops 100 Million in China,"
Xinhua website, July 7, 2008, http://www.chinadaily.com.cn/china/2008-07
/07/content_6825563.htm.

87 *a guilt-ridden Zhang published:* Tania Branigan, "China's Cultural Revolution:
Son's Guilt over the Mother He Sent to Her Death," *The Guardian,* March 27,
2013, http://www.theguardian.com/world/2013/mar/27/china-cultural-revolu
tion-sons-guilt-zhang-hongping.

90 *a group of Chinese and Japanese children on a camping trip:* Sun Yunxiao, "The
Contest in Summer Camp," *Reader Magazine,* November 1993, Gansu People's
Publishing House.
singletons tended to be more self-centered: D. Y. Chen, ed., *The Only-Child
Declaration* (Shanghai: Hainan Publishing Company, 1997).
less self-control: X. T. Feng and X. T. Zhang, "Discussion of the Special

Environment of the Socialization of the Only-Child," *Quarterly Journal of Social Sciences* 5 (1992): 33–37.

91 *academic achievements and sociability:* D. L. Poston Jr. and T. Falbo, "Academic Performance and Personality Traits of Chinese Children: 'Onlies' Versus Others," *American Journal of Sociology* 96, no. 2 (September 1990): 433–51.
poorer eyesight: Hao Keming, *An Empirical Study of China's Only Child Population* (Hong Kong: Guangdong Education Press, 2010), 207.

92 *differences are a result of family structure:* L. Cameron, N. Erkal, L. Gangadharan, and X. Meng, "Little Emperors: Behavioral Impacts of China's One-Child Policy," *Science,* February 22, 2013.

93 *a series of letters from only children:* Mei Zhong, "The Only Child Declaration: A Content Analysis of Published Stories by China's Only Children," *Intercultural Communications Studies* 14, no. 1 (2005).
"all my classmates gave me a nickname, 'Baby'": Ibid., 20.

94 *"we don't have our independent future":* Ibid., 21.

95 *coined the term* ant tribe: Lian Si, *Ant Tribe: A Record of College Graduates' Crowded Life* (Guangxi: Guangxi Normal University Press, 2010).
they make poor hires: China Railway Construction Engineering Group, recruitment advertisement, February 3, 2015, http://www.buildhr.com/company /bf06j/.

96 *"We don't hire two kinds of persons":* Jiang Xiaochun, "Employer Rejected Job Seekers from One-Child Family or Well-Off Family to Make Recruitment More Efficient," *Jinling Evening News* (Nanjing City), June 24, 2014, E06.
slang for "loser": Josh Chin, "China's Communist Party Tells Kids Being a Loser Is Nothing to Be Proud Of," *Wall Street Journal,* December 3, 2014, http://blogs.wsj.com/chinarealtime/2014/12/03/communist-party-paper -warns-youth-on-dangers-of-self-deprecation/.
over 1.5 billion times: "China's Losers," *Economist,* April 16, 2014, www.econo mist.com/news/china/21601007-amid-spreading-prosperity-generation-self -styled-also-rans-emerges-chinas-losers.
"youth cannot be ignored": Chin, "China's Communist Party Tells Kids Being a Loser Is Nothing to Be Proud Of."

101 *put toothpaste on their child's toothbrush:* Vanessa Fong, *Only Hope: Coming of Age Under China's One-Child Policy* (Stanford, CA: Stanford University Press, 2004), 164.
test-taking pressure does take its toll: Zhao Xinying, "School Tests Blamed for Suicides," *China Daily,* May 14, 2014, http://usa.chinadaily.com.cn/china /2014-05/14/content_17505294.htm.

102 *one in five Chinese marriages ends in divorce:* Louisa Lim, "'Lightning Divorces' Strike China's 'Me Generation,'" National Public Radio website, November 17, 2010, http://www.npr.org/2010/11/09/131200166/china-s-me-generation-sends -divorce-rate-soaring.

103 *"that's another matter":* @KAKA不被找到, "12 Chinese Youths Sell Property to Travel the World," Tea Leaf Nation, May 31, 2012, http://www.tealeafnation .com/2012/05/12-chinese-youths-sell-property-to-travel-the-world/.

104 *coined the term* one-child family risk: Du Benfeng, "Population Policy and One-Child Family Risk in China," *International Journal of Social Science and Humanities* 1, no. 1 (April 2012).

107 *will become an Empress:* Liu Ting underwent multiple surgeries for gender reassignment in the spring of 2015. Margaux Schreurs, "Model Citizen Liu Ting Completes Gender Reassignment, Hailed by Media," *The Beijinger,* April 15, 2015, http://www.thebeijinger.com/blog/2015/04/15/model-citizen-liu-ting -undergoes-gender-reassignment-procedures-hailed-chinese-media.

6. *Welcome to the Dollhouse*

108 *"gigantic mass of horny young men":* Quoted in Hvistendahl, *Unnatural Selection,* 109.

109 *30 to 40 million surplus men:* Jane Golley and Rod Tyers, "Gender 'Rebalancing' in China," *Asian Population Studies* 10, no. 2 (2014), http://www.tandfonline .com/doi/full/10.1080/17441730.2014.902159#abstract.
boys born for every 100 girls: World Bank, "Gender Statistics Highlights from 2012 World Development Report," http://databank.worldbank.org/data /home.aspx. The figure of 119 boys for every 100 girls is also given by Chinese Academy of Social Sciences, quoted by many media outlets, including the BBC in this report: "China Faces Growing Gender Imbalance," BBC News, January 11, 2010, http://news.bbc.co.uk/2/hi/asia-pacific/8451289.stm.

110 *most unequal gender ratios:* World Bank, "Gender Gaps in China: Facts and Figures," October 2006, http://siteresources.worldbank.org/INTEAPREG TOPGENDER/Resources/Gender-Gaps-Figures&Facts.pdf.

113 *"Chinese equivalent of Valium":* Elisabeth Rosenthal, "Bitter Roots," *New York Times,* January 24, 1999.
rural men who are increasingly the ones killing themselves: Paul S. F. Yip and Ka Y. Liu, "The Ecological Fallacy and the Gender Ratio of Suicide in China," *British Journal of Psychiatry* 189, no. 5 (October 2006), http://bjp.rcpsych.org /content/189/5/465.
"I wish I had daughters": Mei Fong, "It's Cold Cash, Not Cold Feet, Motivating Runaway Brides in China," *Wall Street Journal,* June 5, 2009.

114 *One in four men was unable to marry at all:* Valerie Hudson and Andrea M. den Boer, *Bare Branches: The Security Implications of Asia's Surplus Male Population* (Cambridge, MA: MIT Press, 2004), 208.
Chinese Academy of Social Sciences: Yi Zhang, "10 Problems Caused by Gender Imbalance of Population," *Red Flag Manuscript,* no. 2 (2005): 13.

115 *heated up to such an extent:* "Could Asia Really Go to War over These?" *Economist,* September 20, 2012, http://www.economist.com/node/21563316.

"virile form of nationalism": Valerie Hudson and Andrea den Boer, "The Security Risks of China's Abnormal Demographics," *Washington Post,* April 30, 2014, http://www.washingtonpost.com/blogs/monkey-cage/wp/2014/04/30 /the-security-risks-of-chinas-abnormal-demographics/.

a third of the overall rise in crime: Lena Edlund, Hongbin Li, Junjian Yi, and Junsen Zhang, "More Men, More Crime: Evidence from China's One-Child Policy," available at SSRN: http://ssrn.com/abstract=1136376 or http://dx.doi .org/10.1111/j.0042-7092.2007.00700.x.

lower self-esteem: X. Zhou, Z. Yan, and T. Hesketh, "Depression and Agression in Never-Married Men in China: A Growing Problem," *Social Psychiatry and Psychiatric Epidemiology* 48, no. 7 (July 2013): 1087–93, http://www.ncbi.nlm .nih.gov/pubmed/23232692.

116 *may stimulate economic growth:* Wei Shang-Jin and Zhang Xiaobo, "Sex Ratios, Entrepreneurship, and Economic Growth in the People's Republic of China," National Bureau of Economic Research Working Paper 16800, February 2011, http://www.nber.org/papers/w16800.

excessive saving: Wei Shang-Jin and Zhang Xiabo, "The Competitive Saving Motive: Evidence from Rising Sex Ratios and Savings Rates in China," *Journal of Political Economy* 119, no. 3 (June 2011): 511–64.

reduced crime: Golley and Tyers, "Gender 'Rebalancing' in China," 143.

Siwan Anderson: Siwan Anderson, "Economics of Dowry and Brideprice," *Journal of Economic Perspectives* 21 (Fall 2007): 151–74.

117 caili *rates across China:* Gwen Guilford, Ritchie King, and Herman Wong, "Forget Dowries: Chinese Men Have to Pay Up to $24,000 to Get a Bride," *Quartz,* June 9, 2013, http://qz.com/92267/in-a-reversal-of-the-dowry-chinese -men-pay-a-steep-price-for-their-brides/.

housing prices in China between 2003 and 2009: Qingyuan Du and Shang-Jin Wei, "A Sexually Unbalanced Model of Current Account Imbalances," National Bureau of Economic Research, May 2010, http://www.nber.org/papers/w16000.

120 *Only 30 percent of marital home deeds:* Leta Hong Fincher, *Leftover Women: The Resurgence of Gender Inequality in China* (London: Zed Books, 2014).

121 *out of sixty-five postings:* Sun Peidong, *Who Will Marry My Daughter?* (Beijing: China Social Science Press, 2012).

China's family structure: Simon Day, "Playing the Dating Game," *Southland Times,* February 6, 2013, http://www.stuff.co.nz/southland-times/life-style /8749732/Playing-the-dating-game.

124 *Parents send back handwritten notes:* Lucy Hornby, "Chinese Tech Groups Turn to Matchmaking," *Financial Times,* February 13, 2015, http://www.ft.com/cms /s/0/d91a8e6a-b1a8-11e4-a830-00144feab7de.html#axzz3eUJVhDq5.

126   *breeding "quality" children:* Hong Fincher, *Leftover Women,* 30.
      "Raise the Quality": Xiaomeng Hu, "China's Inevitable Choice: Raise the
      Quality of the Population, Control the Size of the Population," *People's Daily*
      (Beijing, China), December 20, 2000, http://www.envir.gov.cn/info/2000
      /12/1220794.htm.
      Upgrading population quality: Yu Zhu, "Population's Quality Becoming the
      Main Influencing Factors in China," *Xinhua* website, January 11, 2007, http:
      //news.xinhuanet.com/politics/2007-01/11/content_5594195.htm.
      lamented giving equal rights to women: "Leader Regrets Giving Equal Rights to
      Women," *New Straits Times,* July 31, 1994, http://news.google.com/newspaper
      s?nid=1309&dat=19940731&id=PtxOAAAAIBAJ&sjid=gBMEAAAAIBAJ
      &pg=1931,4668371.

127   *the couple led separate lives:* Malcolm Moore, "China's First Lady Peng Liyuan:
      A Perfectly Scripted Life," *The Guardian,* April 3, 2013, http://www.telegraph
      .co.uk/news/worldnews/asia/china/9969052/Chinas-first-lady-Peng-Liyuan-a
      -perfectly-scripted-life.html.

128   *a September 2014 online poll:* Yang Ding, "About Women Morality Course: We
      Need More Than Just Negating It," *Tencent Web,* September 23, 2014, http://view
      .news.qq.com/original/intouchtoday/n2925.html.
      "violating social morality": "Accused of Violating Social Morality, Dongguan
      Women Morality Class Closed," Sohu website, September 26, 2014, http://news
      .sohu.com/20140926/n404677996.shtml.

129   *"raising a daughter as a son":* Fong, *Only Hope,* 135.
      according to Gallup: Steve Crabtree and Anita Pugliese, "China Outpaces India
      for Women in the Workforce," Gallup, November 2, 2012, http://www.gallup
      .com/poll/158501/china-outpaces-india-women-workforce.aspx.
      more than selling drugs or weapons: US Department of State, "Trafficking in
      Persons Report 2007," http://www.state.gov/j/tip/rls/tiprpt/2007/.

130   *about $1,500 per head:* Lee Tae-hoon, "Female North Korean Defectors Priced at
      $1500," *Korea Times Nation,* May 14, 2010.

133   *most people wanted both a son and a daughter:* Zhou Chi, Zhou Xu Dong, Wang
      Xiao Lei, Zheng Wei Jun, Li Lu, and Therese Hesketh, "Changing Gender
      Preference in China Today: Implications for the Sex Ratio," *India Journal of
      Gender Studies* 20, no. 1 (February 2013): 51–68, http://ijg.sagepub.com/content
      /20/1/51.abstract.

7. *Better to Struggle to Live On, Than Die a Good Death*

139   *five-to-one ratio will shift to 1.6 to one:* Richard Jackson, Keisuke Nakashima,
      and Neil Howe, *China's Long March to Retirement Reform: The Graying of
      the Middle Kingdom Revisited* (Washington, DC: Center for Strategic and

International Studies, 2009), http://csis.org/files/media/csis/pubs/090422 _gai_chinareport_en.pdf.

China's army of pensioners: Dexter Roberts, "China's Brewing Pension Crisis," *Bloomberg News,* August 9, 2012, http://www.businessweek.com/articles/2012 -08-09/chinas-brewing-pension-crisis.

Half of China's thirty-one provinces cannot pay: Ibid.

140 *"If they were their own country":* Ted Fishman, *Shock of Gray: The Aging of the World's Population and How It Pits Young Against Old, Child Against Parent, Worker Against Boss, Company Against Rival, and Nation Against Nation* (New York: Scribner, 2012).

141 *less than a dollar a day:* Jackson, Nakashima, and Howe, *China's Long March to Retirement Reform.*

149 *"Your chances of avoiding":* Atul Gawande, *Being Mortal: Medicine and What Matters in the End* (New York: Henry Holt and Company, 2014), 79.

150 *cemeteries won't sell them burial plots:* "Life After Loss," *China Daily,* December 17, 2013, http://www.chinadaily.com.cn/html/feature/lifeafterloss/.

million of them, and growing: National Health and Family Planning Commission of People's Republic of China, "2010 China Health Statistical Yearbook," National Health and Family Planning Commission of People's Republic of China website, August 8, 2010, http://www.moh.gov.cn/htmlfiles /zwgkzt/ptjnj/year2010/index2010.html.

151 shidu *parents receive reimbursement:* Yao Zhang, Lixin Zhang, and Liying Ren, "The First Shidu Parents Received Reimbursement," *Xinhua Daily Telegraph,* July 12, 2012, http://news.xinhuanet.com/mrdx/2012-07/12/c_131710347.htm.

sharing her quarters with a huge sow: David Moye, "Chen Shoutian Under Fire for Making 100-Year-Old Mom Sleep with a Pig," *Huffington Post Weird News,* December 18, 2012, http://www.huffingtonpost.com/2012/12/17/chen-shoutian -under-fire-_n_2317912.html.

152 *depending in turn on their children's largess:* Associated Press, "Elderly Chinese Woman, 94, Sues Her Daughter for Care as Aging Population Presents New Problems for Governments," *New York Daily News,* October 12, 2013, http: //www.nydailynews.com/news/world/edlerly-chinese-woman-sues-daughter -care-article-1.1483711.

155 *"human reproduction is sacred is no longer accepted":* Yan Yunxiang, *Private Life Under Socialism: Love, Intimacy and Family Change in a Chinese Village, 1949– 1999* (Stanford, CA: Stanford University Press, 2003).

156 *reducing out-of-pocket expenses:* Y. Zhao, Y. Hu, J. P. Smith, J. Strauss, and G. Yang, "Cohort Profile: The China Health and Retirement Longitudinal Study (CHARLS)," *International Journal of Epidemiology* 43, no. 1 (2014): 61–68, http://dx.doi.org/10.1093/ije/dys203.

157 *0.7 percentage points per year:* Jackson, Nakashima, and Howe, *China's Long March to Retirement Reform,* 3–17.

158   *forced nearly a hundred dying patients into the streets:* Coco Liu, "China Death
        Taboo on Its Way Out," *Global Post,* November 15, 2010, http://www.global
        post.com/dispatch/china/101108/hospice-care-health-aging-culture.

164   *karaoke hostesses:* Reuters, "China Bans Tomb-Sweepers' 'Vulgar' Burned
        Offerings," *China Daily,* April 25, 2006, http://www.chinadaily.com.cn/china
        /2006-04/25/content_576881.htm.

165   *40 percent of the world's Parkinson's sufferers:* E. R. Dorsey, Radu Constantinescu, J. P.
        Thompson, Kevin Biglan, R. G. Holloway, and K. Kieburtz, "Projected Number of
        People with Parkinson Disease in the Most Populous Nations, 2005 Through 2030,"
        Neurology 68, no. 5 (February 2007): 384–86, http://www.researchgate.net
        /publication/6715222_Projected_number_of_people_with_Parkinson_disease
        _in_the_most_populous_nations_2005_through_2030._Neurology.

8.   The Red Thread Is Broken

170   *For two decades, over 120,000:* There were 122,661 adoptions from China be-
        tween 1995 and 2013. Australian InterCountry Adoption Network (AICAN)
        and Peter Selman, Newcastle University, http://www.aican.org/statistics.php
        ?region=0&type=birth.

171   *eight thousand China babies:* InterCountry Adoption, Bureau of Consular
        Affairs, US Department of State, http://travel.state.gov/content/dam/aa/pdfs
        /fy2014_annual_report.pdf.
        China continues to be by far the largest source country for adoptions: Ibid.
        "The orphanage asked for more babies": Scott Tong, "The Dark Side of Chinese
        Adoptions," *Marketplace,* May 5, 2010, http://www.marketplace.org/topics/life
        /dark-side-chinese-adoptions.

172   *according to the* Los Angeles Times: Barbara Demick, "Some Chinese Parents
        Say Their Babies Were Stolen for Adoption," *Los Angeles Times,* September 20,
        2009, http://articles.latimes.com/2009/sep/20/world/fg-china-adopt20.
        Caixin *reported a similar case:* Pang Jiaoming, "The Lost Children of Shaoyang
        City," *Caixin,* May 10, 2011, http://english.caixin.com/2011-05-10/100257699
        .html.
        trafficking cases in Guizhou: "Chinese Baby Girls Sold for Adoption," UPI, July
        2, 2009, http://www.upi.com/Top_News/2009/07/02/Chinese-baby-girls-sold
        -for-adoption/UPI-52961246593352/?st_rec=63831376140810.
        Shaanxi provinces: "Doctor, Eight Others Arrested in Chinese Baby-Selling
        Scandal," UPI, August 10, 2013, http://www.upi.com/Top_News/World-News
        /2013/08/10/Doctor-eight-others-arrested-in-Chinese-baby-selling-scandal/638
        31376140810/#ixzz3UEJALYoH.
        foundation Half the Sky: Figures calculated from Half the Sky's financial records
        as posted on HalftheSky.org and verified by Patricia King, chief communication
        officer, July 17, 2014.

174 *constantly violated:* David Smolin, "The Corrupting Influence of the United States on a Vulnerable Intercountry Adoption System: A Guide for Stakeholders, Hague and Non-Hague Nations, NGOs, and Concerned Parties," *Utah Law Review* no. 4 (2013), http://epubs.utah.edu/index.php/ulr/article/viewArticle/1166.

175 *many of those girls could have found loving homes within the country:* Kay Ann Johnson, *Wanting a Daughter, Needing a Son: Abandonment, Adoption, and Orphanage Care in China* (St. Paul, MN: Yeong & Yeong Books, 2004). See also Johnson's forthcoming *China's Hidden Children: Abandonment, Adoption, and the Human Costs of the One-Child Policy* (Chicago: University of Chicago Press, 2016).
practices in Chinese orphanages: Kate Blewett and Brian Woods, *The Dying Rooms,* Lauderdale Productions, 1995, http://www.imdb.com/title/tt0112919/.

176 *little more than places where children were sent to die:* "Death by Default: A Policy of Fatal Neglect in China's State Orphanages," Human Rights Watch report, January 1, 1996, http://www.hrw.org/reports/1996/01/01/death-default.
"some cash with a red birth note": Brian Stuy's blog, http://research-china.blogspot.com/search?q=RED%20BIRTH%20NOTE&max-results=20&by-date =true, as well as interviews with the author.

180 *"an unsettling postmortem":* Brian H. Stuy, "Brian H. Stuy (with Foreword by David Smolin), Open Secret: Cash and Coercion in China's International Adoption Program," *Cumberland Law Review* 44, no. 3 (2014): 355–422, http://works.bepress.com/david_smolin/15.

181 *Families with Children from China:* The FCC has now expanded to be "Families with Children from Asia (FCA)."

182 *"huge part of cultural loss feels physically grafted":* Grace Newton, *The Red Thread Is Broken* (blog), https://redthreadbroken.wordpress.com/.
"kind of joking, kind of not": Interview with the author, September 25, 2014.

188 *"If I start to disbelieve what they [China authorities] told me":* Karin Evans, *The Lost Daughters of China: Adopted Girls, Their Journey to America, and the Search for a Missing Past* (New York: Tarcher, 2008).

189 *a hard-nosed reporter for the* Philadelphia Inquirer: Jeff Gammage, *China Ghosts: My Daughter's Journey to America, My Passage to Fatherhood* (New York: Harper Perennial, 2008).

9. Babies Beyond Borders

191 *first test-tube baby:* "China's First Test Tube Baby to Celebrate 20th Birthday," *Xinhua News,* February 26, 2008, http://www.china.org.cn/china/sci_tech /2008-02/26/content_10784222.htm.

193 *fertility treatments mushroomed:* Jared Yee, "Rising Demand for IVF in China Causes Spread of Unlicensed Clinics," *BioEdge,* November 3, 2010, http://www .bioedge.org/index.php/bioethics/bioethics_article/rising_demand_for_ivf _in_china_causes_spread_of_unlicensed_clinics.

194 *number of twin births:* Qin Xu and Yanhui Wang, "Why Twins Birth Rate Increases," *Fenghuang Web,* January 30, 2013, http://fashion.ifeng.com/baby /haoyun/detail_2013_01/30/21777648_1.shtml.

the one-child policy accounted for at least a third of the increase in twins: Wei Huang, Xiaoyan Lei, and Yaohui Zhao, "One-Child Policy and the Rise of Man-Made Twins," Forschungsinstitut zur Zukunft der Arbeit, Institute for the Study of Labor, August 2014, http://ftp.iza.org/dp8394.pdf.

seven hundred pairs of such "fake twins" in over three hundred villages: "700 Fake Twins Investigated in Yunnan," *People Web,* July 28, 2000, http://www.people .com.cn/GB/channel1/13/20000728/163617.html.

one in every fifty babies born was a twin: Shuang Lu and Yun Luo, "Drugs Lead to Increased Twins Rate," *Sina Web,* January 22, 2013, http://baby.sina.com.cn /news/2013-01-22/084158010.shtml?oda_pick_aid=0&oda_pick_mid=0&oda _pick_pid=3411627&oda_pick_sid=0&oda_pick_st=1&pl=0&kid=0&ct=0.

"To have one family with eight kids": Alexa Olesen, "'Octomom' in One-Child China Stuns Public," *USA Today,* December 30, 2011, http://usatoday30.usa today.com/news/health/wellness/story/2011-12-30/Octomom-in-one-child -China-stuns-public/52284636/1.

195 *five surrogate mothers in a quest for a son:* "Strict Selection Before Surrogacy and 4 Abortions for Bearing a Boy," *Guangming Web,* January 12, 2015, http://life .gmw.cn/2015-01/12/content_14478195.htm.

three surrogate mothers: James Pomfret, "Forced Abortions Shake Up China Wombs-for-Rent Industry," Reuters, April 30, 2009, http://www.reuters.com /article/2009/04/30/us-china-surrogacy-idUSTRE53T04D20090430.

196 *"what does the law mean":* Olesen, "'Octomom' in One-Child China Stuns Public."

forced late-term abortion: Massoud Hayoun, "Understanding China's One-Child Policy," *The National Interest,* August 15, 2012, http://nationalinterest.org /commentary/understanding-chinas-one-child-policy-7330.

linked to infertility: "Study to Assess Impact of Air Pollution on Fertility," *Environmental Technology,* September 10, 2013, http://www.envirotech-online .com/news/air-monitoring/6/breaking_news/study_to_assess_impact_of_air _pollution_on_fertility/26787/.

a five-year study of the relationship between air pollution and female infertility: Ibid.

a "semen crisis": Changfeng Chen, "Shanghai Sperm Bank Investigation Shows 2/3 Semen Unqualified," *Xinmin Web,* November 6, 2013, http://shanghai.xin min.cn/xmsq/2013/11/06/22552119.html.

197 *World Health Organization standards:* Tom Phillips, "Pollution Pushes Shanghai Towards Semen Crisis," *The Telegraph,* November 7, 2013, http: //www.telegraph.co.uk/news/worldnews/asia/china/10432226/Pollution -pushes-Shanghai-towards-semen-crisis.html.

Chinese men's sperm: Weiguang Wang and Guoguang Zheng, *Green Book of*

Climate Change: Annual Report on Actions to Address Climate Change (Beijing: Social Sciences Academic Press, 2013).

With over 60 million females who were never born, killed in infancy, or given away: "Bare Branches, Redundant Males," *Economist,* April 16, 2015, http://www .economist.com/news/asia/21648715-distorted-sex-ratios-birth-generation-ago -are-changing-marriage-and-damaging-societies-asias.

and another 40 million females experiencing infertility: Alice Yang and Jeremy Blum, "Pollutants' Effect on Infertility Rates in China to Be Examined," *South China Morning Post,* September 4, 2013.

exposed by his mistress: Shitong Nie, "Woman Accused Deputy of City Construction Bureau in Changde's Deshan Economic Development Zone," *Zhongyuan Web,* March 11, 2014, http://zx.zynews.com/whzx/134537.html.

Lei was sentenced to death: Jianliang Huang and Xiangsheng Yue, "Former Vice Mayor of Chenzhou City Had Relationships with Nine Lovers," *Sina Web,* May 11, 2006, http://news.sina.com.cn/c/l/2006-05-11/11219831007.shtml.

200 *"but they don't want African American":* Interview with the author, March 5, 2015.

203 *"US and other countries":* Wendie Wilson-Miller, based on an interview with the author, March 6, 2015.

205 *"'anchor baby' industry":* Miriam Jordan, "Federal Agents Raid Alleged 'Maternity Tourism' Businesses Catering to Chinese," *Wall Street Journal,* March 3, 2015, http://www.wsj.com/articles/us-agents-raid-alleged-maternity-tourism -anchor-baby-businesses-catering-to-chinese-1425404456.

"the donor's had eyelid surgery": Wilson-Miller, based on an interview with the author, March 6, 2015.

206 *genetic screening they would prefer:* Niu Yujie, Yang Youmeng, Li Yajuan, Tang Qi, Zhang Yixi, Xu Linyong, and Zhang Helong, "A Study upon Knowledge and Awareness of Genetic Screening and Influencing Factors in Changsha," *Practical Preventive Medicine* 22, no. 1 (January 2015).

207 *"People ought to be free to manipulate their children's IQ":* Bregtje van der Haak, *DNA Dreams* (documentary), Netherlands, 2012, http://www.nposales.com /dna-dreams/.

select embryos that have better genetic markers: John Bohannon, "Why Are Some People So Smart? The Answer Could Spawn a New Generation of Superbabies," *Wired,* July 16, 2013 http://www.wired.com/2013/07/genetics-of-iq/.

forbidding couples who had "genetic diseases of a serious nature": Sun-Wei Guo, "China: The Maternal and Infant Health Care Law," *eLS,* April 16, 2012, http:// onlinelibrary.wiley.com/doi/10.1002/9780470015902.a0005201.pub2/abstract.

208 *"reproduction of the dull-witted, idiots, or blockheads":* Wang Guisong, "Constitutionality Adjustment on China Eugenics Law," *Study in Law and Business,* no. 2 (2011).

Only a tenth of eligible couples: "Only 1/10th Chinese Couples Had 2nd Child After Policy Relaxed."

"selfish and bad parenting to have another child": Lauren Sandler, "Chinese Parents Can Now Have More Than One Child. Why Many Say They Won't," *Washington Post,* January 10, 2014, http://www.washingtonpost.com/opin ions/chinese-parents-can-now-have-more-than-one-child-why-many-say-they -wont/2014/01/10/2c9811de-73c5-11e3-8def-a33011492df2_story.html.

209 *the one-child policy had nothing to do with their decision:* Ma Xiaohong, "Birth Policy's Enlightenment: Child-Bearing Trends in Different Districts," *Population and Development,* no. 6 (2011).

"a case of extreme economic rationalism": Susan Greenhalgh, "Fertility as Mobility: Sinic Transitions," *Population and Development Review* 14, no. 4 (December 1988): 629–74, http://www.jstor.org/stable/1973627.

INDEX